The English Squire
and his sport

Also by Roger Longrigg

Fiction

A HIGH PITCHED BUZZ

SWITCHBOARD

WRONG NUMBER

DAUGHTERS OF MULBERRY

THE PAPER BOATS

LOVE AMONG THE BOTTLES

THE SUN ON THE WATER

THE DESPERATE CRIMINALS

THE JEVINGTON SYSTEM

THEIR PLEASING SPORT

THE BABE IN THE WOOD

Non Fiction

THE ARTLESS GAMBLER

THE HISTORY OF HORSE RACING

THE TURF

THE HISTORY OF FOXHUNTING

not done so. He contrasted with Hesiod's Boeotian bumpkin as Peter Beckford with Squire Western. He was cultured; he was preferably beautiful; but he despised the luxuriousness of the Persians, who even had carpets in their bedrooms, and his education included compulsory games and horsemanship. He was an active sportsman, philosophically encouraged by a range of perfectly modern arguments. He most carefully bred and entered deep-mouthed line-hunting hounds, slow enough to follow on foot, with noses tied to every jink of the hare in poor scenting conditions, and with so little killer instinct that they could be stopped from their quarry by the voice. (The similarity of Xenophon's hounds to the Old Southern harriers of 17th- and 18th-century England is startling.) In the intensively farmed areas of Attica and Elis the sportsman was extremely careful not to do any damage, an attitude familiar to England and so magnificently ignored in France that it was a major cause of the Revolution. He was sportsmanlike as well as sporting: Plato remarked that 'the crafty snaring of little birds is not a gentleman-like pursuit'. (There the English 18th century would not have agreed with him.) The Greek gentleman of the golden age also kept horses, including racehorses, whose success earned him more glory than money. He fished with rod and line: Theocritus has Asphalion hooking and actually playing a big one. He hunted the boar sportingly, the deer less so, but by the 5th century he had to travel a long way to find large game.

Roman manners were stiffer than those of the Greeks, and their pleasures grosser. They preferred dignity to grace and the circus to the covert-side. But the Republic had in 300 BC a land-based aristocracy of about 100 families, in 50 BC perhaps 500, whose rank was strictly hereditary and strictly derived from inherited acres: to these people the Greek idea of the farmer-sportsman-scholar was still real. Below this senatorial rank, but considering themselves (and considered) gentlemen, were the knights, many very rich as a result of wars and the huge growth of trade which followed the destruction of Carthage. To them agriculture was a gentlemanly pursuit as a profession might be, but trade never. Cicero himself, a professional man, made the ennobling jump from town to country exactly as did Elizabethan lawyers and Victorian ironmasters. A squire was the thing to be. Latin consequently has the marvellous pastoral literature of Horace, Virgil and others, and also a fat shelf of hunting treatises not by any means completely derived from Xenophon, though in form imitative of his *Cygeneticus*. But as the Empire aged, a taste for indolent luxury and bestial spectator sports grew, and at the

ΑΥΡΑ

same time game almost disappeared from Italy. It was not the Roman landowner who rode to harriers in the manner described by Arrian and Oppian, but transplanted officials and local notables in the remoter parts of the Empire: the Gaulish Celts, who hunted hare, fox and deer with their Segusian hounds (*above*), and the Britons, whose celebrated rough-coated Agassaeans were probably the ancestors of both Welsh and Breton hounds. The Romano-British land-holding official, whose villa had its own stables, kennels and hunt staff, as well as its large well-run farm, was probably the nearest thing to Xenophon's Ischomachos, and to the English squire of 1,500 years afterwards, that the later Empire could show.

(iii) Noble and Knight in the Dark Ages

The barbarian invasions gradually filled Western Europe with uncouth tribesmen, who in some places – notably Britain – entirely destroyed the civilization they found. Most brought with them a passion for field-sports, especially hunting. They adopted with joy the excellent Italian horse, which had vastly improved the breed all over the empire and made riding (as against driving) everywhere normal for hunting and war, and which was itself principally indebted to North Africa. Here and there they took to racing. They appreciated, and continued to breed, at least some of the hounds they found, although the very best survived only in the unconquered outlands of Wales and Brittany.

There were wide differences between the various Goth, Vandal, Lombard, Saxon and other newcomers. They started with different tribal organizations. Some had been more or less influenced over a long period by contact with the marches of the empire. Some were so deeply influenced by the society of which they became overlords that they were, as in Italy, effectively absorbed into it. Some adopted or adapted aspects of Roman Law, which included the notion, unknown in their homelands, of hunting certain beasts or in certain places as a matter of minority privilege; to others, such as the English, such limitations only existed as an aspect of the rights of property: status did not come into it. In spite of these and other variations, in most of Western Europe a consistent stratification emerged which survived into feudalism and beyond. There was a court, sometimes brilliant and often international and polyglot. There was a scattering of great lords, gross and illiterate, living and sporting in the countryside. When levies were raised for war or policing, a small minority were horsed: this élite eventually acquired a distinct and hereditary status (as it had in republican Rome) and was more and more sharply differentiated from the classes below. When feudalism was systematised – incompletely, except in Normandy and Norman Sicily, and with large regional variations – the horse-soldier held a knight's fee, a manor, which provided his horse, sword and retinue, all available to the lord from whom he held the fee. He was armigerous: a gentleman. He was part of chivalry in the age of chivalry, and subject to its curious laws. From him, when conditions came right in 14th-century England, developed the country gentleman.

The latter's sport was the child of developments begun six centuries earlier. The great war-horse, Flemish or Burgundian, was from the 8th century the winner of battles and tournaments; but with Saracen blood from North Africa by way of Spain the palfrey became handier and more docile at the same time, and was the hack and sporting horse. An achievement of seminal importance, also at the same time, was the development in the Ardennes, allegedly by St Hubert himself, of the first great French scenting hound (*overleaf*); long before 1066 the black St Hubert spawned the black-and-tan or tricolour Norman as a distinct breed, and soon afterwards the blue-mottled Gascon as another. There were also grey- or gazehounds of various sizes and coats, mastiffs (alaunts) and terriers. Meanwhile the broken-coated hounds of Brittany and Wales, and a small indigenous breed – beagle or brachet – of Ireland, Scotland and the North of England, continued to develop. If Sir Roger de Coverley descended from the knights of the Teutonic levies, his hounds descended from these progenitors. Falconry had been known to the late Roman Empire as a diversion of the barbarian East,

St Hubert Hound: woodcut from Turberville's *The Book of Falconrie and Hunting*, 1611.

Anglo-Saxon falconry and boar hunting.

and it is said to have been brought to Western Europe by the Lombards. (But the earliest European accounts of it are derived from Latin translations of Persian.) The later Anglo-Saxon kings were as devoted to hawking as to hunting, and it is mentioned in the *Colloquy* of Archbishop Aelfric of Canterbury about AD 995.

Between Alfred the Great and the Norman Conquest, England was rather unlike the rest of Europe, owing to what seems to have been an exceptionally relaxed and tolerant society. It would be absurd to call it democratic, but it was peaceful, prosperous, sporting, and not at all tyrannical. It was very unlike Normandy. But from 1066, for nearly three centuries, England became an integral part of Europe and not greatly to be distinguished from other parts. The specialness of England in Chaucer's time grew from special conditions, the uniqueness of the English gentleman from unique circumstances. But the squire's attitudes, and especially his sport, grew so firmly from their early medieval roots – French as much as English – that it is worth looking at the latter.

(iv) Feudalism and Exclusive Sporting Rights

By AD 1000 most of Europe was comparatively settled and peaceful, and most of it was, or was becoming, more or less strictly feudal. In feudal theory all land belonged divinely to the king, and all tenure of it was granted by him and conditional on the performance of the appropriate services. The right to bear arms was also in the gift of the king. The right to hunt was the child of land-holding and arms-bearing, and was therefore royal also; it could be delegated, but the delegated rights were subject to whatever limits the king chose.

Political philosophy thus produced the feudal forest laws; it codified, as practically divine, a class stratification which when applied to hunting produced the distinction between high and low game, between venery, chase and warren; and it justified the savage penalties for encroachments on royal and noble prerogatives. When the rigidities of this system were imposed on the free-and-easy society of England they were, said the *Anglo-Saxon Chronicle*, 'violently unpopular with all classes' – not only with peasants who liked venison, but with knights and nobles also. Consequently when the great nobles were able to browbeat the king they extracted the *Carta de Foresta* (1217) as well as *Magna Carta;* and when the country gentry were in a comparable position of power 150

years later they grabbed the hunting rights for themselves. Ever afterwards, well into the 19th century, game laws of varying ferocity protected the property and privilege of the landed gentry, and they were
the direct heirs, and consequence, of the Norman forest laws.

Until the beginning of this period the castle was almost everywhere a
moated wooden structure round a courtyard, which often harboured
farm-stock and peasantry as well as stables, kennels, mews, huntsmen,
falconers and men-at-arms. The castles of the great became stone in the
11th century, but the fortified manors of knights were mostly still
wooden until the time of the Crusades.

Attached to the manor was its demesne: beyond this the open field and
the common. The serfs were bound to the land, and they were able to
farm their strips of the open field by virtue of giving a part of their
yield to the lord and a part of their time to his demesne. The minor lord
had no other source either of income or of goods. All kinds of livestock
were tiny; there was no way of feeding any but a breeding nucleus
during the winter; the winter diet depended on meat salted at the
October slaughtering. Life was not only rough and comfortless but also,
in peacetime, extremely dull. All these circumstances made hunting,
hawking and fishing important to the small manor, the great castle,
the monastery, and the peripatetic court. Thus, while feudal theory
provided the rationale for the stratification of hunting rights and of
game, these practical considerations occasioned their enforcement. The
king declared huge areas of forest his and his only. Inside or outside his
forest he granted rights of chase to certain lords and religious houses; a
chase became a park if enclosed. A person thus enfranchised could grant
a right of chase or park within his chase or park, or the much humbler
right of warren. The beasts huntable under these franchises varied from
time to time and place to place; broadly, deer and boar were noble
game, and the hare was also worthy of a great man's disport owing to the
fascination and difficulty of catching it; roe, hare and the major vermin
(fox and badger) were the normal beasts of chase; and rabbits were the
staple of warren. To a knight's fee might be attached any of these rights,
as reward or bribe or by time-out-of-mind custom: but the lesser land-
holders were often deprived of any but the humblest warren-hunting,
either by contiguity to royal forest or by the jealousy of the local magnate. In such cases the knight's organized sport (as so often today)
depended on invitation. He could hunt any beast he liked (outside the
fence months, the close season) in completely wild country, unclaimed

and unreclaimed waste: but this was often a hollow privilege, as much of the primeval hardwood forest was impassably boggy and impenetrable with fallen trees and undergrowth.

(v) Elegant Sport in the Age of Chivalry

Life continued brutish, and sport graceless, until the invention of chivalry in Provence in the mid-12th century.

Chivalry transformed the life-style of the upper classes of Europe, reviving the long-dead ideal of the gentleman who combined physical courage and strenuous activity with good manners and gentle emotions. A major consequence of the idea of chivalry was the Crusades – international Christianity militant, as had been the paladins at the court of Charlemagne – which also fed it with the trappings of daintiness and luxury discovered by Europe in the Middle East.

Everything was now altered. Manors became stone houses instead of wooden castles; they were furnished with carpets and tapestries. Diet was varied. Clothes were richer. Music and recitation from troubadour and jongleur filled the halls, into which women made a civilizing entry. Hopeless, courtly love was felt, or fashionably assumed. Chess was much played. The romances gave every man of gentle blood an ideal not very far from the Athenian (except that pederasty was deprecated) and not very far from the modern. For two centuries – about AD 1150 to 1350 – the education of a gentleman's son was normally in the household of a grandee, where he learned manners and sport. Instruction in the latter became quite as much a matter of terminology and behaviour as of technique; to commit errors in the Terms of Art of Venery and the even more complex and whimsical language of hawking brought far more

odium than adultery, which became, for the first time in Christian
Europe, an acceptable minority sport objected to only by the curmud-
geonly, or that figure of ridicule the horned husband.

Against this background, the changes made to hunting were greater
than any in continental Europe ever since, and than any even in Britain
until the reign of Elizabeth. Four circumstances especially directed
things: the quality of the hounds of France, and thence of England; the
density of the forest; the size of sporting households; and the chivalric
concern with forms. Put together, these created a style of hunting virtually unknown before AD 1000 and virtually unchanged after 1300, and
described in a little treatise (*La Chace dou Serf*) of about 1250 which
substantially anticipated the great hunting literature of the following
centuries. The huntsman harboured the stag early in the morning, and
submitted a fewmet (dropping) in his horn to the lord. After a feast, the
stag was unharboured by a single lymer, and part of the pack was uncoupled and laid on. The relay hounds were uncoupled as the stag
passed them. Death, undoing and quarry followed strict rules, and a
language of the horn, already complex, communicated exact information to men and hounds out of sight of each other in the woods.

Where a champaign country permitted it, coursing recovered some of
its ancient popularity in France (it never lost it in England), the crusaders
having relearned this sport in the desert. Other results of the Crusades
of enduring sporting importance were the rediscovery and importation
of the Eastern horse, and the refinement of hawking.

Western Europe knew the desert horse only in the persons of its im-
pure descendants of Andalusia and Lusitania, and the Barb-descended
horses of Limousin and the Camargue. There was no importation of
the North African horses which had dominated the classical racecourse

Unearthing a Fox: England, about 1300.

from the earliest Olympics to the fall of Rome, except by the Saracens into their own territory in Spain. But Richard I and Tancred were two of many crusaders who admired the horse they saw in the desert for its stamina and docility; a few were certainly brought home to continue an ancient but long-interrupted process of improvement.

Of hawking before the Crusades it is difficult to say much with certainty. Many references declare that it was highly regarded as an art, and not unimportant for food, so there must have been competent falconers (handlers of the more esteemed long-winged hawks) and austringers (those who had charge of the plebeian short-winged goshawks and sparrowhawks). It appears that they hawked birds rather than ground-game, especially cranes and duck. The crusaders met experts far beyond their own attainments, and from their return date an entirely new dimension of elegance and sophistication in the sport,

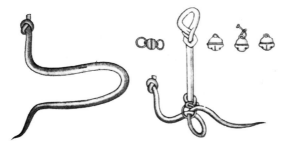

The falconer's leash, jess and bells.

Mounted hawking.

Falconers at work in the Mews. (Above and previous page: Miniatures from the *Falkenbuch* of the Emperor Frederick II, about 1240.)

its elaborate language, and the use of exotic species. Hares and rabbits were taken in quantity, which increased the value of a franchise of warren, and partridges – also available to warreners – were the most useful flying quarry. The rigid stratification of the age impelled a grading of hawks proper to rank; in France this became a long list, reading down the degrees of nobility and knighthood; even in England the falcon (female peregrine), gerfalcon and their males were reserved for the great, the goshawk for yeomen, the sparrowhawk for the humble; the merlin – pre-eminently a lark hawker – was the ladies' bird, and the hobby the priests'. It should be added that the sparrowhawk was the most freely available and quite the hardest to train, and that it caught great numbers of flying partridges and young pheasants on the ground. (The pheasant was introduced to England a little before the Norman Conquest, and began the steady climb which made it, by 1900, the unquestioned lord of much of sporting England, to the rage of fox-hunters, the contempt of rough shooters, and the profit of large land-owners.) It was already normal for the falconer to be mounted in open country, and to mount on the wrong (off) side if he held his hawk, as Europe did, on the left wrist.

A certain amount of game of all kinds is shown, in very early pictures and illuminations, being shot: but the prey must either have been bayed by hounds or stalked to point-blank range, as the early longbow (*below*) was neither powerful nor accurate. The crossbow was introduced to Europe in the 11th century, and used with real effect in the first Crusade, but the taking of game with it was probably limited to poachers until the 14th century. Its sporting development, like that of the fowling piece, grew out of military improvements.

Fishing had been a sport to the Romans – Oppian's battles with big fish were as inspiriting as his gallops after the harriers – and this spirit was still alive or reborn in the 11th century: the good Archbishop Aelfric, teaching Latin, preferred river to sea fishing because it was more fun. But as fishing became important to the domestic economy of riparian owners, and the delvers of stewponds, its sporting charm was forgotten, hardly to be mentioned for centuries. Ponds and moats were stocked with fish for the table, probably at every manor that ran to hounds and hawks: and religious houses are accused of having introduced grayling into trout streams, to the wounding of their remote successors. Much river fishing was strictly private (though fishing-rights were far less valuable than milling), but much was quite free: *Del' Houstillement au Vilain* says that the French villein of the 13th century had a mortar, ladder, hedging-gloves, plough, billhook, spade, knife, shears, harrow, little cart, and fishing tackle as the tools of his livelihood, and this list will serve for England too.

The tournament was, from perhaps AD 1250, the most important vigorous diversion for a gentleman, after hunting and hawking. It was, of course, the image of war, and like the archery contests of English villages in a later age it was part of military training. But as early as 1300 the military supremacy of the mounted armoured knight was coming under threat – from the arrow, not from gunpowder – and in a curious way, typical of sporting history, its great age as sport and spectacle coincided with its disappearing military relevance.

One other major outdoor sport was fitfully alive, here and there, during the early middle ages: racing. In Ireland it was hugely popular, as law and folklore copiously show, until the Anglo-Norman invasion destroyed the ancient Irish civilization. In Brittany it was a living tradition among the exiled heirs of the Romano-British, but probably not for long or on a large scale. In a few French towns it was a merry and knockabout local amusement of the tradesmen, which is probably the most that can be said of the sport in London. In rural England in Richard I's reign it was, if we believe the metrical romance *Bevis of Hampton*, conducted among knights for substantial prizes. *Bevis* gives the impression that the Whitsun races were a regular event, and that a high value was put on fast horses. This marks the beginning of an association between English gentlemen and racehorses which has lasted ever since, interrupted only by those periods when persons who were not gentlemen owned the horses. (We are partly, but only partly, in such a phase today; gentleman owners are heavily outnumbered and vastly outspent by the Rest, but they are still well represented in the Jockey Club.)

The foregoing dizzy gallop through three millennia brings us to the 14th century AD, when many things, long brewing, combined to create the English country gentleman and his yeoman neighbour, and equip them for their sport. The squire had scenting hounds from Normandy, and latterly blue-mottled from Gascony, as well as small brachets, mastiffs, and excellent greyhounds. He had horses successively improved in Roman times, at the Norman Conquest, and as a result of the Crusades. He had a good many deer – red, fallow and roe – and a great many hares; he had pheasant and partridge, bustard and woodcock, plover and goose. He had long- and short-winged hawks, and was expert in their use. He had a military crossbow, accurate, powerful, portable, easy to shoot. He had fisheries, public and private, in still water and running, with a long background of successful stocking. He had a strong tradition of jousting and a flimsy but real one of racing. He now acquired prosperity, national power and local pre-eminence which at last enabled him to make proper use of all that history had provided.

CHAPTER TWO

The Later Middle Ages

(i) The Enthronement of the Squire

Chaucer's England was sharply different from France and from its own immediate past. There were many reasons for the difference, many aspects of it, many results from it: and nearly all favoured the country gentleman.

The country, though an island, had not previously been insular. There was first an intimate association with Normandy, then one with Gascony. From the former had come, as a military aristocracy, most of the great families; from the latter came many more soldiers and officials, and such courtiers as Piers Gaveston, Edward II's ambiguous and detested favourite, the son of a Gascon knight. An archaic kind of French remained the language of the court and of official documents, and it was natural that William Twici wrote (or rather stole) the first English hunting treatise, in about 1328, in bastard French. But during the next two generations national self-consciousness grew mightily, partly as a result of wars fought in France by Englishmen under a great English king: and when William Langland and Geoffrey Chaucer wrote, English had become not only an educated man's literary language, but also the tongue of court, business and speech in a gentleman's household.

The wars of Edward III in France had a number of other important consequences.

One was that England, not being a battleground, was able to adopt the postures and indulgences of assured peace, while enjoying the vigour and profit of successful war. Of the Hundred Years' War a Frenchman said, '*Les bois sont venus en France avec les Anglais*', meaning that farming land reverted to waste as it was fought over. Destructive predators so greatly increased that there were a long series of royal proclamations (1355, 1356, 1413, etc.): 'We give leave and licence to anyone who can hunt and take without any penalty' wolf, fox and badger. (This was a crisis measure indeed: the wolf had been the principal beast of venery in several parts of France, as strictly preserved as it was again in the 17th century, and probably the main reason for the special development of the Gascon hound.) French deer were still energetically protected, but in new waste and overgrown old forest, and in a countryside disturbed by armies and deprived of law, poaching was rampant. Poaching was, as it happened, rampant in England too: but it was done slyly, in green garb for camouflage, with greyhound and longbow, bringing loss to the lord but not contempt to his law.

The king's expeditions had to be massively financed. In theory the army was still a feudal levy, but in practice military service was so largely commuted that the king had to pay wages to professionals. He raised the money in two main ways, more or less alternately: from Parliament, which meant the landed interest; and from the towns. Each extracted more and more concessions in return for their money. The result was that by the end of the 14th century the lord of a good manor was, as M.P., in a position of national political power which went far to take sovereignty from the crown: hence such legislation as the Statute of Labourers, which kept down agricultural wages. At the same time government was decentralised as feudalism crumbled; the country gentleman administered the law as Justice of the Peace at home which he enacted as Knight of the Shire at Westminster. His executive and judicial power in his own neighbourhood was increased to a level approaching omnipotence with the destruction of part of the great aristocracy by the Wars of the Roses, and the loss of the power of the rest under strong Tudor government. It all left the squire a local god, sometimes the godlier (though often no better a landlord) for being an abbot or prior. The independence and privilege equivalently won by the towns worked to the same end, because rich townsmen moved out and became country gentlemen. This process accelerated in the 15th and more still in the 16th centuries, but it was well started in the 14th.

Country and town both financed Edward III's wars from the immense profits of wool. There were prodigious flocks in the pasture areas – the Yorkshire dales, the Cotswolds, the Sussex downs, the drier parts of the fens; there were also a great many sheep in arable areas, many owned by serfs and grazed on communal pasture or common waste, many more on the demesne. The export trade brought wealth to the countryside, and to the towns where various monopoly arrangements created the convert landowners of the next generation. In the 15th century weaving moved from towns to countryside, largely in search of running water. Parts of the process of weaving were a cottage industry, and cloth brought new wealth to all rural classes. In the towns, cloth merchants largely replaced wool merchants as the commercial aristocracy. Many, like the celebrated Thomas Paycocke of Coggeshall, Essex, married into and joined the landowning gentry, and from the Yorkist kings (as from the Tudors) coats of arms were readily bought; Daniel Defoe, 150 years later, traced many of the landed families of the West Country to cloth merchants in towns like Bristol. To Poggio Bracciolini (in *De Nobilitate*) the process was simply impossible; everywhere but England it was.

Changes in the structure of power coincided with equally important changes in the manor itself.

It used always to be taught that the transformation of the late 14th-century English agricultural economy resulted from the Black Death of 1348–9, which by halving the working population put the serf in a seller's market for his labour and thus, at a stroke, destroyed the old manorial system. But the Black Death was reported from monasteries, where a lot of infirm old men lived close together in dripping stone cells, and got a false idea of fatalities among healthier people in healthier places; examination of parish records has shown that hardly more village holdings changed hands than at other times; it is now clear that the changes, though large, were gradual, and arose from other causes.

The central change was the commutation of service to rent. This began in a small way in the 12th century; it was accelerated by the fact that anyone, of any class, who sold wool got money for it. The wool trade, and still more the cloth trade, put even the remotest village on a money economy. This suited everybody. Peasants had rather pay rent than undergo the indignity and inconvenience of tenure by servitude; lords got willing labour which they could control because they paid for it, rather than sulky hinds doing the minimum. The land hunger of lords for more sheep-walks was another reason for their taking rents. Sometimes they could simply grab a neighbour's estate, with soldiers home from France and domination of the local bench; sometimes they had to buy it.

An effect of all this was that a tough and able peasant was able to amass enough money to buy out his once land-tied neighbours, and become an employer of their labour. He became the yeoman, either tenant or freeholder, economically independent – sometimes pretty rich even in the 14th century – but without the legal power or social pretension of a gentleman. The jump into gentility was then made by as many yeoman as cloth merchants: Clement Paston was a yeoman in Richard II's reign; his son was William Paston Esquire of Paston Hall, Norfolk, a Justice and without qualification a gentleman. (This too would have been incomprehensible to Poggio Bracciolini.) The distinctions are clear in Chaucer. The knight and his son were literate, accomplished, travelled, mannerly, gentle. It appears that they were landless – members all their lives of a great man's military household – and the knight himself perhaps a younger son. The franklin was clearly their social inferior, yet he was a Justice and had been Knight of the Shire; he had a fine house, where he kept an hospitable table laden with partridge and pike of his fattening. We can assume that the franklin's wealth was wool-based, and be certain that his son or grandson acquired a coat of arms. Certainly this was the last moment in England when a rich and influential landowner like the franklin would be deemed the inferior of a landless professional soldier; thereafter, and for ever, land was the badge of gentility or the passport to it.

The franklin doubtless bought his house from an improvident or extravagant gentleman. There were many such in the late middle ages, as the newly powerful gentry aped the excesses of great men, emulated the splendour of Edward III's court, bought luxuries looted from France, and observed, as had their betters who could better afford it, the daunting chivalric rules of hospitality. A high proportion of the manor-houses were rebuilt from about 1350 onwards: the new seat was normally a two-storey building, partly castellated and often moated, surrounding a courtyard on to which gave rooms (not simply a hall) with tall windows. Chimneys replaced a hole in the roof. Formal gardens were laid out for herbs, bowls, and dalliance, all growing in popularity. Brick-kilns were introduced from Holland to areas like East Anglia where there were few quarries or trees, and in the 15th century many new manor-houses were built of this comfortable material. Only the castles of the Welsh marches and the peel-towers of the Borders were still military buildings.

All this clearly overstretched the rents of a great many lesser gentry (as gambling and agricultural improvement did those of the 18th century), letting in the prudent yeoman and merchant. But other gentry, cleverer or luckier, greatly enriched themselves by marriage, legal chicanery, assiduous service to king or magnate, or successful farming and trading. The class gap thus greatly widened, not between gentleman and yeoman, but between rich and poor: the successful 15th-century landowner added a local economic stranglehold to his almost limitless legal powers.

This made life very pleasant indeed. 'The nobles of England', said Poggio with dismay, 'think themselves above residing in cities. They live in retirement on their country estates amid woods and pastures.' This bizarre preference, more even than social mobility, divided England from the continent, the gentleman from the *gentilhomme*.

(ii) Game Laws of the Gentry

The gentry 'living in retirement on their country estates' used their power in Parliament not only to keep their labourers' wages low but also, and more particularly, to protect their own hunting rights. The time had been when even lords of manors living within or near royal forest were debarred from hunting, forbidden to keep greyhounds except by special royal licence, and obliged to have their guard-dogs expediated – the middle toes struck off with mallet and chisel, rendering the dog 'lawed' or *mutilatus*, unable to hunt. In the new political climate, game laws protecting the rights of the gentry effectively replaced forest laws protecting the rights of the king:

> [In 1390] If any layman, not having in lands 40 shillings *per Annum*, or if any priest or clerk, not having 10 pounds living *per Annum*, shal have or keep any hound, greyhound, or other dog for to hunt, or any ferets, hays, harepipes, cords, nets, or other engines, to take or destroy deere, hare, conies, or other gentlemens game, and shal be thereof

convicted at the session of the peace, every such offender shal be imprisoned for one whole yeare.

The 'qualified' person – qualified simply by income – remained privileged in this regard until 1830. This was preposterous, even bestial: but the bestiality needs to be qualified by two important points. First, from the beginning in 1390 to the end in 1830 there was no *class* qualification such as that which bedevilled France and Germany, but one which, in practice as well as theory, allowed the substantial yeoman to hunt as freely as his armigerous neighbour. This has a good deal to do with the special character of English field sports. Secondly, although poor men might not own hounds, there was nothing to stop them riding to someone else's: in sharp distinction, once again, to the continent, tradesmen and small tenant farmers could and did follow the hounds of the gentry, on equal terms with all but the Master of Hounds. This had even more to do with the character of English sport, and sometimes still does.

(iii) Late Medieval Hunting

Hunting was a major attraction of residence 'among the woods and pastures'; it remained a major source of food in the meatless winter; it was also a major source of ostentation. Deerhunting grew more elaborate and expensive in the 14th century, which may go far to explain the popularity of informal harehunting.

The new manor-houses had new and bigger kennels housing Talbots, Gascons, brachets, greyhounds and terriers.

The Talbot was the black-and-tan Norman, which probably got its new name from an Anglo-Norman family. It had been the pre-eminent pack staghound, but its qualities – superb cold nose, sonorous cry, great slowness as a matter both of physique and of meticulous line-hunting – increasingly suited it only to the role of lymer. The lymer (kept on leash, by definition) was the sagacious single hound taken by the huntsman to harbour a huntable stag in the dawn, and circumambulate the thicket so that its ring of scent kept the deer where it was; one lymer or a couple later unharboured the deer for the pack. The Talbot survived, in rather small numbers and mostly in the North of England, as the old-fashioned leggy pack bloodhound; and also as the rare, disease-prone, inbred bloodhound of modern dog-shows.

The Gascon was a less pure descendant of the black St Hubert of the Ardennes, imported into England in large numbers by such immigrants as the Brocas family; this eminent but sometimes raffish clan joined Edward III's court from Gascony in 1363 and became hereditary Masters of the Royal Hounds, replacing the Norman Lovels and de Borhuntes. The Gascon was another line-hunter, far more notable for nose and cry than for drive or pace, but it was lighter-built and faster than the Norman, and somehow acquired a characteristic (though by no means universal) blue-mottled colour. Probably colour and build both came from outcrossing to breeds developed north of Gascony, which may themselves have had an admixture of Breton blood. The Gascon developed, without great change, into the Old Southern hound of England, associated latterly with Sussex, the West Country and Lanca-shire; until tastes changed it was the pre-eminent harehound and so, from perhaps 1350 to 1800, the most usual hound of the gentleman's private pack. Incapable of catching a fox fairly above ground, it was wholly displaced in the 19th century by the foxhound and dwarf-fox-hound harrier. It survives now not at all in England, but in America as the old New England hound – shot over – and the Penn-Marydel pack foxhound of Eastern Pennsylvania, Eastern Shore Maryland, and Delaware.

The brachet was a much smaller and more active hound, perhaps ultimately derived from the Irish beagle mentioned in all the ancient sagas – beagle simply means small. (Sometimes 'brachet' or 'brache' meant bitch, and a doghound was a 'rache'.) Brachets were packed with Talbots or Gascons for forest deerhunting, their value being ability to smeuse below dense undergrowth. They also hunted hares in the open, with or without Gascons. Their drawback was a shrill, unmusical cry, and they were sometimes almost mute. The 16th century knew a small Ribble hound, the 17th the light fast Northern hound, the 18th the fox-beagle; these were all the same and all descended from the brachet. The fellhound is its purest modern descendant (but for its considerable dip of greyhound); but the foxhound owes more to the brachet than to any other ancestor.

Mastiffs were still kept as guard-dogs, but their value in hunting disappeared with the wild boar. Greyhounds coursed hare out of half-cut corn, roebuck started out of covert by scenting hounds, and fallow deer in parks. Terriers were used for rabbiting, bolting foxes, and fighting badgers.

English hunting methods were described about 1328, briefly and incompletely, in *Le Art de Venerie le quel Mestre Guyllame Twici, venoeur le Roy d'Engleterre fist*. Twici, Edward II's huntsman, copied a lost French original and added little to the *Chace dou Serf* of seventy-five years before. It is evident that forest deerhunting was exactly like that of France; it is also clear that harehunting, while less noble and less useful for the table, was considered at least as much fun.

Documentary evidence of the next eighty years is confined to France, but it can be applied, with few qualifications, to England. *Le Livre du Roy Modus et de la Royne Racio* is a Norman treatise of about 1338 devoted principally to staghunting. The methods described have not significantly changed, but protocol and ceremony have been elegantly elaborated. Hunt servants, for example, are now divided into *veneurs* (harbourers and huntsmen), *piqueurs* (mounted whippers-in) and *valets de chien*, varlets, foot-servants who hold the coupled hounds at unharbouring and relay, and uncouple them at moments determined by exact new rules. Harehunting *à force*, across country with scenting hounds, is still esteemed. The fox is normally smoked or beaten out of his earth and netted, but sometimes hunted for sport with hounds. In England these must have been the brachets.

Fifty years later Gaston Phébus, comte de Foix, wrote his fascinating and deeply practical *Livre de la Chasse*; it has the additional merit of copious contemporary illustration, vivid and exact, which is as relevant to England as the text. Like all good sportsmen then and since, Gaston was an observant student of natural history, and his pages about the lives and habits of animals were plagiarised even more frequently than the rest of his book. He loved the beauty of nature, especially early on a hunting morning. Staghunting is described in detail, and the details are already quite familiar. Hare- and foxhunting are also fully described, and depicted in some of the most charming of the miniatures. The hare is shown coursed and hunted. One picture shows a wheatfield half cut, strips of standing corn having been left. The hare is beaten out of the crop or the stooks, and huntsmen with crossbows ride after their small greyhounds. The foxhunting pictures – *Comment on doit chascier et prendre le Regnart* – show two horsemen and running *valets*; the former have belted tunics, thigh boots, and rowelled spurs; they ride long, with heavy curb bits and high pique saddles; the footmen have spears or staves, and lead coupled hounds. Horns are a foot to eighteen inches long, natural cow embellished with metal, and carried on a sash over one shoulder. Four or five couple of hounds, variously coloured, are in full cry: they are close to the brush of their fox in a country which is part grass, part covert. Gaston's hounds were as carefully bred and as lovingly looked after as those of Will Goodall himself; although some of his veterinary counsel strikes a chill, his account of kennel design might have been written yesterday.

The almost total relevance of Gaston to England was demonstrated about 1407: Edward Plantagenet, 2nd Duke of York, wrote *The Master of Game* to instruct the future Henry V in the whole art of hunting, and he found it proper (as well as easy) simply to translate Gaston. The only major departures are that the *Master* has harehunting before stag-hunting, as Twici did, which suggests that it was apt to be of greater general interest in England; and it makes no mention of the nets and snares with which Gaston sometimes took deer. This suggests a degree of self-denying sportsmanship which the English 15th century was hardly likely to feel. If deer were not snared in royal circles, they were un-doubtedly so caught in all others: so were hares and rabbits, in their private warrens by the gentry, and there as well as elsewhere by others. Birds of all sizes – even those which scarcely made a mouthful – were limed and netted, and by the sporting gentry as well as by their labourers.

(The liming of small songbirds was still regarded as good sport in the early 19th century.)

(iv) Monks and Ladies

A kind of sporting country gentleman inviting special and dubious mention is the religious. Two large factors pulled in opposite directions. On the one hand, the early Fathers, and a thousand years of popes and bishops, forbade the regular clergy to hunt or keep hounds, and stricter persons continued to think it deplorable in them to do so. On the other hand, the larger communities took a great deal of feeding all through the year, for which reason many houses were given extensive chases within royal forest, and almost all had deerparks; even the estimable Abbot Samson of St Edmondsbury preserved his chase and employed his huntsmen, although he never, says Jocelyn of Brakelond, took part in the chase himself.

The chases provided an irresistible facility, and led to the shameless ignoring of the rules: and in the late 14th century monks were more worldly and secular than ever before. Many dressed as laymen, lived richly, entertained munificently, hunted assiduously. William Langland in *Piers Plowman* describes a monk as:

> A pricker on a palfrey from manor to manor,
> An heap of hounds at his arse as he a lord were.

Chaucer's monk was an 'outrider', his house's estate manager, which gave him the opportunity if not the excuse to behave likewise: he loved hunting, and kept a stable of fine horses and a kennel of hounds. Such unseemly conduct gave Thomas Cromwell ample excuse to dissolve a number of the monasteries which he pillaged for Henry VIII.

Some ladies hunted: perhaps many (*below*). *Roy Modus* suggests there

were plenty of Dianas in 14th-century Normandy. Breviaries show ladies riding astride to hounds, or with their merlins on their wrists. The Wife of Bath sat her ambler easily; since she wore spurs (a pair) she, too, clearly rode cross-saddle. Tapestries and miniatures show ladies assisting at the alfresco feast before a hunt and the gory ceremony of the *curée* after it (though one or more are usually occupied with lovers). Probably many late medieval ladies enjoyed the meet, and a few the run, as in Victorian England.

(v) Hospitality and Hawking

When the prosperous country gentleman wanted to honour a guest, or impress a neighbour, he arranged either a deerhunt in his wooded chase or a course in his park.

The hunt allowed, even demanded, the utmost in display, the most awesome in ceremony. The huntsman, in his new dress of short coat and hose, would make formal presentation of the fewmet of the harboured deer, in the courtyard, to his master; after a solemn colloquy, in which only the most expert or the most indulged dared join, the company mounted small, easy-paced palfreys and proceeded gently to the rendezvous. There the feast would already have been spread, with benches and trestle-tables brought in a cart; its centre would almost certainly be venison pasty, and with enough prevision there would be wine ordered months before from France. (Nothing could be got locally that was not grown or made locally.) Two relays would be placed as experience directed, and to each place varlets would take four or five couple of hounds. After the unharbouring the hunt would take an extremely long time, owing to the denseness of the woods and the melodious unhurriedness of the pack; most of the hunt staff would be on foot throughout. Anyone competent to blow the proper motes on his horn would continually do so – the number of motes had climbed from a necessary minimum of eight or ten to several dozen by 1400, from those which declared at the unharbouring the quality of the stag's attire to the various recheats and to the triumph, death, undoing and quarry. When the stag turned at bay it was the privilege of the highest-ranking person to kill it with his hunting-knife, an honour often graciously delegated. The ceremonial butchery of the undoing was also customarily taken over by a professional, like the gralloch of a stag shot on the hill today. Blood and guts would then be mixed with bread from the pouches of the hunt servants, and given to the hounds *sur le cuir*. Ladies in headdresses which would not have survived overhanging branches would join the party and listen to the concerto of the horns, which not only expressed gratification but also recalled missing hounds. The haunches would be carried home on a packhorse to be roasted or salted, and the head to be mounted over the stable door.

The course was more nearly a spectator sport, though not yet as conveniently arranged as the hunting 'within the toils' beloved of the bloodthirsty renaissance. Fallow-deer, sometimes red also, were kept in the park for the larder. When sport was proposed, brachets started the deer out of the trees and chivvied them into view; two or three brace of greyhounds (never 'couple', because never coupled) were then slipped. The deer were sometimes coursed, sometimes shot, and often shot, wounded, and then coursed. This sport was an indulgence of Edward IV, and it is described in detail by Malory in the *Morte Darthur* (a mine of vivid and unreliable material about 15th-century hunting). Less ceremony was attached to it, but it was convenient, and the quantity of game taken could be prodigious.

After hunt or course, the gentle part of the company would dine: no longer in a reeking great hall, with uncouth retainers lower down the table, but in a tapestried dining room with the fire decently in a chimneyed fireplace. The party would behave with decorum, though not yet sunk to the effeminacy of eating with forks; all present, including the women, would know how to read and write, which must have improved the quality of the discourse. All would stay for the night or many nights, sleeping in beds (having cautiously bathed) and making demure use of new sanitary facilities.

This was the high level of a country gentleman's entertainment, expected of him, and his heaviest expense. But he found his most serious sport, his best loved art, in the skilled mystery of hawking. 'In these dayes', says a 15th-century MS, 'manye gentlemen wil do almoste nothing els, or at the leaste can do that better than any other thing.'

The mews would be in the courtyard, south facing through vertically slatted windows. ('Mews' properly means the quiet, dark place where a hawk is put while it moults, but its use was extended to the whole hawkhouse.) The falconer was a servant as important as the huntsman, though commanding a smaller corps; according to a 14th-century MS he 'must be noe comon drunckarde; he must not be colloricke; he must not be a sluggarde; he must not be a sloven.' Hawks required infinite patience, kindness, cleanliness, long hours, and the delicate treatment of damaged feathers. Their keeper had a pharmacopoeia of medicaments, a workshop of tools, a treasury of bells, swivels, varvels, and the ornate, plume-crowned hoods in their owner's livery which Europe had brought back from the East.

The gentleman might have in his mews (the males are named second): gerfalcon and jerkin, falcon and tiercel (or tassel, tarcel, tiercelet etc.), lanner and lanneret, saker and sakeret, hobby and jack, merlin and jack-merlin, goshawk and tiercel-goshawk, sparrowhawk and musket, and kestrel.

The gerfalcon or gyrfalcon (which turns in a gyre) was the big Greenland, Iceland or Norway falcon, expensive, hard to come by, but well known in England through contact with Scandinavia; most came from Denmark. The falcon (peregrine) was by far the most important hawk to all English falconers; she was flown at grouse, partridge, pheasant, duck, and all but the very biggest other birds, as well as hares and rabbits. Her tiercel's quarry included all smaller birds. The lanner was a little smaller, and imported in large numbers from Italy, Greece and North Africa; she was temperamental but flown very successfully at partridge. The saker, rather larger than the falcon, was almost as much imported as the lanner, though from remoter places in Central Europe and South Asia; she was flown at birds as large as kites, and often at hares. The hobby was sometimes flown at partridges, the jack only at larks. The tiny merlin killed all small birds, including quail and possibly snipe. The goshawk was humbler because her low-flying chase-and-pounce was less beautiful than the mount, gyre and stoop of the long-winged hawks, but she was big, powerful, savage and fast; her feet were often armed. Both she and her still humbler cousin the sparhawk or sparrowhawk were just as effective for the pot. Both were commonly followed on horseback, and brachets were used to drive the game out of covert for them. The purpose of the kestrel was the hawking education of the son of the house; although a true falcon in the naturalist's sense,

GERFALCON

PEREGRINE

MERLIN

HOBBY

GOSHAWK

SPARROWHAWK

it was considered useless for killing game in the field, but could be taught very easily to come to the lure (*below*).

Falconer's Lure: gaudy feathers surrounding a piece of raw meat tied to a block of wood.

The English species were normally let out in time to breed, and the young captured from the nests as eyesses. Adult hawks trapped wild were called haggards (hedge-birds) or passage-hawks, and presented quite different problems to the trainer. The short-winged hawks could be trained to return to the hand, but the long-winged were retrieved after flying by the lure, which was a live bird, dead bird, or imitation bird. Any number of hawks might be taken out; if a cast (two) or more, they were carried on a cadge, a frame of wooden poles. Though a hawking party might be large (as witness many tapestries and pictures), hawking was the frequent sport of the gentleman when he was not entertaining; he went out with a companion or two, his expert staff, a number of markers or beaters, and varlets with coupled brachets. Or, which some most enjoyed, he went out quite alone with a single hawk on his wrist.

It was as necessary as in hunting for a gentleman to master the terms: the large 15th-century manuscript literature of hawking, in all languages including English, is invariably insistent on this point. And the vocabulary grew enormous: no hawk, part of a hawk, natural process, piece of equipment, or phase of the sport was known by the obvious word. As in hunting, this had a good deal to do with the proliferation of books in a socially-mobile age; as in hunting, most of the English books were taken from the French.

(vi) The Sporting Bow

Fleeting mention has been made of shooting. This was barely possible before about 1350, although we can imagine soldiers illicitly shooting parked deer with their military crossbows as Indonesian troops now shoot the amiable orang-utan with Russian automatic rifles, and as North East Kenya is poached by Somali gangs armed with similar weapons. The bow as a sporting piece depended on two completely different technologies, and techniques, both with a military basis.

The longbow had never been a weapon of much importance, its only merit being the speed at which it could be used. But in the 14th century, in England, there was somehow developed a very long unrecurved yew-wood bow with a formidable effective range, a considerable degree of accuracy in the hands of an expert with well-fletched arrows, and disabling or even lethal penetration of man or horse. The levies of Edward III's armies carried this home-made bow (though his mercenaries had crossbows) and won battles by dint of the awesome clouds of arrows they despatched, each man shooting every few seconds. As the learned parson Gilpin explained in *Remarks on Forest Scenery*, 'the Englishman did not keep his left hand steady, and draw his bow with his right; but keeping his right at rest upon the nerve, he pressed the whole weight of his body into the horns of the bow.' Hugh Latimer was later taught 'not to draw with the strength of arm, as divers other nations do, but with the strength of the body.' Early success inspired the statutory ownership of the long-bow by every English yeoman, and competition shoots on every village green: the marks were straw targets at fifty yards and popinjays (*below*),

gaudy artificial birds on poles or in trees. The longbow was not used by gentlemen for sport, but it was most widely used for 200 years by others for poaching.

The crossbow meanwhile grew extremely powerful and accurate, being made of composite materials including whalebone, and even of steel. Various mechanisms – cranks and levers – enabled immensely stiff bows to be bent. The result was a truly formidable weapon, but cumbersome and slow to use. About 1350 a light crossbow with a simple mechanism was developed for sporting use; examples are shown in the illustrations to Gaston Phébus. When used for shooting hares out of standing corn, the arrow was not pointed but a birdbolt (*below*), with a clublike end which knocked down without piercing or lacerating. By perhaps 1400 a sporting crossbow was in every English country gentleman's house, so effective a game-piece that it was limited by law – like hound, snare and net – to persons of property.

The sporting crossbow was used in two ways, respectively comparable to the stalking rifle and the shotgun. In the first case a prowl was attempted in a camouflaged cart or behind a stalking-horse (sometimes real, sometimes two men ludicrously enshrouded as in a pantomime, and requiring close understanding between them). As in deerstalking, the closer the shot and the stiller the quarry the better, and the stalk had to be upwind. Greyhounds were kept in reserve in case a wounded beast ran: a very good system once normal but now unfortunately rare in Scotland. In the other case game was pushed out of covert by hounds (not yet spaniels) and shot running. Many deer, some hares, and a few birds were killed, or at least hit, in this way.

The great value of the sporting crossbow to the country gentleman was that it enabled him to enjoy a day's sport on his estate – and fill his larder – on his own, without giving anybody any warning, without the paraphernalia of hounds and huntsmen: and especially on days when his hawks were in moult or suffering from cramp.

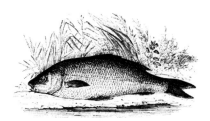

(vii) The Renaissance of Angling

At an uncertain date fishing recovered the sporting esteem it had lost for four centuries. About 1440 the *Treatyse of Fysshynge wyth an Angle* (printed in 1496) was compiled from earlier writings - some French – which suggests a widespread interest.

Everything was home-made. The rod is to have a six-foot butt of hazel or willow, baked in an oven and then dried for a month, the pith taken out with a hot iron: then a yard of white hazel similarly treated: then the top a 'fair shoot' of blackthorn or crab. The butt is banded with iron hoops and the top armed with a noose. The sections are jointed and spliced, but can be taken down: this makes it 'so preuy that ye may walke therwyth: and ther shal noo man wyte where abowte yee goo'. To the noose is looped a horsehair line, coloured and plaited, tapered to a massive nine strands. The hooks are forged, the smallest made from needles, and spliced to the line.

Paste, worms and such are obviously the baits for those fish still caught with such things, but twelve flies are given for trout and grayling. The bodies are of wool of various colours, and the wings taken from specific feathers of various named birds. The dressings remained in regular use for centuries, as they were repeated, often word for word, in much later books, including Walton's.

Fishing continued to have an economic value, which led to strenuous preservation, and to the fining of poachers caught on such important fisheries as that of Romsey Abbey on the Test. It had a special value to the religious, not only as being ennobled by St Peter, but also because it did not disturb, as hunting did, the duty of continual contemplation of divine matters. This points to a fundamental difference between fishing and all other field sports. The heartiest sporting squires have been keen fishermen – Sir Roger de Coverley's neighbour Will Wimble, and a century later those real, very different contemporaries Colonel Peter Hawker in Hampshire and Jack Mytton in Shropshire: but your essential angler is solitary and contemplative, a little despised by the foxhunter and despising him, his enjoyment coming from natural sights and sounds, spiced by triumphs in which he runs no risk and strains no thews. All this is clear in the *Treatyse:* the angler

> schall have his holsom walke and mery at hys owne ease, and also many a sweyt eayr of divers erbis and flowres that schall make hym ryght hongre and well disposed in hys body. He schall heyr the melodies melodious of the ermony of byrde: he schall se also the yong swannes and signetes folowing ther eyrours, duckes, cootes, herons, and many other fowlys with ther brodys, whche me semyt better then all the noyse of houndes, and blastes of hornes and other gamys that fawkners or hunters can make, and yf the angler take the fyssche, hardly then is ther no man meryer then he in his sprites.

Most country gentlemen were much merrier in their spirits riding to hounds, coursing, hawking or shooting.

(viii) Tilt-yard and Tourney

In battle, the armoured knight and his horse became increasingly vulnerable to an arrow from the bow of a single, frail, unarmoured footsoldier: as the tank and its tracks, towards the end of the Second War, were vulnerable to one-man infantry rocket-launchers. The knight armoured his horse, too, which made the two of them almost immobile with weight of metal; heavy medieval cavalry became obsolete during the Hundred Years' War.

But the knight's powerful trotting horse became more rather than less valuable; the magnificent convoluted plate-armour, the emblazoned shield, the fancifully crested helm became more rather than less expensive. The reason was the tremendous 14th-century popularity of tilting as a sport (*below*). It naturally belonged particularly to courts and cities, where permanent grandstands were built above the tilt-yards, and valuable prizes were won; semi-professionals made pothunting tours, palely echoing the knight-errantry of the romances. Special armour was devised and at huge expense constructed, with sharply convex forward surfaces to deflect the point of the lance; a special tilting-helm was used, very large, often cylindrical, resembling an opulent dustbin, heavily padded inside.

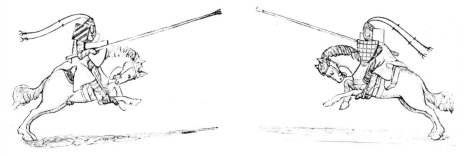

The expense made the tourney a minority sport, like staghunting, but many of the richer country gentry were enthusiasts. Manor-houses had their own jousting-fields, often with small wooden grandstands, and their stables housed a Great Horse or two for this single purpose. Horsemanship was primitive so that much practice was needed (*below*): this was provided by running at the ring and the quintain, a target usually painted like a savage which swivelled and whacked the pupil if he struck it wrongly.

The whole thing died, of expense and irrelevance, but before it did so it inspired the re-invention of scientific horsemanship in renaissance Italy; it also kept the Great Horse alive for the High School of the 17th century.

CHAPTER THREE

Tudor England

(i) The Wealth and Status of the Squire

Through most of the 15th century there were still magnates with great estates, wealth and power. The estates were in parcels spread over several counties, hard to administer and occasioning progresses like those of kings. Most of the wealth derived ultimately from wool; much of it was spent on building, immense households and hunting establishments, and private armies. The power, both central and local, was tremendous, owing to the fragility of the royal government under the Lancastrians and the extent to which the Yorkists had to buy support from their feudatories. Among the greatest magnates were churchmen, whose cloth increased rather than reduced their hold over their own countrysides. Where this state of affairs operated, and while it lasted, the lesser nobility and gentry were severely hampered in their own avid grabbing.

But the Wars of the Roses, and Henry VII's prudent and glamourless government, virtually destroyed the great lay magnates. Private armies disappeared. There was peace in the countryside, and it was the king's peace; the law was the king's law and that of Parliament and Justice. Only in the Borders was peace-keeping still delegated to the lords, until Elizabeth curbed their power and took over their function in 1571. Elsewhere castles were allowed to fall down because they were no longer needed (or proof against gunpowder), and their stones were used for palaces and mansions. Peace and prudence meanwhile allowed a great recovery of trade, and cloth enriched town and country as never before.

Early in the 16th century Reformation was added to Renaissance to transform the face of Europe. In England, as nowhere else, it was peaceful. Doctrinally its effects were tentative and gradual, but economically they were immediate and dramatic. If Henry VIII had been able to keep the lands and wealth of the monasteries he dissolved, he would have given himself a base for a royal power more despotic than any since William Rufus's; but being short of money he sold. Some went to magnates whose own circumstances compelled them to resell; some to speculators who bought for resale. The beneficiaries were the landed gentry and yeomanry, who within less than a century had absorbed the whole of the ecclesiastical holdings.

In these conditions of new wealth, new peace, the fragmentation of great estates, more townsmen than ever moved out to the country and more yeoman than ever moved from farmhouse to manor. John Winchcomb, 'Jack of Newbury' of the ballad, was a clothier who had founded a county family by the time he died in 1520. For him and his like a coat of arms was not expensive. 'As for gentlemen,' said Sir Thomas Smith in 1583, 'they be made good cheape in England.' Nicholas Bacon's father had been sheepreeve to the Abbey of Bury St Edmund's; Nicholas went into politics by way of law, becoming Elizabeth's first Lord Keeper, and ended owning most of the farms his father had managed for the brethren. His son Francis noted (in the essay *Of Kingdoms*) that 'the device of king Henry the seventh . . . was profound and admirable: in making farms, and houses of husbandry, of a standard; that is, maintained with such a proportion of land unto them, as may breed a subject to live in convenient plenty'. Tudor policy, as well as woollen cloth, peace, destruction of great estates, dissolution of monasteries and social mobility, was fighting for squire and yeoman.

Bacon, interpreting this policy, said that its merit was military: and William Harrison's supplement to Holinshed's *Chronicles* (1586) remarked that every village in the realm could raise a posse of archers (*overleaf*), pikemen, and at least one 'gunner' with caliva or arquebus. From 1557 this territorial army was under the command of the Lord Lieutenant of the county. Elsewhere (*Of Empire*) Bacon urges reliance on the 'second nobles'; 'There is not much danger from them, being a body dispersed. They may sometimes discourse high, but that doth

little hurt: besides, they are a counterpoise to the higher nobility, that they grow too potent: and lastly, being the most immediate in authority with the common people, they do best temper popular commotions.' The central government deliberately used them in this role instead of, as in France, sending out officials to hear local disputes and keep local peace. The Elizabethan J.P. carried out royal policy (to which, as M.P., he had often subscribed), administered petty justice, and was the local government in regard to the Poor Law and the regulation of wages and prices. Although he was awesome locally, his hands were tied by statute and he was far less whimsical and arbitrary than the 18th-century Justice.

The squire was therefore not an ogre in the countryside: not even, in all cases, when he enclosed. 'Sheep,' said Sir Thomas More, contrasting England with Utopia,

'which are naturally mild, and easily kept in order, may be said now to devour men, and unpeople, not only villages, but towns . . . the nobility and gentry, and even those holy men the abbots, not content with the old rents which their farms yielded, nor thinking it enough that they, living at their ease, do no good to the public, resolve to do it hurt instead of good. They stop the course of agriculture . . . and enclose grounds that they may lodge their sheep in them. As if forests and parks had swallowed up too little of the land, those worthy countrymen turn the best inhabited places in solitudes.

Francis Bacon endorsed this view late in the century, being 'vehement in parliament against depopulation and inclosures'.

It is true that many peasant holdings were amalgamated into viable farms, by means of a purchase price the peasant could not refuse, which created classes of landless labourers, new townsmen and sturdy beggars. But much reclamation of waste and reorganization by fencing of open field was done with the full cooperation of the villagers, who equally profited from more efficient farming. Polydore Virgil said in Henry VII's reign:

> Almost the third part of England is uncultivated, and possessed only by stags, deer, or wild goats; which last are found chiefly in the northern parts. Rabbits too abound everywhere. You everywhere meet with vast forests, where these wild beasts range at large; or with parks secured by pales. Hunting is the principal amusement of all the people of distinction.

The countryside has been compared to an archipelago – thousands of little civilized islands in a sea of waste and wilderness. It profited everybody to cut down trees for ships and smelting, and to increase the nation's available pasture. The scale of enclosure of open field and of grazed common and waste was, *pace* More, pretty small: there was an immense amount left for the late Georgian landowners to grab.

In one regard the Tudor squire took on an ogreish aspect, following the precedent set in the late 14th century when he first emerged. The statute I Henry VII ch. 7 re-enacted that 'unlawful Hunting by Night, or with painted Faces' was a felony. V Elizabeth ch. 11 enacted, 'He who enters a *Park* to *chase* Deer, without the *Licence of the Owner*, must suffer three Months Imprisonment, and be bound for his Good Behaviour for seven Years.' The squires' game was protected by the squires' statute: but the penalties were mild indeed compared to continental Europe, or to England in 1820.

In earlier and later times there was enmity between town and country – the one was taxed to subsidise the other owing to the composition of Parliament; the 19-century squire despised trade – but in Tudor times there was no such feeling. Hundreds of village monuments record squires who were proud of their mercantile origins; because of the priceless historical accident of primogeniture, younger sons went into trade or the professions and rejoined the country gentry only when they bought their own estates. This had evident cultural as well as economic and political results; the Tudor squire was not always uncouthly isolated among his sheep and hounds. Relations between squire and burgher, as between squire and yeoman, were far more relaxed than on the continent for another reason: a very small minority of the gentry was noble. And most of the lords were new men, risen in the royal service from the ranks of gentry and lawyers. This explains the absence of another divisive factor much noticed abroad at the time and in England later: foppishness, court manners, were derided and detested even at court. Shakespeare continually said so, and he depended on the patronage of the court; Francis Bacon continually said so, and he was a successful courtier. The gentry were not at odds with their contemporaries sideways, downwards or upwards.

Joining the gentry, from beside or below, involved acquiring certain skills as well as a coat of arms. 'It becomes a gentleman,' said Richard Pace in *De Fructu* (1525), 'to be adept at blowing hunting horns, to be skilful in the chase, and elegantly to train and carry a hawk. The study of letters should be left to the sons of rustics.' The socially ambitious had to learn what bastard French phrase to shout to their new hounds, and what mysterious names to give the feathers and accoutrements of their new hawks. This explains the enduring popularity of the *Boke of St Albans*, produced by the 'schoolmaster-printer' in 1486, and unconvincingly ascribed to a lady called Dame Juliana Berners or Barnes; the *Boke*'s little treatises on hunting, hawking and heraldry are manuals of behaviour and terminology, not of technique: and the *Boke* was consequently reprinted far more than any other work of its time except the Bible. Gentlemen began to wear swords during the 16th century, and to fight duels instead of calling up a gang of servants; fencing – a new art imported from Italy and later France – became another thing a probationary gentleman had to learn.

The study of letters was not wholly left to the sons of rustics. The sons of the gentry were still sent for their education to the houses of greater nobles – a custom dead on the continent, and deplored for its unnatural cruelty, as English public schools still are, and may be for a few more years; Sir Thomas Cockaine, a substantial Derbyshire squire, spent his youth in the household of the Earl of Shrewsbury: he learned sport and manners, and literacy if not deep scholarship. But this practice was dying in England too, and by 1600 it was more usual to have a tutor and then to send your son to a university. Certain books were immensely influential during the century: the *De Civilitate* of Erasmus (1526); *The Courtyer* (1561), Sir Thomas Hoby's translation of Baldessare Castiglione's *Il Corteggiano* (1528): but scholarship was not highly regarded among the gentry. Ben Jonson *(Everyman in his Humour)* echoed Pace: 'Why you know, an a man have not skill in the hawking and hunting languages now-a-days, I'll not give a rush for him; they are more studied than the Greek or the Latin.' G. M. Trevelyan concludes that most squires read very little but a few read a great deal.

(ii) Comforts of the Manor

The prosperity of the landed gentleman and yeoman grew and grew throughout the 16th century; it showed itself, especially in the second half of Elizabeth's reign, in an immensely higher standard of living.

How a Kennel ought to be situated and Trimmed for Hounds: from Tuberville's
The Book of Falconrie and Hunting, 1611.

This was visible above all in the manor house itself. Thousands were built, many incorporating masonry and lead from ruined abbeys, more and more of brick. Half timbering remained usual where there were plenty of trees. Good glass, previously imported, was manufactured domestically in Elizabeth's time, and windows as well as ceilings grew high. No fortifications being needed, light and air came in from all sides instead of only from a closed and defensible courtyard. Assured peace also allowed stables and kennels *(above)* to be built well away from the house, an arrangement recommended by Bacon *(Of Building)* and probably usual. There were many more chimneys; in the grates much more coal was burnt. Ceilings were decorated with plasterwork, walls with tapestry and panelling, on which pictures were beginning to hang. Silver and pewter appeared on tables instead of wood, and the gentry used forks. Fabrics became richer and furniture more comfortable, partly as great quantities of both were imported, partly as domestic imitations of foreign luxuries were made. Lords 'peradventure lay seldom in a bed of down or whole feathers' in William Harrison's father's time, but by 1586 they slept in well stuffed four-posters. Some houses were even plumbed: 'When Sir Nicholas Bacon the lord keeper lived, every room in Gorhambury was served with a pipe of water from the ponds, distant about a mile off.'

(iii) Deerhunting in Forest, Park and Toil

The wild red deer had been largely removed from large parts of England because of its destructiveness; more than any other beast it also suffered from four centuries of energetic poaching. Hunting it at force with hounds was, according to George Gascoigne in about 1575, 'A sport for noble peeres, a sport for gentle bloods'; it was very expensive, not from technical necessity but because of the display, retinue and feast which custom required. Method as well as manner was still French, with lymer and relays and elaborate language of the horn. No rules now restricted stag-hunting to 'noble peeres', but increasing rarity and continuing lavishness effectively did so.

There were exceptions, areas where plentiful red deer were hunted informally by the gentry and their tenants. The most notable was North Devon. Exmoor was still royal forest in Elizabeth's reign, and Mr Hugh Pollard, the ranger, kept a pack of royal hounds at Simonsbath. These were the lemon-pies, of French royal origin, which remained the Devon and Somerset Staghounds until their dispersal in 1825. The breed greatly influenced other North Devon kennels including, no doubt, that of Mr Coffin of Portledge; with these hounds (in Kingsley's *Westward Ho*) Amyas Leigh and his friends hunted 'a hart of grease' about 1580. (Leigh is a fictional squire almost as informative as Western or Sir Roger; he was literate but little and locally educated; he spoke broad Devonshire; he was a member of the 'best society' of old North Devon families; he was horseman, falconer, angler, archer, jouster, and expert in the new French game of fencing.) Sir Thomas Cockaine's Derbyshire staghounds were probably more nearly Talbot (*below*); he laid on ten couple and kept five for a relay, a small pack by any standards, to which rode small fields of neighbours.

These staghunting squires started at five in the morning in late summer. Sir Philip Sidney's Kalander (in *Arcadia*) says that 'the sun (however great a journey soever he had to make) could never prevent him with earliness, nor the moon, with her sober countenance, dissuade him from watching till midnight for the deer's feeding'. According to an old hunting song (quoted in Nares's *Glossary*):

> The hunt is up, the hunt is up,
> And now it is almost day;
> And he that's abed with another man's wife
> It's time to get him away.

An alternative to the normal method of deerhunting was proposed by Sir Thomas Elyot (in *The Governour*, 1531) who recommended using the hounds only as tufters and riding down the game in the Persian fashion:

> In the huntyng of redde dere and falowe mought be a great part of semblable exercise, used by noblemen, specially in forestis which be spaciouse, if they wold use but a fewe nombre of houndes, onely to harborowe or rouse the game; and by their yornyng to gyve knowlege which way it fleeth; the rememant of the disporte to be in pursuying with javelyns and other waipons in maner of warre.

This method was in fact widely used, as it always had been, but in parks rather than 'forestis'.

Parks, once the subject of special royal grant to privileged nobles and abbeys, were by the 16th century attached to every considerable manor-house. There were often two, for red and fallow; the purpose, as always, was sport and food. Fynes Moryson, just after Elizabeth's death, remarked that 'England, yea perhaps one County thereof, hath more fallow deer than all Europe'. They were nearly all in parks, and nearly all ended in venison pasties, to which there was no continental equivalent. The parks were either converted demesne farm or enclosed common. If the latter, it was less often a cause of genuine local misery than was the creation of a new sheep-walk, but it caused greater ill feeling.

> My lord of Leicester, favourite to queen Elizabeth, [remembers Bacon] was making a large chace about Cornbury Park, meaning to enclose it with posts and rails; and one day was casting up his charge what it would come to. Mr. Goldingham, a free-spoken man, stood by, and said to my lord, 'Methinks your lordship goeth not the cheapest

way to work.' 'Why, Goldingham?' said my lord. 'Marry, my lord,' said Goldingham, 'count you but on the posts, for the country will find you railing.'

Parked fallow deer were usually coursed or shot: 'Kylling of dere with bowes or grehundes serveth well for the potte,' said Elyot with contempt. But they were sometimes hunted, and to this chase belongs the earliest use (by Cockaine) of the word 'tufter'. Roe were unlodged by a lymer and hunted with a single relay.

An exotic method of deerhunting had a limited vogue in the second half of the century: hunting 'within the toil'. This was first described in English by George Cavendish, who accompanied Wolsey on an embassy to France and wrote, about 1530, a *Life* of the Cardinal. The toil was a semicircular screen on the edge of a forest, up to which were drawn carriages and into which was driven game. Guests could thus go hunting without leaving their seats. In France the participants tackled boar *dedans les toiles* at genuine personal risk; in the English version – at Hampton Court, Kenilworth, and a few other places – fallow deer were hunted by bassets into the range of crossbows or the sight of greyhounds. At best it was something like a bullfight; at worst it resembled the orgy of slaughter which the Germans confuse with sport.

(iv) Harehunting and Coursing

Outside their parks, for sport behind hounds, the vast majority of the gentry already depended on the hare. Every squire of sporting tastes kept a cry of harehounds, mostly of the blue-mottled sort derived from the Gascon. Their merit was cry, nose, slow line-hunting, and indifference to blood; they could be followed by a nervous man on a placid horse (or on foot), and they could be stopped from their quarry by pole or voice. It was as normal as at any later period for a gentleman to ride to his harehounds surrounded by tenants and tradesmen: and harehunting was cheap enough, notes Gervase Markham, to be 'easilie and equalie distributed, as well to the wealthy farmer as to the great gentleman'.

Hare coursing in open country remained as popular as ever, and ownership of greyhounds (*below*) was freed from all its medieval limitations. As many squires owned sight- as scenting-hounds, and it was to them that their wives and daughters commonly rode. Bustards were also coursed.

'The Hare Dog': a coursing greyhound, drawn by Dr Caius, 1603.

A new sport – probably as foreign as the toil, but from Spain rather than France – was codified in Elizabeth's reign: competition 'paddock coursing'. This was a race between greyhounds after a deer down a screened avenue a mile long; prizes were large and betting heavy. One can imagine few squires setting up a mile-long alley in their own parks, but many entering their greyhounds in courses in the 'paddocks' of great houses. The dogs were carefully trained and most carefully fed, and for many gentlemen the sport was a betting medium at least as hazardous as the turf.

(v) Fox, Badger, Otter and Rabbit

The fox was still a cunning and treacherous thief, to be killed how you might. Spade, smoke, net, trap and terrier were all used almost everywhere.

But as early as 1531 Sir Thomas Elyot said, 'I dispraise nat the huntynge of the foxe with rennynge hounds . . . it wolde be used in the deepe wynter, whan the other game is unseasonable.' George Turberville (*The Noble Art*, 1576) also hunted the fox from January to March – above ground, having stopped the earths – in the absence of other sport; he normally coursed it with greyhounds, having tufted it with hounds, because his bassets and bloodhounds were too slow for it. To Gervase Markham the scent of the fox as of the badger was 'stinking' and too easy for hounds; he used 'shag-haired' hounds – evidently Welsh – which he followed on foot in covert. Thomas Blundeville, a Norfolk squire, also hunted the fox on foot in his woods.

Elizabethan foxhound: from the title page of Sir Thomas Cockaine's *Short Treatise on Hunting*, 1591.

This lukewarm attitude to foxhunting was usual but not universal. William Harrison records that in 1586 there were a few places where both fox and badger were 'preserved by gentlemen to hunt and have pastime withal'; elsewhere they were 'rooted out'. Sir Thomas Cockaine does not say (in his *Short Treatise* of 1591) if he preserved foxes in Derbyshire, but he did hunt them there for most of the second half of the 16th century. His 'small Ribble hounds' (*above*) were bred specially for fox and entered solely to it. His walking and cubhunting were conducted in the modern fashion; the only oddity is that his pack went to the covertside in couples, and were only uncoupled when 'the trailers of an olde Foxe and finders of him' had him unkennelled. Cockaine expects his reader to have foxhunting neighbours: the beginner is to borrow a couple of old foxhounds, from a local gentleman or yeoman, for his cubhunting. In fact, over most of England, no neighbour would have had such a thing.

The badger was not considered to reek as pungently as the fox, but it was still easy for hounds to find. It was almost always tackled underground by strong terriers.

The otter was much more authentically destructive and much harder to kill. About 1545 Sir Henry Savile of Sothill, Yorkshire, complained in a letter to his cousin that otters 'do me exceeding great harm in divers places. My folks see them daily, and I cannot kill them: my hounds be not used to them.' He had to send for a professional otter-killer. Other gentlemen whose estates included rivers with desirable fishing went otterhunting with three breeds: the otter's drag was hunted up to the holt by Southern hounds, it was bolted by terriers, and it was tackled by lurchers. Most otters were probably not killed by hounds at all, but by the spear, used when the quarry vented. True otterhounds were almost certainly confined to Wales; if Sir Henry Savile's hounds were Northern, not Southern or Welsh, it is doubtful if they could ever have been entered successfully to otter.

Rabbits were here and there a scourge in the new formal gardens which extended the amenities of manor-houses. They were attacked with terriers, smoke, traps and ferrets; it is impossible to doubt that the squire's sons had as much fun with their ferrets as their descendants did.

(vi) Racehorse and Great Horse

Apart from hunting, there were three sorts of horse-sport which occupied the Tudor gentry: racing, the High School, and jousting.

At the beginning of the Tudor period the English horse was in a bad state, and suitable for none of these activities. The Wars of the Roses had reduced the number, and the remainder were ineptly bred, stallions being allowed to run haphazardly with mares to produce all kinds of ill-assorted hybrids. Many of these were too small. Henry VII and VIII tackled this situation with legislation. The export of horses was forbidden; stallions under thirteen hands were forbidden to run with mares (in pony breeding areas like Devon the bottom limit was twelve hands); and all men of rank were obliged to keep horses of potential cavalry value.

Henry VIII also imported horses on a considerable scale, especially from Francesco Gonzaga, marchese di Mantova, and from Spain. In this as in his breeding policy he was followed by a large number of individuals; by Elizabeth's reign many horses of many types came annually to England. Harrison in 1586 noted 'Such outlandish horses as are daily brought over unto us . . . as the genet of Spain, the courser of Naples, the hobbie of Ireland, the Flemish roile, and Scottish nag.' The jennet was the part Barb Andalusian, the European horse then most nearly resembling the thoroughbred; the courser was the pre-eminent heavy cavalry horse; the hobby, Spanish-descended, was a dainty little horse, often a natural ambler, ideal for travel and hawking; the Flemish was a heavy horse, used in the town coaches which, in imitation of the queen, a few grand persons were having built, and also beginning to replace the ox for draught; the nag was very like the hobby: known latterly as the Galloway it was the principal racehorse until Eastern stallions created a new breed.

A sporting squire of reasonable means would have had in his stable the coursers required of him by law, and needed for the tilt-yard; hunting geldings; ambling nags or hobbies for hawking; pack-horses; perhaps stalking-horses; latterly heavy draught-horses; and, increasingly, running-geldings which were racehorses. He would, by 1600, have bred them selectively and to their own kind only, fed them carefully, and been aware of specialised schooling and training.

Racing as we know it began in Henry VIII's reign, in three ways: at court, in towns, and among country gentry.

The king kept his racehorses at Greenwich and ran them mostly in matches at Hampton Court. (His sport is copiously if incompletely documented in the Wardrobe Accounts.) With few exceptions, English monarchs have raced horses ever since. Like many of his subjects, Henry was hotly competitive and liked betting; his example undoubtedly stimulated match-racing for wagers throughout the kingdom.

The first town to establish municipal racing was Chester, which made the decision in 1511 and put it into operation an uncertain number of years later. Rich townsmen may have owned the first few runners on the Roodeye, but the gentlemen of the neighbouring countryside provided them soon and always. Chester's example was followed in Elizabeth's reign by a number of towns including Croydon, Salisbury, Carlisle, Richmond (Yorkshire), Doncaster and Boroughbridge. Initially the finance came from corporations and guilds, but increasingly the races relied on subscriptions as well as horses from the neighbouring gentry.

There were also races got up by the gentry without a municipality being involved at all. Such were Kiplingcotes, Galtres and Sapley. '6

April 1602,' recorded an anonymous diarist. 'This day there was a race at Sapley neere huntingdon: invented by the gents of that Country: at this Mr. Oliver Cromwell's horse won the syluer bell: And Mr. Cromwell had the glory of the day.' (He was the uncle of the namesake who spent his time less innocently.)

It is not at all certain that the Elizabethan squire bred a horse specially for racing, but he did feed and train it in order to win wagers from his neighbours. In his *Masterpiece*, Gervase Markham advised boiled raisins and dates, aniseed, liquorice and sugar-candy as well as the normal diet of dry bread, oats, beans, hay and short grass. In *The Complete Jockey* the same writer recommended readying a horse for a race with eight or ten weeks strong work for a gross horse, six for a lean one, with two gallops a week. The owner rode his own horse, and in jockeyship Markham advised him:

> Now I shall give you another instruction worth observing, that is, the day you are designed to run the Race when you come within a mile or less of the starting gate or post for that purpose assigned; take off his cloaths, which being done clap your Saddle upon his Back sending some person, with his cloaths to the end of the Race intended, and ride him on gently until you come to the weighing or starting post; show him the post, and make him as far as he is capable, sensible of what he is designed for to be done withal.
>
> The Signal for the start being given put him on or near three quarters speed, or if his Strength will allow it more, but be sure you put him not to more than he is able to perform, hold the Rains pretty streight in your hand but by no means check him in his Course, but let him run on chearfully and give him all the encouragement you can, and so let him run the whole Race through.
>
> If you, during the Course find his strength to fail him, or that he begin to yield, give him what ease you can and do not force him to two [*sic*] great a swiftness, but use him so that he may be at all times well-pleased with his courses and free to run on.

There is clearly, in this race, not only a starting and a finishing post, but also a rule about fixed weights which involves weighing out and in. But there were other races between neighbours, of unguessable place and frequency, in which there were no rules, weights, or fixed marks, and the wager was often a quartern of oats or a cow.

Gervase Markham's 'Perfect Saddle', about 1600.

Except perhaps in Spain, where a Saracen tradition survived, European horsemanship was everywhere clumsy and inept in 1500. Soon after this date Frederico Grisone began teaching in Naples, and to his school came gentlemen from all over Europe, including a few from England. One of these was Robert Alexander, who went home to become Henry VIII's riding master at Hampton Court. What he taught startled the English; his horsemanship was 'the most honourable exercise' to Sir Thomas Elyot in 1531. The effect was elegant and noble, but the methods were cruel: whips and cudgels were used to break the horse's spirit, and curbs with 15-inch arms to jam his chin onto his chest.

The horse involved was the massive trotter – Neapolitan, Burgundian or Flemish – which had carried thirty stone of knight in armour, which was now of no military use, but which in the early 16th century all gentlemen were obliged by law to keep. Most continued to keep them in the late 16th century for the tilt-yard, and some for the riding-school also. Grisone's own book, *Gli Ordini di Cavalcare* (1550) was several times plagiarised in English, notably by Thomas Blundeville in *The fower chiefest offices belonging to Horsemanshippe, That is to saye, the office of the Breeder, of the Rider, of the Keeper, and of the Ferrer* (first part 1565); Blundeville expounded the merciless precision of Grisone's method to a readership of squires, who mostly still owned horses of the appropriate kind, and many of whom toyed with his techniques in extemporised *cavallerizze*.

The manorial tilt-yard itself remained in use, but the lances were aimed at rings and quintains (*above*) rather than living opponents.

(vii) Hawk, Crossbow and Gun

The sports so far described were all communal, but even the festive Elizabethans went off by themselves in their fields and woods to take game. They used hawks, crossbows and guns.

Falconry in England, like staghunting, was conducted almost wholly in imitation of the continent, and all advances in it were learned from abroad. Elizabeth's subjects imported from Italy new refinements in the art, as they imported fantastical clothes and scientific horsemanship: the most comprehensive writer on falconry was Turberville, who relied on Italian originals as heavily as did Blundeville when writing about horses. There were also, however, a number of domestic treatises of equal practical value and less pretension, such as the MS of 1575 called *A Perfect Booke for Kepinge of Sparhawkes or Goshawkes* (addressed by

'How necessary a thing a Spaniell is to Falconrie': Turberville, *The Book of Falconrie and Hunting*, 1611.

'How one may catch all kinds of Birds with Hawks and Nets': engraving by J. A. Lonicer, 1584.

definition, at least in theory, to the yeoman rather than the gentleman). For a squire to carry a falcon as he rode about his land had always been usual; in Elizabeth's time it was practically universal. It was pothunting as well as sport: Squire Cary of Clovelly took a leash of partridges out of two coveys while he did his morning's tour of the 'housefarm'.

The crossbow was dead as a weapon of war, but it remained important in sport (*above*). It killed a lot of deer in parks, some hares, and a few sitting birds. By the end of the century it was being rapidly and permanently replaced by the gun.

Gunpowder and cannon were first used in the 13th century, the handgun (its powder fired by a hot coal) in the 14th. The matchlock was invented in the 15th: 'match' meant fuse; originally a glowing fuse was thrust onto the powder, then a trigger lowered it. Competition target-shooting with matchlocks (*opposite, 1*) was a popular sport in various parts of Europe in the early 16th century, and may have penetrated England. The wheellock (*opposite, 2*) was invented in Nuremburg in 1515; its mechanism produced a shower of sparks by means of

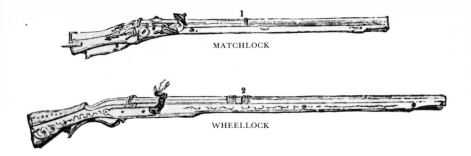

MATCHLOCK

WHEELLOCK

friction (as do some of the less satisfactory types of cigarette lighter) some of which with luck landed on the charge. It was expensive, and therefore from the beginning a sporting rather than a military weapon. A few came to England in Henry VIII's reign, and they and the match-locks killed many deer and a few birds with single lumps of lead.

In the second quarter of the century 'hail-shot' became available to the English sportsman and poacher (*below*), so much more lethal to birds than a single pellet that a statute of 1549 enacted thus: 'Whereas . . . there is grown a customable manner of shooting of hail-shot, where-by an infinite sort of fowl is killed and much game thereby destroyed to

the benefit of no man . . . be it therefore enacted that no person under the degree of Lord in Parliament shall henceforth shoot with any hand-gun at any fowl.' This statute was widely ignored, and when Mistress Ford's husband in *The Merry Wives* went 'a-birding' it was probably hail-shot he discharged.

The snaphaunce, which substituted concussion of steel on flint for the less predictable friction of the wheel, is said to have been invented for, or even by, Dutch poachers in the late 16th century. It quickly developed into the first flintlock, which remained, essentially unchanged, the sporting gun of the English squire, and of everybody else, for over two hundred years.

Gun Dogs: 'Perfect Water Dogge' and 'The forme and proportion of the Setting Dogge': from Gervase Markham's *Art of Fowling*, 1621.

(viii) Fishing

Fishing as a sport had been re-invented in the late middle ages; it remained a minority enthusiasm throughout the Tudor period and made, more quietly, technical advances like those recorded in foxhunting, falconry and shooting.

To most people what mattered was the table; this was true all over Europe. Italy and Germany produced large numbers of books on husbandry and country life, and nearly all included sections on fishing (French books of similar type tended to ignore the subject, which is surprising); what was described was the management of stews. When Edmund Spenser said of the fish of the Thames (in *Epithalamion*)

'Those trouts and pikes all others doo excell' he was talking gastro-
nomically rather than sportingly.

But the spirit of the 15th-century *Treatyse* lived on among a minority,
for whom Leonard Mascall published *A Booke of Fishing with Hooke &
Line* in 1590. Much of it follows the *Treatyse* – including the fly patterns
– but there are notable developments. The Elizabethans fished fine:
the massive nine-strand horsehair point has shrunk to three strands or
even one. Flies are sometimes given cork bodies, presumably to float
them. Double hooks have been invented. Most interesting of all, Mascall
shows that Elizabethan fishing proprietors had transferred to their
rivers the skills of stocking and preservation which they had learned from
their stew-ponds. The gentry had been preserving wild deer and breeding parked deer for centuries; from the mid 16th century they were preserving pheasant and partridge, previously taken freely by the humble
as creatures of warren; by 1580 a few were preserving foxes and
badgers for hunting; by 1590 they were stocking their trout-streams. A
modern attitude to the sporting estate has become, here and there,
almost complete.

(ix) Diversions of House and Garden

Outdoor games were subject to rigid social classification, as were dances
and clothes.

The grandee's game was tennis, a late medieval importation from
France. There were very few courts outside London, and those few
were attached to royal hunting boxes or to the houses of courtiers who
had learned the game at Hampton Court. At the opposite extreme,
handball, football and hockey were played everywhere, following or
breaking a thousand local codes of rules, under the patronage but never
with the participation of the squire. Elyot said football was 'Nothyng
but beastely fury and extreme violence, whereof proceedeth hurte, and
consequently rancour and malice.' (Few remarks of the 1530s are so
perfectly applicable to the 1970s.) More, in *Utopia*, linked football,
tennis and quoits with dice, cards and 'tables' as pursuits 'in which
money runs fast away': from which it appears that Tudor gentry betted
as well as patronised or played. Wrestling had even more various rules:
with running, and throwing the stone or 'barre', it was another large
medium of betting.

Almost every Tudor manor had a bowling green. The game had

become popular among the great in the 13th century, and among towns-men in the 14th (the first recorded municipal bowling green was Southampton's, in use in 1299). From manor and corporation the game spread to taverns, thousands of which had greens in the 15th century; by the 16th this amenity was accused, credibly enough, of encouraging idleness, drinking and wagering.

A sport of the humble revived among the gentle was archery. This was apparently the personal achievement of Roger Ascham, a scholar appointed by Henry VIII as tutor to the future Queen Elizabeth. According to Dr Johnson, he took up the longbow at Cambridge, purely as recreation; his book *Toxophilus*, the only treatise on the subject in English until the late 19th century, recognizes the sporting and competitive aspect.

Both cock-fighting and skittles were ancient; for both Henry VIII was enthusiastic; Westminster had a cockpit and most of the king's houses had skittle-alleys. The king was imitated in both regards at a few country houses: but skittles joined bowls at taverns, for wet-weather carousing, and while every country town came to have a cockpit, only a small minority of private houses ever did.

CHAPTER FOUR

The Stewarts

(i) *The Squire under the Early Stewarts*

Between the death of Elizabeth and the outbreak of the Civil War England saw large changes at the top and in the centre of things. The Stewart kings and their greatest servants tried to change the position of the crown in the constitution, and thus destroyed the consensus with which the Tudors had governed. Puritanism arrived with black coat, steel buckles and canting voice. The Church of England acquired its glorious literature and liturgy, envied by the whole Christian world (but now replaced by a drab modernism designed by the smallminded for the benefit of the illiterate). Domestic letters and imported painting sustained their Tudor magnificence. But in the countryside very little changed, and the life of the country gentleman was that of his father and grandfather.

Part of the reason was negative: there was no Fronde in England. The countryside remained peaceful, and the peace was kept by unpaid Justices. The gentry could afford the burden of local government partly because the laws they administered benefited themselves, they having helped to make them; partly because they continued prosperous. They feathered their own nests, but without scandalous rapacity, and in interpreting the laws of game, trespass, wage and price they still allowed themselves to be bound by statute. They were thus a stabilising factor of immense importance, and were so perceived by James I as clearly as by Henry VII:

King James [said Bacon] was wont to be very earnest with the country gentlemen to go from London to their country houses. And sometimes he would say thus to them, 'Gentlemen, at London you are like ships at sea, which show like nothing; but in your country villages you are like ships in a river, which look like great things.'

The ethos of these great things in their country villages was sympathetically explored by Richard Brathwaite in his *English Gentleman and English Gentlewoman* of 1630. Brathwaite represented what he described: he was born in Westmorland, studied at Oriel College, Oxford, was called to the bar, and settled down as gentleman and Justice at Catterick, Yorkshire. He was insistent, like the king, that the gentleman and his wife should spend far more time at their own place among their own neighbours, their tenants and servants, than in the city where they were idle, extravagant, and without importance. Their virtues were honesty, good nature, compassion, tolerance, their duties hospitality and charity; they were also to admire the beauties of nature. The lady's 'constant reside is in the country, where hospitality proclaims her in-bred affection for the workes of piety. The open fields she makes her gallery'. As in Tudor society, a natural manner was admired, devoid of cringing or of arrogance, free of the foreign mode of foppish artificiality. Moderation was urged in dress and wine, and also in hunting and shooting: too great a devotion to field sports weakened the brain. (Hawking, for reasons apparently personal, Brathwaite derided: he warned his reader not to become 'besotted' with it.)

The worst state, to Brathwaite, was idleness, which was a major reason for preferring country to city life: but what a gentleman did to occupy his time was up to him and to his taste and personality. There was room for infinite individuality; although the great majority of country gentlemen were sportsmen, those eccentrics were tolerated who spent their time in study, observatory, herbarium or cowhouse. In his manner towards the world, as in the way he spent his energy, a gentleman was to be true to himself, to ape no one, to act and speak as his authentic self; in this philosophy Brathwaite and his readers agreed exactly with Montaigne, himself followed much later by la Rochefoucauld and Voltaire. The French essayists wrote against a context of an unremittingly artificial society orbiting slavishly round a court; they yearned for the natural manners and vigorous independence of the English country gentleman.

Continued prosperity showed in continued building, in a style in which opulence was apt to be made a little more obvious. The courtyard went behind the house instead of between the wings which fronted it, so that a formal and even a pompous façade was offered to the world. There was much more panelling, decorated with many more pictures; statuary invaded country houses; ceilings were lavishly, and sometimes unhappily, embellished with heavier plasterwork. The garden, following continental models in its geometric hedges and parterres, was more than before a part of the scheme of the house; a large number of the exotics still commonplace in English gardens were introduced in the first two Stewart reigns.

Manor-houses of any size were still almost totally self-sufficient in their day-to-day needs – they had to be – although luxuries such as wine and tapestries still came from London or from France. The Tudor gentry – not, perhaps, the richest – made extensive use of their local inns for entertaining, taking a private room and moving into it after dinner; the reason was probably the superiority of the landlord's wine. Both William Harrison and twenty years later Fynes Moryson describe this custom, and both remark on the excellence of many of the inns. This remained the practice of 17th-century squires in some areas, and of some squires in all areas; the major drawback lay in the fact that the inn's staff was often in league with footpads. The inn's wine aside, the manor fed itself; the letters of various members of the Verney family of Claydon, Buckinghamshire, show that their farms, mills, creameries and gardens provided what appeared on the table. Meat was still salted after the autumn slaughtering (there was no technique for feeding stock during the winter except for a breeding nucleus); this kept in undiminished importance the stewpond and dovecote, the decoy for waterfowl, the partridge-net, snare, hawk and 'long gun'. Penshurst, Kent (in Ben Jonson's ode) got its deer from 'Gamage's Copps', 'When thou would'st feast, or exercise thy friends.' On Penshurst's lower ground were bullocks, calves and cows; on its middle ground the horses and mares, with rabbits in the banks; its woods and hills

provide
The purpled pheasant, with the speckled side:
The painted patrich lyes in every field,
And, for thy messe, is willing to be kill'd.

(ii) The Gentry in Civil War and Commonwealth

The Civil War did a good deal of damage to a number of country estates, especially to deer-parks and stables. The latter continued to be pillaged under the Commonwealth: John Evelyn noted in his diary (speaking of July 1650) that 'the country was much molested by soldiers, who took away gentlemen's horses for the service of the State, as then called'. But on the whole the life of the countryside and its resident gentry went on much as before; the royalist gentry kept their heads down, took no part in the political life of the country, and left local government to the Major Generals and their officers. Very few estates changed hands because of the war; under Commonwealth and Protectorate the gentry paid fines, economised, and with few exceptions survived. Dorothy Osborne's long and loving series of letters to William Temple, from whom politics divided her, described an unchanged life in Bedfordshire; it was still possible for a neighbour in 1653 to be 'drunk with joy that he had a wife and a pack of hounds'. Walton's Venator and Auceps – countrymen as Piscator was not – spoke in that same year as though life and sport were quite unaffected by a government odious to their author.

Puritanism much inconvenienced the great nobles, who were used to weighty influence and flamboyant junketings. They lost their power; they were forbidden to put on masques or indulge in their other revelries. The government spoiled the fun of humble rustics, too; it cut down the maypole on the village green, and forbade the bear-baiting in the local town. But the hunting, coursing, fowling, angling and even racing of the fortunate gentry in the middle went on as before and as afterwards. Only a minority of crazed extremists disapproved of field sports, as of the innocent diversion of bowls (in fact a heavy and hazardous gambling medium), and they were repeatedly overruled. Cromwell himself was compared to a huntsman and his troopers to hounds; Andrew Marvell (*An Horatian Ode upon Cromwell's Return from Ireland*) represents the Pict huddling under his 'plad',

> Happy if in the tufted brake
> The *English Hunter* him mistake;
> Nor lay his Hounds in near
> The *Caledonian* Deer.

(iii) Wisdom and Folly in the Restoration

The Restoration therefore made less difference to the life of the sporting gentry than to most other English lives. All that happened was that they took up the reins of local government which they had been obliged to drop: this probably helped them, though not in a crudely obvious way, to recover at last from the fines extracted by Cromwell.

An example, well documented by his own *Memoirs*, is that of Sir John Reresby of Thryberg, in the West Riding of Yorkshire. His father died in 1646, in debt because of the fines he had had to pay in the Civil War; Sir John was then twelve. The debts were paid off by the widow, evidently an excellent manager, principally by selling the timber of extensive woodlands. By 1668 – eight years after the Restoration – Sir John was able to begin improvements to his patrimony: he refaced the house, enlarged the deer-park, laid out new gardens with fountains in the French style, and restored and beautified the church. All this was done slowly, carefully, economically. Sir John left an estate more valuable and more beautiful than the one he inherited; in this regard it is relevant that he was a highly educated man, much travelled, a Knight of the Shire and to a minor extent a courtier. He was, of course, a serious if conventional Anglican. In Yorkshire and the rest of the North there were a few Catholic gentry but no puritans. The nonconformists lived in towns; successful nonconformist merchants, unlike their Anglican rivals who joined the gentry, remained deliberately urban and middle class.

There is much in this that is typical, as witness the life and opinions of Sir Roger de Coverley. This Worcestershire squire was the creation of Joseph Addison, Richard Steele and Eustace Budgell (in that order of importance); he was represented as born in 1654, inheriting in 1676, becoming High Sheriff in 1677, serving as Knight of the Shire in Parliament twice (and thus knowing London, and belonging to a London club), and taking the chair at Quarter Sessions. In his village church he was master or landlord of the whole congregation; his servants never left him and his tenants were of many generations' standing. This was another estate managed with the mixture, approved by Brathwaite, of generosity and prudence, unaffected by the libertinism or the ruinous extravagance of the Restoration court. But one of Sir Roger's neighbours was spendthrift, deep in debt, unable to bring himself to sell, unable to bring himself to economise because he had to keep up his state. This was, said Addison, a dreadfully common folly. The pathological meanness of another neighbouring squire, who even did manual work on his farm, was less common.

In contrast to Sir John and Sir Roger – substantial and provident men – there were thousands of ill-educated small squires who had neither the resources nor the wisdom to recover from the extortions of the Commonwealth. 'Our gentry are grown ignorant in everything of good husbandry,' said Pepys (with the complacency of a man in the middle of a city), but what undid them was lack of capital. In 1660 really began the process, which continued steadily into the 19th century, of the polarisation of agricultural land into big estates; this was inevitable as soon as agriculture became a capital-hungry business dominated by land-hungry millionaires.

(iv) Country Politics

From 1688 onwards – the year of the 'Glorious Revolution' which installed William and Mary in the Protestant interest, in place of the latter's Catholic and gravely ill-judging father – the lesser and remoter squirearchy was almost solidly Tory. Partly this was a matter of tradition – the royalist squire or his father had fought for Charles I against the Parliament-men, and James II, Catholic as he was, was Charles's son (less isolated gentlemen – those with fingers in urban and commercial pies, in the good Tudor fashion – were often Whig); it was for this reason that Sir Roger de Coverley was a much stronger Tory in Worcestershire than in London. But as his smaller, remoter, less wordly-wise neighbours held to Toryism from sentiment, so Toryism became the party of their interest against the Whiggery of townsmen and the great landed aristocracy. So it was Toryism which raised a furious voice against the dispossession (albeit by purchase) of small squires by agricultural magnates, and Toryism which bitterly opposed the Land Tax levied to finance Marlborough's wars in Queen Anne's reign. All this survived into George I's time in the kind of perfervid Tory countryman represented by Fielding's Squire Western.

Already politics – on these partly emotional and partly practical lines – divided and bedevilled the countryside. Sir Roger lamented

the Mischief that Parties do in the Country; how they spoil good Neighbourhoods, and make honest Gentlemen hate one another;

besides that they manifestly tend to the prejudice of the Land-Tax, and the Destruction of Game. The Spirit of Party reigns more in the Country than in the Town. It here contracts a kind of Brutality and rustic Fierceness.

Tory and Whig gentlemen would not even go to a cock-match together; 'This Humour fills the Country with several periodical meetings of Whig Jockies and Tory Fox-Hunters.' (We shall return to jockeys and foxhunters.)

(v) Game Laws and Qualification

The Whig magnates were landowners at least as conscious of the fact as the Tory squires they were trying to gobble up; the two came together in Parliament, constituting 90% of its membership, and agreed on the Game Laws if on little else.

Landowners were concerned with all their edible game – deer if they had any, hares, rabbits, pheasants: but above all with partridges, which were of the greatest economic importance owing to their immense numbers and the comparative ease, in the countryside and with the methods of the time, of taking them. (It became sharply easier from 1600 as the shotgun replaced the hawk.) The complaint was that out of the squire's preserves, onto the yeoman's farm, wandered these dinners of fresh meat, otherwise scarcely obtainable; hence the miserable statute produced in 1671 by the Cavalier Parliament (22–23 Charles II ch. 25) which enacted that even a freeholder could not kill any game, even on his own land, unless he had at least £100 a year. (That this law had late medieval and Tudor precedent does not take away from its cynicism.) Understanding the significance of the statute requires a statistical context. Gregory King in 1688 drew up tables calculated from the hearth tax and other sources which showed that there were:

300,000 yeomen and farmers with less than £100 a year
12,000 gentlemen with an average of £280 a year
3,000 esquires   with an average of £450 a year
600 knights   with an average of £650 a year
800 baronets   with an average of £880 a year
160 peers   with an average of £3200 a year

16,500 landowners were 'qualified', 300,000 were not. Of course a few yeomen had more than £100 a year and they, whatever their crudity of manner or brutality of origin, were 'within the Act'. Sir Roger de Coverley had such a man in his country whom he esteemed – 'a very sensible man, shoots flying; and has been several times Foreman of the Petty Jury'. But he killed hares and pheasants, and 'would be a good neighbour if he did not destroy so many partridges'. There was also a large if diminishing number of undoubted gentlemen who did not have rents of £100 a year; however ancient their families and resplendent their quarterings they were debarred by the Act from killing game on their own acres. The irony was that Sir Roger's prosperous yeoman lived far more cheaply than his poorer neighbours because he could shoot hares and birds.

(vi) The Changing Countryside

The Reresbys destroyed extensive stands of hardwood in order to pay their debts; this was one of many reasons why deforestation accelerated during the 17th century. The principal one was fuel. In places far from the sea or from navigable rivers, coal could only be brought, very expensively, in small parcels by packhorse. Those parts of Oxfordshire remote from the Thames, for example, were almost entirely stripped of trees: the change was seen to have taken place between the first publication of William Camden's *Britannia* in 1594 and Gibson's edition of it in 1695.

The result, of course, was more sheep-walk. Enclosure of common and waste continued, with the same object, deplored by Bacon at the beginning of the century and Defoe at the end. But the scale was still very limited. Macaulay's *History* compares 17th-century drawings made of the English countryside for the Grand Duke Cosimo with the England of his time: great stretches of land under heavy cultivation in 1870 were then 'as bare as Salisbury plain'. 'Between Biggleswade and Lincoln there was scarcely an enclosure; nor from Abingdon to Gloucester (forty or fifty miles).' Ogilby, the Cosmographer Royal, showed most of England to be 'wood, fen, heath and marsh' in his *Itinerarium Angliae* of 1675.

An agricultural revolution was begun by William III, who introduced Flemish husbandry to East Anglia. There were two consequences of the utmost importance to the squire's economy and to his sport: hedges, and drainage. But it was a long time before either came to most farming or sporting areas.

(vii) Henry Hastings and the Passion for Hunting

Hunting continued the principal diversion of the great men of all Europe; it was, said Robert Burton in the *Anatomy of Melancholy*, 'the sole almost and ordinary sport of all our noblemen ... 'tis all their study, their exercise, ordinary business, all their talk; and indeed some dote too much on it; they can do nothing else, discourse of naught else.' This was as true of England as of France, Germany, the Netherlands, Hungary or Poland: but from the elegant protocol of French hunting and the huge slaughter of German the English sport, in all its varieties, was growing more and more remote. James I himself – a tricky and complex character, not unconcerned with his dignity – hunted the hare with an informal vigour unthinkable to his continental contemporaries, even the sensible Henri IV of France: but the great difference was that English hunting was as much the sport of squire and yeoman as of king and noble.

This is abundantly clear in the copious writings of Gervase Markham (especially *Country Contentments*) as in Ben Jonson, Brathwaite, and many others: and in the life-style of a sportsman coeval with Markham, Mr

Henry Hastings, second son of the Earl of Huntingdon, who lived in
Dorset. He was described by his neighbour the Earl of Shaftesbury:

> Mr Hastings was low of stature, but strong, and active; of a ruddy
> complexion, with flaxen hair. His cloaths were always of green cloth.
> His house was of the old fashion, in the midst of a large park, well
> stocked with deer, rabbits, and fish-ponds . . . He kept all sorts of
> hounds (*opposite*), that ran buck, fox, hare, otter, and badger; and he
> had hawks of all kinds, both long, and short winged. His great hall
> was commonly strewn with marrow-bones; and full of hawk-perches,
> hounds, spaniels, and terriers. The upper end of it was hung with fox-
> skins of this, and the last year's killing. Here, and there a pole-cat
> was intermixed; hunter's poles in great abundance . . . The parlour
> was a large room, compleatly furnished in the same style. On a broad
> hearth, paved with brick, lay some of the choicest terriers, hounds and
> spaniels. One or two of the great chairs, had litters of cats in them,
> which were not to be disturbed. Of these three or four always attended
> him at dinner, and a little white wand lay by his trencher, to defend it,
> if they were too troublesome. In the windows, which were very large,
> lay his arrows, crossbows, and other accoutrements. The corners of
> the room were filled with his best hunting, and hawking poles . . .
> He lived to be an hundred; and never lost his eyesight, nor used
> spectacles. He got on horseback without help; and rode to the death
> of the stag, till he was past four-score.

(It is curious that Mr Hastings had no guns, although he lived well
into the reign of Charles I.)

It is not clear to what extent all those hounds were entered solely to
the different chases: perhaps only the fox and otterhounds. Other packs
in the South West hunted nearly everything: 'the hounds that hunted
Cranborne Chase', said its historian the Revd William Chafin, 'hunted
all animals promiscuously, except deer, from which they were necessarily
kept steady, otherwise they would not have been suffered to hunt in
the chase at all.'

(viii) Deer, Hare and their Hounds

Although in intensively cultivated parts of England, such as Kent, red
and fallow deer were confined to parks, there were still less disciplined

'DOG WITHOUT
HAIR'

'RUST-COLOURED
GREY HOUND OR
TURKISH HOUND'

'ENGLISH FIGHTING DOG OF
HORRID ASPECT'

Dogs of Mr Hastings's time. All by Aldrovandus, 1637.

areas where they were common. They became much more common when park fences were flattened in the Civil War. Enfield Chase in 1685 was a 'region twenty-five miles in circumferance, which contained only three houses and scarcely any enclosed fields. Deer wandered there in thousands, free as in an American forest'. A few years later, 'The red deer were then as common in Gloucestershire and Hampshire as they now [1870] are on the Grampian Hills. On one occasion Queen Anne, on her way to Portsmouth, saw a herd of no less than five hundred.'

Feral fallow deer here and there also teemed. They were still often coursed instead of hunted: 'How will a right greyhound', says Venator, 'fix his eye on the best Buck in a herd, single him out, and follow him, and him only, through a whole herd of rascal game, and still know and then kill him!' Irish wolfhounds were esteemed for this sport although, as Dorothy Osborne wrote to Sir William Temple, they were quite inconveniently large.

Harehunting was the gentleman's principal chase in most parts of England, as it had been since the days of *The Master of Game*. When Sir Roger de Coverley grew too old to ride to his fox-beagles he got a pack of slow, steady Southern hounds (*below*) – 'stop hounds' – and went sedately out with them 'encompassed by his tenants and servants'. A good hare was frequently saved and put into an orchard, where it lived with many others 'in a very comfortable captivity'. The captivity probably ended in the cooking-pot. It is also likely that, when wild hares were elusive, a resident of the orchard would go out in a basket to be hunted.

Old Southern Hound

The gentleman's pack, for stag, buck, roe or hare, varied according to his country – not only the latter's actual requirements, but also its tradition and the breeding stock locally available. Markham (in *Country Contentments*) associates the slowest and heaviest hounds with Lancashire, Cheshire and the West Country; the fastest and lightest with Yorkshire, Cumberland, Northumberland; and a middle-sized hound, bred between these two, with Worcestershire, Bedfordshire, and other places 'where the Champain and Covert are of equal largeness'. Beagles were bred almost everywhere, small enough to be 'carried in a man's glove'; they were considered amusing to watch at work, but very seldom killed anything.

(ix) The Growth of Foxhunting; Otter and Vermin

From Sir Thomas Cockaine's Elizabethan *Short Treatise* it is clear that some gentlemen and yeomen – certainly in Derbyshire, doubtless elsewhere – had in their kennels hounds bred solely for and entered solely to the fox. Foxhunting remained the unpublicised sport of deeply rural squire and yeoman, too scurried and undignified for great nobles, too unpredictable to fit in with their feasts and rituals. No doubt, given the amount of waste and wood, the great majority of foxes throughout the 17th century were killed near villages in the ancient way: the drag of the fox when he returned from his midnight sortie was hunted up, in the dawn, by a bloodhound; when unkennelled he went to ground; he was bolted out with terriers, or smoked or dug out, and netted or knocked on the head. To Oliver St John, speaking in the Long Parliament of his most hated enemy, 'Strafford was to be regarded not as a stag or hare, but as a fox, who was to be snared by any means, and knocked on the head without pity.' This is often quoted as demonstrating the mid-17th-century attitude to foxhunting, and by and large it did: but there were certainly dozens, possibly scores, of foxhunting men of Mr Hastings's stamp to whom St John's views were as odious as they would have been to George Osbaldeston himself. Foxes were actually preserved for sport, in a few places, as early as the 1580s.

In the second half of the century foxhunting acquired royal and ducal glamour. The 2nd Duke of Buckingham, expelled at last from court, hunted the fox on his Yorkshire estates with his tenants; the Duke of Monmouth joined Lord Grey in Sussex to hunt the Charlton (later the Goodwood) country; the Duke of York (James II) wore a Tory red coat and went foxhunting with his Tory friends. At the same time more squires turned to foxhunting – still a small minority but an ever larger one – as did Sir Roger de Coverley in about 1680. Among the real-life gentlemen whose foxhunting is on firm record are Mr Nicholas le Strange in West Norfolk from 1641; Mr Monson of Burton, Lincolnshire, from 1672; Mr Pelham of Brocklesby, in the same county, from well before 1700; Lord Arundell of Wardour Castle, Wiltshire, from 1696; Mr Thomas Boothby of Tooley Park, Leicestershire, from 1697; Mr Richard Orlebar of Hilnwick Park, Northamptonshire, from 1702. It is not to be supposed that this list is more than a fraction of the total. As early as 1689 Thomas Shadwell described (in *Bury Fair*) the 'strict order of hunters, such as keep journals of every day's hunting, and write long letters of fox-chases from one end of England to the other'.

The method of foxhunting was described by Nicholas Coxe in *The Gentleman's Recreation* of 1674:

> To this purpose you must draw with your hounds about groves, thickets, and bushes near villages, for a fox will lurk in such places to prey on young pigs and poultry. But it will be necessary to stop up his earths, if you can find them, the night before you intend to hunt. At first only cast off your sure finders; as the drag mends so add more as you dare trust them. Let the hounds kill the fox themselves. Foxhunting is very pleasant, for by reason of his strong scent he maketh an excellent cry.

(This represents no advance whatever on the method of Cockaine: which does not make late Stewart foxhunting absurdly antique, but Elizabethan foxhunting astonishingly modern.)

It is generally supposed that this early foxhunting was a slow affair – a start before dawn, when the drag was fresh and the fox gorged, and a morning spent mostly in covert without a gallop or a jump. Usually, no doubt, that was just how it was: but Cockaine in the late 16th century recorded a fourteen-mile point and a kill above ground; the Duke of York said after a hunt that he 'kept pretty close to the hounds, though the hedges were wide and the ditches deep and wide'; Sir Roger de Coverley, vaingloriously fanciful, killed one fox 'which took him above fifteen hours' riding, carried him through half a dozen counties, killed him a brace of geldings, and lost above half his dogs'; and Bernard de Mandeville (in *The Fable of the Bees*) records that 'foxhunters who have all day long tried to break their necks, join at night in a second attempt on their lives by drinking'. Already the attraction of foxhunting, over any other sport of the field, was the physical excitement; it enlisted more and more sporting squires until the golden age of the early 19th century, by which time, for all but a few of them, a private pack of foxhounds was far too expensive.

The otter was a pest on many English rivers, especially (of course) those with good fishing. Izaak Walton's Venator was told that otterhunting (*above*) was 'much pleasanter than any other chase whatsoever', but the otter was destructive vermin, and was not yet credited with the charm perceived by later and more sentimental generations. It is possible, but not probable, that gentlemen entered tall, rough-coated hounds solely to otter; most otterhounds were foxhounds or harriers earning their broth in the summer.

Mr Hastings in Dorset killed badgers and polecats in the way of sport (*below*). So did all his contemporaries. Martens were another occasional

chase. Terriers, lurchers and traps were used, even by the most sporting, far more often than hounds.

Otterhound.

(x) Creation of the Thoroughbred

Robert Burton at the beginning of the century approved vigorous cures for the affliction of Melancholy: 'Riding of great horses, running at rings, tilts and tournaments, horse-races, wild-goose chases, which are the disports of greater men, and good in themselves, though many gentlemen, by that means, gallop quite out of their fortunes.' Every considerable gentleman had, indeed, a Great Horse or two in his stables, for the quasi-military games still popular, and for the High School exercises invented in Italy and now being vastly refined in France; he had running-geldings, often 'Galloway nags', for racing for wagers; he had hacks, hunters, pack-horses and sometimes carriage-horses. Of all these the hack was the most important – Galloway or hobby, when possible an ambler – because even the greatest gentleman did most of his travelling on horseback: few roads were good enough for the wheel, even in summer.

Successive government attempts to improve the general quality of the English horse for military reasons had not worked very well, the main cause being haphazard breeding of hybrid with hybrid with unpredictable results.

Two lessons were then learned by the English, both from abroad.

One was the superiority of North African or Arabian stallions (*opposite*) for breeding, not only because of the absolute excellence of these horses – their docility, elegance, soundness and stamina – but more particu-

larly because, as French and Italian travellers had observed, the desert
horses bred true. Thomas Blundeville knew this, probably only from
his reading of Italian treatises, as early as 1565; a generation or two
later Gervase Markham knew it from personal experience, and it may
well have been he who sold the first Arabian in the royal stables to
James I.

The other lesson was the necessity of careful and selective breeding.
This had been taught to Elizabeth and the Earl of Leicester by the
Neapolitan, Prospero d'Osma, in 1576, in a report he was commis-
sioned to prepare on the condition of the royal stud. The advice may
not have been taken by Elizabeth's servants, but its essence filtered
through to the English countryside. 'An husbandman', said Burton,
'will not rear a bull or a horse, except he be right shapen in all parts, or
permit him to cover a mare, except he be well assured of his breed.'
This assurance meant records, and a treatise of 1605 instructed the
horsebreeder to 'keep a note in a booke when everie mare is coverede
and with what horse'. The careful selection of stallions and the compila-
tion of a stud-book were a large advance on the slapdash methods of the
Tudor countryside, and they became general. Sir George Reresby was,
said his son, deeply concerned about 'his breed of horses, in which he
was very exact': and by Charles I's reign he was in this typical of the
more enlightened gentry.

Selective breeding and the use of eastern stallions were both imported
ideas, but a third and crucial factor in the improvement of the horse was
home grown – or, if learned, learned from classical antiquity rather than
contemporary Europe. This was the racecourse test. Speed, stamina,

soundness, courage, were all qualities needed for hack and hunter as well as racer, but the racecourse was the only place where they were reliably revealed as a guide to the selection of breeding stock. This was a major reason for the growth of racing among the 17th-century gentry. The nobles and riding-masters of Italy and France had been far ahead of the English: but because the English had racing, England invented the thoroughbred. And not the thoroughbred only but, even more important in the life of the countryside, the halfbred hack and hunter of thoroughbred character, and the superior light harness horse, part thoroughbred, such as the Cleveland Bay and Norfolk Trotter.

All this was the greatest contribution of the English 17th century to sporting history; it was the work of kings and their servants, of great nobles, and of private country gentlemen; the part played by the last, principally in Yorkshire, was at least as important as the others. It was also at least as early. On 1 December 1609 a man called Deleto wrote from Orléans to the Earl of Rutland:

> My lord of Cranbourne is returned . . . He baught at Marseilles one Barbarye horse, and Sir Thomas Howard too, and Sir Johan Shefillde baught asnother which is beather then eny of the outher: but as I heare he payed well for hime, for it cost Sir Johan Shefillde before he had hime braught to Paris on hundred and fortie pound.

These Barbs went to their owners' English studs, and by the middle of the century 'Barbarye' or 'Barbine' stallions, and a few mares too, are recorded in the ownership of dozens of noblemen and gentlemen.

Civil War and Commonwealth broke up many private stables because the cavalry needed remounts, but on the whole the process of improving the English horse was accelerated. Cromwell himself imported horses which contributed to the nascent thoroughbred. The great royal stud at Tutbury, Staffordshire, was dispersed and its horses – the best in England – spent years in various private stables, covering private mares, until some of them were reassembled in 1660. And many gentlemen who had spent part of their time and much of their money in London withdrew entirely to their country seats, both royalists keeping out of trouble and moderate Parliament-men disgusted by the excesses of regicides and puritan fanatics. Thus we find the 3rd Lord Fairfax, a Parliamentary cavalry commander, living at home in Yorkshire and covering his Barb mares with his Morocco Barb and Helmsley

Turk; we find Sir John Pelham in the 1650s sending his mares to the Barb stallions of the Earl of Northumberland, Mr Huett and Mr Masters.

The atmosphere of the Restoration, and especially its vigorous racing, caused a great new wave of horses to be imported; by the time Queen Anne died almost all horses recorded at the beginnings of thoroughbred pedigrees had arrived in England. For political reasons the source was the Middle East rather than North Africa – Syria, the Lebanon, Turkey – and the horses were desert Arabs imported by those countries or looted by the Turkish cavalry. Charles II probably, William III certainly, imported horses for themselves: but most of the horses that arrived were imported privately and stood at private studs. The significant ones were still nearly all in Yorkshire (although Captain Byerley's 'Turk' stood in Northumberland) – in Charles II's time those of Messrs Curwen, Croft, Darcy; in William III's and Anne's those of Mr Leedes, Colonel Childers, Mr Gilbert Routh, Sir Marmaduke Wyvill, Mr Darley of Aldby. (The Darley Arabian was found in Syria by a roving younger son, obliged to go away and seek his fortune: the English rule of primogeniture helped create not only the squirarchy but the thoroughbred too.) Some of these families are remembered for other things – the Darcys were courtiers, the Darleys were Masters of Hounds – but most for nothing else: yet their immortality is assured until the last *Stud Book* is burned.

(xi) Gentlemen on the Turf

At the beginning of the process just described, the racecourse was already seen to have a value, as providing the test which breeders needed for their guidance; but there are few indications that importing or selective breeding was done primarily with the racecourse in mind. But Sir John Sheffield in 1609 had to pay £140 to get his new Barb only as far as Paris, and investment on this scale, however richly rewarded in the long term, invited some return in the short term. This, as much as pure sport and breeding guidance, must have inspired the growth of English racing in the 17th century and the participation of horsebreeding squires in it.

The major race meetings of 1600, such as Doncaster, Chester, Salisbury, were typically put on by city corporations on their own land, the intention being to stimulate trade, and were partly financed by subscriptions from the local gentry, whose horses were the contenders. This remained true of most new racecourses, such as Brackley and Harleston in Northamptonshire and Tarporley in Cheshire. Considerable improvements were made, many in James I's reign, in such things as the building of grandstands, the marking and measuring of courses, railing the finishing straights, care of the turf, and the provision of bigger prizes to attract more and better runners.

There were also race-meetings, as in the previous century, but of greater historical importance, got up entirely by local gentry with the involvement of no municipality at all. One of these was Hambledon, Yorkshire, a superb natural race-ground far from anywhere, which was run essentially as a trying-ground for local breeders. Another was Kiplingcotes, where the gentry in 1619 drew up the first comprehensive rules of racing; these covered subscriptions, weights, fouls and disqualifications. The Kiplingcotes rules probably inspired those of the Duke of Newcastle at his private meeting at Worksop, nearby, and the duke's rules probably inspired those of his ex-pupil Charles II at Newmarket. Edward Webbe, in *His trauailes*, described Wallasey, Cheshire, on the Mersey opposite Liverpool: 'These fair sands, or plains upon the shore of the sea at Walsey, which for the fitnesse of such a purpose allure the gentlemen and others oft to appoint great matches, and venture no small sums in trying the swiftness of their horses.' Thomas Heywood in the *English Traveller* saw the same thing at Barnet, Hertfordshire, in 1620: 'Heere all the countrey gentlemen appoint a friendly meeting . . . some for pleasure, to match their horses.'

The meeting which squires as such did not attend was Newmarket. Racing started there because it was James I's favourite area for hunting: the court followed him there: racing followed the court. It consisted entirely, until well after the Restoration, of matches between courtiers, often for heavy wagers. These were copied. The squire, far from 'headquarters', had been for a century accustomed to gamble on cockmatches, the bowling-green, various card games, and village wrestling and running contests; in the very early 17th century he began serious betting on the racecourse. This led inevitably to cheating of most of the normal modern kinds, described in the clearest terms by Ben Jonson (in *The Alchemist*) and James Shirley (in *Hyde Park*), and sententiously deplored in his *Autobiography* by the tetchy Lord Herbert of Cherbury.

Cheating and heavy losses gave the puritans their excuse for forbidding racing, by annual edict, throughout the Commonwealth, although the real reason was that they were afraid of large assemblies of over-excited royalists. Either the law was ignored, or exceptions were made, because when Salisbury races were threatened in 1650 the trouble came not from the government but from the non-payment of subscriptions by the gentry of Wiltshire.

The Restoration – licence after repression – naturally saw a great resurgence of racing at all its traditional centres (and above all at New-market) and at many new places, of which subsequent history made Epsom the most important. Towards the end of the Stewart period York and Ascot were started. The organizational pattern was commonly the same as ever – corporations staging meetings which the local gentry financed. As at Salisbury in 1650 this was sometimes a frail arrangement. A manuscript memoir records of Chester races that, in 1665, the High Sheriff of Cheshire

> borrowed a Barbary Horse of Sir Thomas Middleton, which won him the plate; and being master of the race, he would not suffer the horses of Master Massey of Puddington, and Sir Philip Egerton of Outon, to run, because they came the day after the time prefixed for the horses to be brought, and kept in the city; which thing caused all the gentry to relinquish our races ever since.

Without the patronage of the gentry even Chester races, the oldest in England, could not have survived; but the gentry relented.

Whig jockeys, like Tory foxhunters, disturbed Sir Roger de Coverley's Worcestershire with their sectarian turmoil, and about 1700 the country racecourse saw specifically political contests. This was above all the outrageous work of the 1st Marquess of Wharton, who owned Careless. Wharton, the first great political manager, was the supreme Whig 'jockey' (jockey meaning simply a person concerned with or expert in horses; it was used pejoratively, of cheats or horse-copers, but only in certain contexts). Careless, of pure Eastern blood, was the son of Spanker, himself the best horse in England of the previous generation; Spanker was by Mr Darcy's Yellow Turk (probably a chestnut Arab) out of a 'natural' (home-bred) Barb mare of Lord Fairfax's breeding. 'Sometimes,' said Macaulay, 'when, in a distant county, it was fully expected that the horse of a High Church squire would be first on the course, down came, on the very eve of the race, Wharton's Careless, who had ceased to run at Newmarket merely for want of competitors.'

(xii) The Squire's Horses and Stables

Importation and selective breeding immediately influenced, as they were intended to, hunter and hack as well as racehorse. As early as 1618 Michael Barrett's *Hipponomania, or the Vineyard of Horsemanship* thus describes the ideal hunter:

> Let him be of a meane [i.e. average] stature, some sixteene hand of height . . . his head of a mean bignesse, his chank thin and wide, his eare not too little, and if he be somewhat wide-eared, it is a sign of toughness, so they be sharp; his forehead broad, having a bunch standing out in the midst like a hare; his eye full and large, his nostril wide, with a deep mouth; all his head lean; a long, straight neck; a firm thin crest, well reared; a wide throstle, a broad breast, deep-chested; his body large, his ribbes round and close, shut up to his huckle-bone; a good-filled, long buttocks, not very broad, well let down in the gascoyne; his limmes clean, flat, straight, but not very bigge; his joints short, especially between the pastern and the hoof, having little hair on his fetlock, a straight foot, black hollow hoof, not over big.

Barrett unmistakably declares plenty of blood in this animal; but the size – far bigger than Galloway, hobby or Barb – insists that at least one grandparent was a Courser or Friesland: so Barrett's hunter was comparable to a modern Cleveland Bay cross heavyweight hunter or eventer, than which few more spendid animals can be imagined.

It was doubtless a horse of this kind that a gentleman rode, if he dared, in a wild-goose chase or pounding-match, a kind of wild cross-country follow-my-leader. (To 'pound' means, in the hunting field, to leave your rival far behind or to go where he cannot follow.) Another contest involving this kind of horse was the hunting match, a race behind hounds chasing stag, buck or train-scent (drag). Both these continued until displaced by steeplechase matches in the late 18th century.

The Great Horse itself continued to be valued and bred, more particularly after the Restoration. The cavaliers in exile had seen the horsemanship of the pupils of the great Parisian master Antoine de Pluvinel, and many had attended riding schools which taught his *Haute École;* this was a truly scientific system, far removed from the

crudities of Grisone. The Duke of Newcastle at Welbeck (*above*) was the greatest English exponent, both in practice and as a writer, and he made a fair number of converts. But the great expense of the right sort of horses deterred some gentlemen, while the difficulty of getting expert instruction in remote places excluded others. Probably more for these reasons than from differences of taste, scientific equitation never had the following among the English gentry that it commanded abroad. Evelyn, travelling in Europe in 1644–5, saw Schools and *Cavalerizze* in every town and attached to every great house, but there were never many in England: and in 1680 Thomas de Grey complained in *The Compleat Horseman* that the 'Noble Science' of High School horsemanship was quite abandoned in favour of racing.

A more general use for larger horses – of slow growth in the early 17th century but rapid after 1660 – was between the shafts. A fine turn-out became, for the first time, part of every gentleman's display if he could afford it. When Sir Roger de Coverley in about 1677 wanted to impress the capricious widow he was courting, he 'made new Liveries, new paired my Coach-Horses, sent them all to Town to be bitted, and taught to throw their Legs well, and move all together'. The cost of coach-horses did not compare with that of imported Barbs or Arabians, proved racehorses, or Great Horses for the *manège*, but it was not inconsiderable. The Earl of Bristol, as appears from his accounts and letters, paid the Earl of Lichfield £150 for seven brown coach-horses, and Lord Dover £64 10s. for three Dutch geldings: good harness horses cost about 20 guineas in 1700. (The same source reveals that dairy cows were somewhat under £4 each, 'six score wethers' cost £51, making each sheep worth a little over 8s., and 'fine coloured deer' for the park a little over a guinea each.)

The gentleman's stable, like his kennel, had moved away from the house in Elizabethan times; it was usually built to a very low standard. Thomas de Grey said, 'Your stable ought not to have any unsavoury gutter, channel or sewer near it. The windows must be fitted with handsome casements and shutters, as well to keep out cold and wind as to let in cool fresh air.' At such great establishments as Welbeck, hygiene and ventilation, heat and convenience were all most carefully looked after, but de Grey's good counsel was generally ignored in his own time and for long thereafter. (Kennels, by contrast, seem to have been pretty good. The requirements of fresh air and fresh water, sunlight, room to move, room to sleep, dry ground and good drainage, cleanliness, and cooking facilities had been clearly understood by Gaston Phébus in the 14th century, and repeatedly restated in English as well as other languages. The hound fared far better than the horse in the English squire's establishment.)

(xiii) Gun, Net, Decoy and Hawk

Mr Henry Hastings took birds with hawk and crossbow, but after 1600 he was quite unusual among sporting gentlemen in not owning a gun. Hawking continued the elegant diversion of a smaller and smaller minority. In 1621 the Archbishop of Canterbury aimed his crossbow at a buck, but impaled a keeper; archery then became (in the tradition of Roger Ascham) purely a country-house or country-town game, comparable to the croquet and lawn tennis of later ages, and engaging as

many ladies. Shooting grew into the squire's premier sport, as much as
– even more than – hunting.

This was a matter of technology and of fashion, and both – like
scientific horse-breeding and horsemanship – came from abroad.
Snaphaunce and flintlock were foreign inventions, and examples of
both brought to England were far better than any domestic guns. It was
reported that birds were shot on the wing in many countries as early as
1560, but it is most doubtful if any Englishmen shot flying before 1600;
extremely few attempted it before 1660, and comparatively few for a
hundred years after that. Neither guns nor shooters were in the early
days good enough. The best of the former continued to be imported
from France and Italy, but some really bad guns came from abroad
too, many of which were unsafe. This impelled the Gunmakers Company
to 'proof' guns by firing a larger charge than would ever normally be
used.

Gervase Markham described, probably accurately, the normal
method of shooting birds in 1621. You were to shoot them on the ground,
as many as possible with each shot: choose 'the longest and largest rank
or file of fowl you can find'. A retriever comes out with you: 'By all
means you must have your dog in such true obedience that he may not
stir from your heels or let so much as his shadow be perceived till you
have shot and yourself bid him go.' A stalking-horse was also often used,
as it had been with the sporting crossbow.

By 1640 London gunmakers were copying continental models faithfully enough so that really good fowling pieces were being made,
expensively and in small numbers: but they were still inferior to the
French, as were their users. The exiled Cavaliers saw Frenchmen shooting flying as a normal thing, which impressed them as deeply as did
French scientific equitation. (In 1644 a Spanish writer noted that far
fewer partridges were killed since it became the fashion to shoot them
flying.)

In spite of returned Cavaliers and the awestruck tales of other
travellers, Nicholas Coxe made no mention of shooting flying in the
first edition of *The Gentleman's Recreation* in 1677; but in the edition of
1686 William Blome shows a sportsman on horseback shooting into a
covey of partridges on the wing. The recommended piece for this difficult practice had a 4′ 6″ barrel and a large bore; the gun was kept cocked,
even while you rode, on the chance of a snap shot. Two of Sir Roger de
Coverley's neighbours shot flying at about this time – the substantial

yeoman who was tactless enough to be 'within the Act', and Will Wimble. (The latter was an unusual figure in that, the younger brother of a baronet, he lived at home with his brother as 'Superintendent of his Game'; he hunted the harriers, constructed fishing tackle and shuttlecocks, and made setting dogs.) In Sir Roger's own house, 'A little Room adjoining to the Hall is a kind of Arsenel filled with Guns of several Sizes and Inventions; with which the Knight has made great Havock in the Woods, and destroyed many thousands of Pheasants, Partridges and Woodcocks.'

These species, with hares, were the gentleman's game, protected by law against poorer neighbours, protected by gamekeepers against poachers and vermin. The second Game Law (IV William & Mary ch. 23) added grouse and black game owing to the importance of these birds in the North. Neither heather nor bracken was allowed by this law to be burned, except at certain times of the year; shepherds breaking this provision to increase their grazing were whipped.

In spite of the popularity of shooting and the improvement to guns, and in spite of the estimable example of Frenchmen and Spaniards, game was too valuable to be shot only. 'It is usual for a Man who loves Country Sports', said Addison, 'to preserve the Game on his own Grounds, and divert himself upon those that belong to his Neighbours.' Sir Roger himself went to the extreme edges of his estate to shoot hares and partridges. Those he preserved were netted for the table. The method was to use a pointer or setting dog, which held the birds to ground while a net was delicately drawn over them by two men; or else the dog worked the covey very gradually into the net. Sometimes a hawk was flown to keep the birds on the ground, or a kite-hawk on the end of a string. Sir Roger, 'in his youthful days, had taken forty coveys of partridges in a season'; 'taking a covey', it has been pointed out, suggests the net (*opposite*).

Duck were lured into decoy nets at the edges of any ponds where the fowl flighted. Wild duck were as esteemed then as now, and all manors where they were possible probably had decoys. They were usually in the form of tapering tunnels. Tame birds, tied and pinioned, decoyed the wild birds into the mouth of the net; they were often worked up it to its narrow end by a dog; it was considered good sport. In Lincolnshire, where the fen country had virtually no resident gentry at all, this was big business, and wildfowlers violently resisted the first suggestions, by the Duke of Bedford, to drain the fens for agriculture.

'The Setting Dogg & partridge': taking a covey with a net, from Blome's *Gentleman's Recreation*, 1686.

Snaring and liming birds, as well as trapping various animals, was also considered thoroughly sporting by gentlemen, as well as useful by humble folk. Thrushes and fieldfares were frequent victims, as well as partridges and pheasants.

Hawking was still an important country sport in 1600, and for a generation after that. Gervase Markham's *Country Contentments* (the first edition appeared in 1611) treats fully of it; so does the closely similar *A Jewell for Gentry: Hunting, Hawking, Fowling and Fishing* of 1614, anonymous but ascribed to Thomas Snodham. Simon Latham wrote two good books on the subject in 1615 and 1618, and Edmund Bert one in 1619; this quantity of literature argues a healthy market. In some regards the sport developed. Walton's Auceps in 1654 listed all the long-winged hawks of earlier times, and additionally such exotics as the Stelletto of Spain, the Blood-red Rook of Turkey, and the Waskite of Virginia. The French Pye, of two sorts, joined the short-winged hawks, and the Eagle and Iron were flown. So were, though apparently neither often nor very successfully, the Raven, Buzzard, Kite and Hen-driver (harrier).

The sport went into almost total eclipse in the Civil War and Commonwealth (notwithstanding Auceps) and it was revived only by a few enthusiasts after the Restoration. The gun was king. Hawking never recovered wide popularity; but it never died either.

(xiv) Angling in Water and on Paper

Angling, on the contrary, grew immensely in popularity during the 17th century, and developed a good deal in tackle and technique. The popularity is demonstrated, and the advance made clear, by the flood of angling literature which began to pour off English presses.

The *Treatyse* had been followed by Leonard Mascall's book in 1590, this by John Taverner's *Certaine Experiments concerning Fish and Fruite* in 1600. Then came John Dennys's poetical *Secrets of Angling* in 1606, the considerable fishing part of Gervase Markham's *Country Contentments* in 1611, William Lauson's *Secrets of Angling* in 1620, Thomas Barker's

Barker's Delight; or, the Art of Angling in 1651 and Walton's *Compleat Angler* in 1653. Barker went into a third edition by 1659 and Walton into a fifth by 1676. In 1658 Richard Franck wrote (and in 1696 published) his *Northern Memoirs*. 1662 saw both Colonel Robert Venables's *The Experienc'd Angler* and Charles Cotton's *How to Angle for a Trout or Grayling in a Clear Stream*. There was James Chetham's *Angler's Vade Mecum* in 1681, and the following year Nobbes's *The Compleat Troller*. These are a few of the most important books, all successful and most best-sellers, all instructional, many original; fishing was growing as lustily as shooting, and was not limited, like shooting, to gentlemen of £100 per annum.

The reason was the growth of fishing for fun. The pot or slab was still important, but so increasingly were the sport and science of angling. Ben Jonson's tribute to Penshurst shows that the stew was called on only when the river had failed:

> And if the high-swolne *Medway* fail thy dish,
> Thou hast thy ponds, that pay thee tribute fish.

Rods remained fifteen to eighteen feet long; most were of various traditional woods, but Dennys mentions cane in 1606. Walton prized a good top, and was careful to protect it from damp: he painted it with size, then with lead and oil paint, then with two coats of colour, preferably green. Chetham's eighteen-foot rod in 1681 had a fir butt and a hazel top tipped with whalebone. Casting was devised early in the century: Lauson in 1620 threw a line two or three times the length of his rod.

The line was still usually horsehair, the strands chosen for strength and uniformity. The line was dyed with soot, alum and walnut-juice to give a clear greenish result for invisibility. Sir Roger de Coverley, about 1675, 'tired many a salmon with a Line consisting but of a single Hair', which is frankly incredible: but for smaller fish caught on a fly, a single hair was Barker's point in 1651 – 'You shall have more rises.' Silk lines are mentioned by Walton (for bream); they were normal to Nobbes in 1682 but not to most people for another century and a half.

Sir Roger probably used a reel. Barker had a 'winder' on his 16′ 'stiffe and strong' salmon rod; and 'Some use a wheel', says Walton of salmon fishing, 'about the middle of their rods or near their hand, which is to be observed better by seeing one of them, than by a large demonstration of words.' By the time Walton died in 1683 the reel was in fairly general use, for salmon at least and perhaps for other heavy fish like carp and barbel.

Will Wimble 'makes a *May-fly* to a miracle; and furnishes the whole Country with Angle-Rods'. But it is clear from *Barker's Delight* that there were already established tackle-makers; besides rods and reels they sold hooks, creels ('of willow twigs' in 1606) and landing nets. Cotton had his trout-rods made in Yorkshire, and kept them up all season for his fishing on the Derbyshire Dove.

The vast majority of fish were caught (as they still are) by bottom fishermen with paste or worms. Quill and cork floats were used (though despised by the Yorkshireman Lauson as a Southern trick: he relied on his eye). Much magic and superstition still attended the composition of pastes; ghoulish 'oyntments' incorporated such ingredients as powder of mummies. Every serious fisherman had his own receipts for improving his paste with cheese, honey, egg-yolk, heron-fat, cat's fat, man's fat and turpentine. Worms were scoured through all kinds of things to increase their allure, and ground-bait included sweet paste, barley malt, garbage, offal and cowdung. The important natural baits beside worms were grasshoppers, wasp-grubs, caddis, snails, frogs and minnows. Lauson in 1620 used new-born puppies and kittens for pike: 'A young Whelpe, Kitlin, or such like, is a good bait for a Luce.' Barker mentions salmon-roe as a newly discovered and almost infallible bait for trout in 1651. Walton liked a dead mouse on a pale night. Robert Howlett, in *The Angler's Sure Guide* (1706), reports that he has recently been told about glow-worms as bait for catching carp at night.

Walton hid behind a tree to dap for chub with a grasshopper, and painted his rod-top and dyed his line for camouflage; but of fly-fishing he reported casting down-wind and down-stream. But Robert Venables shows that many people were already fishing upstream, with worm or fly, and this is confirmed by Cotton and by John Worlidge in his *Systema Agriculturae* of 1669: 'If you cast your Fly up against the Stream, the Trout that lies upon the Fin in such strong Currents, and discerns you not, being behind him, presently takes your bait.'

Until about 1650, and by some people for long afterwards, the flies used were essentially those of the *Treatyse* – twelve patterns, careful and deliberate imitations; they were the flies of Mascall, Barker and Walton, who quotes the *Treatyse* word for word. (Walton was no fly fisherman, but it can be assumed that he accurately reported the methods of men who were.) Most of these flies had wool bodies, sometimes 'lapped' with a rib of silk or herl; the mayfly, uniquely, had a palmer-tied cock's hackle (spiralling up the shank from bend to eye) secured by a gold twist, and a wing of mallard breast feathers: a dressing in use today. (Natural mayflies, hawthorn, and oakflies were also used.) While Walton was writing, many more dressings were being devised; Charles Cotton on the Dove had patterns unknown to the *Treatyse*, and Chetham in 1681 had a wide variety of flies, many with the modern names.

Walton recommended the fly fisherman to have with him hooks and fly-tying materials – wool, various feathers, tinsel and silk – so that he could imitate on the spot a fly the trout were rising at. It is practically certain that Walton himself never did this, but it is certain that Richard Franck, fishing in Yorkshire at the same time, did always take his dubbing bag to the river bank; there is nothing to suggest that he thought himself unusual in inventing an imitation *ad hoc* during a rise.

Salmon bred in many south-country rivers from which they have now long disappeared, including the Thames. Minnows (real and artificial) and fly were used, but to Walton a worm well scoured in moss was best. He did not use a reel, but sometimes had a ring at the tip of his rod through which the line ran; he held the end in his free hand. Grayling or umber were already widespread in the 17th century, and were mostly caught at the same time and in the same way as trout. There were a few distinct grayling flies, gaudier than trout flies: 'He has been taken with a fly made of the red feathers of a paroquet, a strange outlandish bird.' Though 'very pleasant and jolly after mid-April, and in May, and in the hot months', the grayling was not esteemed, for sport or table, as highly as trout.

Certain methods even of the gentle Walton cause modern eyebrows to go up. A favourite way of catching pike was to attach a twelve-yard line with a live fish or frog to a pinioned goose or duck, and then to chase the bird across the pool: or tie the line to a bladder or bottle which drifted down-stream; or fix it to a bundle of straw which drifted in the wind across the water; all these were ways of covering the water without casting. 'Barre netting, and night-hooking, where you love Angling,' said Lauson in 1620; but night-hooks were widely used, and considered permissible by Chetham to owners of private fishing; otherwise they were 'unwholesome, unpleasant, and very ungentiel'. Will Wimble wove casting-nets, and in suitable waters they remained popular well into the 19th century. Torch and spear had gone out of use on the best Hampshire trout waters, although Walton had seen torchlight spearing in Hampshire; John Evelyn (22 July 1654) enjoyed it with his uncle Hungerford at Darneford Magna. It became an important way of catching salmon in Scotland, and was not generally forbidden until 1862. Mr Nicholas Segrave in Leicestershire had a tame otter to catch fish for him in 1653; this method never became widespread.

A branch of the sport known to and approved by Walton was fly-casting for swallows and martins. He also fished for herons, baiting a large hook with a live gudgeon, and tying a very strong line to a heavy branch.

This diversion relates more closely to bear-baiting, or to the cruder amusements of the most uncouth countrymen, than to the contemplative donnishness which continued to characterize the angler. Walton was a scholarly London merchant descended from Staffordshire yeoman stock: a pretty typical angler then and since. Venator, before his conversion, said, 'Many merry Huntsmen make sport and scoff at Anglers,' and Auceps called fishing 'a heavy contemptible, dull recreation'. Among Walton's exemplars of brothers of the angle was Dr Nowell, Dean of St Paul's, who wrote the Church of England catechism, spent one tenth of his time fishing, and had himself painted with Bible and fishing tackle. Anglers are 'quiet men, and followers of peace'. The angler is, already, represented as spending the winter thinking and talking and reading about fishing; he does not shoot or hunt. A man of city, college or close, he normally travels to his sport. Once there he looks after himself: *Gilbert's Delight* (1676) advises the fisherman: 'If you have a Boy to go along with you, a good *Neat's-Tongue* and a Bottle of *Canary* should not be wanting.'

Clearly, however, squires with fishing did fish; some of them bought some of the fishing treatises, and a handful contributed to fishing literature. Gentlemen with rivers and ponds were also better informed about preserving and better capitalised to improve their fishing. Pike were systematically taken out of ponds for carp and bream fishing, and out of rivers to protect the trout. Trees were cut back from banks to make room for back-casts, even at the expense of reducing the covert for game. New pools for carp and tench were still dug, with running water in and out if possible; they were drained and cleaned periodically. Waters were restocked from a 'nurse-pond', and the health and numbers of fish were taken seriously by John Taverner as early as 1600.

The attitude to salmon, trout, grayling, carp and sometimes other species thus began to resemble that to partidge, pheasant, grouse, blackgame and hare: it was also noted that trout taken in summer tasted a great deal better than those in the middle of spawning. These factors, put together, created the idea of fence-months for fish; it has been said that Walton's insistence on this point was more influential than other parts of his largely derivative instruction. But sportsmen had not yet appreciated the extent to which species differ, and May was absurdly suggested as a fence-month for trout as well as for coarse fish: while trout were habitually caught at Christmas, by Walton as by everybody else, on worm or minnow.

(xv) Games and Spectator Sports

Robert Burton lists the plebeian country sports, as 'ringing, bowling, shooting, keelpins, tronks, coits, pitching bars, hurling, wrestling, leaping, running, fencing, mustring, swimming, wasters, foiles, foot-ball, balown, quintains, &c., and many such, which are the common recreations of the country folks'. Other sports mentioned during the century include single-stick, boxing and cricket. The squire looked on, sometimes played cricket, often wagered. He also wagered on his own skill on his bowling green; every manor had a green – something frequent in the 16th century became invariable in the 17th – and ladies played as much as gentlemen. In country towns the green was a great place of resort.

The cockpit was another. It was not normal for a gentleman to breed his own gamecocks, as some did with such passion in the 18th century, but it was very normal for him to join the unseemly and democratic bedlam at a main of cocks. Wild behaviour and heavy betting were described with pitying (and prudish) wonder by both Evelyn and Pepys.

Equally popular spectator sports, without the betting element, were bull- and bear-baiting. A puritan's journal of 1643 (quoted by Macaulay) recorded that Henrietta Maria, returning from Holland to England, brought a shipment of bears: 'The bears were left at Newark, and were brought into country towns constantly on the Lord's day to be baited.' Victims of the Commonwealth, these amusements, like the theatre and gambling, were welcome additions to Restoration fun.

CHAPTER FIVE

The Georgians

(i) Growth of the Large, Death of the Small

The Hanoverian countryside was transformed, irretrievably and beyond recognition: but when Victoria climbed demurely onto the throne of her uncles, the squire was still squire, still a local divinity, still a passionate sportsman. Where the old squire had survived and the new had changed his urban spots, their life of paternalism, husbandry and hunting had changed less in 200 years than ours in the last thirty. At least they were allowed to exist.

The first great change that historians notice was the shift of political power from the whole landowning interest to a narrow oligarchy of magnates, territorial and financial, who controlled through their rotten and pocket boroughs a large slice of parliament, and through sinecures and 'places' much of the rest. The policies and legislation which followed benefited all landowners, but the great more than the small, and the smallest very little. Sir Roger de Coverley's neighbours among the small gentry – those with, perhaps, under £200 a year – had been savaged by the Land Tax, and some had never recovered from Cromwell. Squire Western's poorer contemporaries had no capital for agricultural improvements. And landowners rich and poor, as much as merchants, burned their fingers in the South Sea Bubble: 'fine Parks and new-built Palaces', said Defoe in 1722, 'are taken under Forfeitures and Alienations by the Misfortunes of the Times, and by the Ruin of their Masters Fortunes in that *South-Sea* Deluge'. But the very rich survived, as they always do.

Small estates therefore came onto the market, all over England, throughout the 18th century. The general impression early in the century was that new-rich merchants were buying the places. 'Merchants', said Adam Smith, 'are commonly ambitious of becoming country gentlemen.' They could afford it after the Whig wars and the great growth of trade in the early 18th century. 'The present encrease of Wealth in the City of *London*', said Defoe, 'spreads itself into the Country, and plants Families and Fortunes, who in another Age will equal the Families of Ancient Gentry, who perhaps have been bought out.' And elsewhere: 'It is observable, that in this part of the Country [Essex], there are several very considerable Estates purchased, and now enjoyed, by Citizens of *London*, Merchants and Tradesmen.' In areas further from the centres of trade the richer yeomen profited from the bankruptcy of their former landlords. In Leicestershire, 'the Grasiers are so rich, that they grow Gentlemen'. As the century advanced, the biggest acquisition of land was by existing big estates. The 3rd Duke of Richmond inherited only 1,100 acres. He began to increase his holdings as soon as he succeeded, buying from embarrassed or undercapitalised neighbours not only small but considerable estates – 1,000 acres and upwards – until he had 17,000 acres.

In some areas this polarisation was well advanced by 1750; in most the small gentry were not swallowed up for another two generations. William Cobbett reported that thirty miles of the valley of the Wiltshire Avon had fifty 'manors and mansion-houses' in 1760; in 1826 there were eight. Between Salisbury and Warminster five manors were left out of twenty-five. The same could be seen in Hampshire, Berkshire, Cambridgeshire, Lincolnshire, Norfolk. Two or three hundred acres, £200 or £300, could no longer sustain a gentleman's way of life; he was better to sell up and use the capital another way. If he sold to outsiders the effect, said Cobbett, was calamitous:

Forty years ago [1780], there were *five* packs of *fox-hounds* and *ten* packs of *harriers* kept within ten miles of Newbury; and now there is *one* of the former (kept, too, by *subscription*) and *none* of the latter, except a few couple of dogs kept by Mr Budd! 'So much the better,' says the shallow fool, who cannot duly estimate the difference between a resident *native* gentry, attached to the soil, known to every farmer and labourer from their childhood, frequently mixing with them in those pursuits where all artificial distinctions are lost, practising hospitality without ceremony, from habit and not on calculation; and a gentry, only now-and-then residing at all, having no relish for country delights, foreign in their manners, distant and haughty in their behaviour, looking to the soil only for its rents, viewing it as a mere object of speculation, unacquainted with its cultivators, despising them and their pursuits, and relying, for influence, not upon the goodwill of the vicinage, but upon the dread of their power.

A surprising factor, gravely prejudicial to some landowners, was the variation in rents. According to Arthur Young in 1768 the highs and lows derived quite as much from local tradition as from the profitability of the land or the earnings of its tenants. The national average per acre per year was 12s. 7d., but some excellent land that should have been let far above this average was let far below it: and the least financially powerful, least sophisticated squire was the one most bound by a local usage fatal to his own survival.

(ii) The Agricultural Revolution

Cobbett preferred a race of sturdy yeoman and squireens, and emotionally it is easy to agree: but the big estates made many of the agricultural advances, and educated gentlemen made them all.

> I am sensible [said Arthur Young] that not one *farmer* in five thousand reads at all, but the country abounds in gentlemen farmers, whose ideas are more enlarged, and whose practice is founded less on prejudice . . . All the well known capital strokes of husbandry are traced accurately to gentlemen: From whence comes the introduction of turnips in *England?* But from *Tull.* Who introduced clover? But *Sir Richard Weston.* Marling in *Norfolk* is owing to Lord *Townshend* and Mr. *Allen.*

Jethro Tull invented drill husbandry: the first drill ever used was on his farm Prosperous, near Hungerford, to which he moved in 1709.

'Turnip' Townshend (advanced to Marquess in 1787) was one of the proprietors who took farms in hand so that they themselves improved enormous acreages; his marling of light soil with limy clay immensely increased its productivity. Mr Thomas William Coke was another; enclosing, marling, growing roots, rotating correctly, he increased the rents of the Holkham estate from £2,200 p.a. in 1776 to £20,000 in 1816.

Some of the social effects of new enclosures like those in Norfolk are treated below; the agricultural effects were of immense value. There were two above all: proper rotation, and manuring. Rotation was perfectly well understood by educated farmers in the late 18th century, but fatally ignored or mismanaged by the crass; the commonest error was to follow cereal with cereal on the same land, instead of intervening seasons of root or fallow. The value to arable of fenced or folded sheep was clearly visible to Defoe in 1720, but manuring was carried much further late in the century, and dissuaded many good farmers from stall-feeding their beasts. Nor was the farm's own manure enough for improving landlords: 'There is no town', said Arthur Young in 1768, 'in the kingdom of any size, but what yields a considerable quantity of manure annually; ashes of wood and coal, horse dung, the cleaning of streets, the riddance of privies, poultry, and hog dung, shambles offal, soot, and a variety of other manures.'

Simple tenant farmers did not understand rotation; they resisted valuable new feed-crops like turnips, carrots, clover and lucerne; they would not weed sufficiently; they used an absurd number of horses – six to a plough when two would have been enough – abiding by local custom; they made flimsy dead-wood fences instead of planting quickset thorn; but by the late 18th century they did, generally, understand drainage. They dug their ditches about two foot wide and deep, filled them with brushwood or straw, and sometimes covered them with earth; the job cost 'twopence a rod and small beer' for the labour, an outlay often recouped by the first crop.

Meanwhile Robert Bakewell in Derbyshire was adapting the philosophy and exactness of thoroughbred breeders to farm stock, and by the end of the century cattle, pigs and poultry had improved beyond recognition. The Smithfield Market records show that stock of all kinds sold to the butcher increased, on average, to twice the weight between 1700 and 1800.

Some farms improved by the owners were kept in hand; most were relet at far higher rents. In spite of these, the new tenants could make a great deal of money. Arthur Young analysed the accounts of a typical 1,100-acre tenant farm in Norfolk, employing six servants and six labourers, and with forty people 'in the field' at harvest time; the annual outgoings were £1,002, the price achieved for cash crops, meat, wool and dairy products £2,265, the profit a clear £1,263. This tremendous prosperity naturally created the warmest relations between landlord and tenant, which were energetically fostered by good landlords. William Howitt (in *The Boy's Country Book*) remembered 'Rent Nights' on his father's Derbyshire estate in the 1780s. Every tenant (which included the whole village) was given supper by the squire after paying his rent each May and November: 'The supper was a regular old English one of roast beef, plum-pudding, pigeon-pies, roast fowls, fruit-tarts, when the season permitted, and plenty of ale and pipes.' The squire's wife was with the party until the pipes were lit.

Arthur Young's startling figures depended on heavy investment by the landowner, especially in marling, fencing, draining and building. Squire Howitt in Derbyshire was a coal-owner, which gave him finance for agricultural improvements from his own resources. From the middle of the 18th century it became easier for other landowners to make the investment because, with the establishment of joint-stock banking, they could do it on credit. It is probably also relevant that many improving landlords had business connections or business backgrounds. A well documented example is Mr Richard Sykes of Sledmere, Yorkshire. His was a cadet branch of an old Cumberland family who became, as cadets should, successful merchants. Richard inherited Sledmere from his mother's family in 1748, and only then became himself a squire. It was both fashionable and profitable to be an improver, and he approached the business like a businessman, keeping full accounts and records, and relating investment to return. But he was no less a sporting squire for this counting-house philosophy: he kept a private pack of harriers, and in spite of severe gout (he drank expensive port) followed them energetically in park and countryside.

(iii) Transport

Farming made money if the produce sold. Defoe remarked again and again in the *Tour* that much local prosperity, even in quite distant places, depended on shipments carried to London: even fish were carried alive in barrels of water to London, by coach, from the East Anglian fishing ports. But in areas of deep clay soil road transport was very difficult; parts of Sussex were cut off in winter, the roads being virtually impassable even to pack-horses. There was no finance to improve the roads because they were a parish responsibility: 'in *England* it is the Tenant, not the Landlord, who pays the Surveyors of the Highways.' The solution was turnpike or tollbar, of which the first were licenced by statute late in the 17th century. By 1725 a good deal of England was served by turnpike roads, although a good deal was still untouched by them. The charges were low: a horse one penny, a coach threepence, a cart fourpence to eightpence, a wagon sixpence to a shilling, cattle a few pence a score. The engineering was adequate, and included many new bridges; people were thankful to pay to get their wagons through, far more heavily laden than before, and bring their cattle to market in better condition.

The six-horse coach of Queen Anne's reign, drawn always at a walk, became a faster and lighter two- or four-horse stage by 1750 (though it was springless, often in accidents, and often held up by highwaymen); comfortable private carriages and fast post-chaises began to appear in numbers at the very end of the century.

Water had been an important means of carrying farm produce – especially grain – for centuries, and the late 17th century saw a few rivers made navigable by locks. The partial canalization of rivers increased enormously in the early 18th century; Acts of Parliament often provided the finance. Barges were by this time carrying wool, wheat, coal, iron, and quarry-stone. In 1759 the Duke of Bridgewater, a great coal-owner, built the first major canal which was an entirely artificial waterway to carry his coal from the colliery to Manchester; it was widely and wisely imitated during the next fifty years, first in Lancashire and the West Midlands, then all over England. Some landowners deplored the canals (as they later execrated the railways) on the simple ground that they stopped horses, though not foxes or usually hounds. But they brought income to places where the people had previously found it impossible to carry their goods to market, and comforts which had previously been too expensive to bring. This sometimes had a direct effect on the physical countryside from a sporting point of view. In Northamptonshire the blackthorn hedges were planted threefold as soon as the country was enclosed, one row only being needed to contain the stock, the other two being cut eventually for fuel. The result was a gridiron of huge bullfinches which could be jumped neither over nor through. Canals brought coal, the enclosures were surrounded by normal oxers, and the Pytchley country became huntable. Cottages were more comfortable with tiles or slate brought by canal than with local straw thatch; stock-raising areas got straw by canal and arable areas muck, which increased specialised farming and so farming profits.

Agricultural improvements enriched some landowners and effectively dispossessed others. Better transport helped them all. Both these developments were of great benefit to the humblest people in the countryside, who were already in 1700 (as they had been since the 14th century) generally prosperous and contented. But two other large changes of this period enriched most of the rich and reduced many of the poor to indigence and misery. These were enclosures and machines.

(iv) Enclosures

It is estimated that two million acres of waste, wood and common were enclosed between 1696 and 1795. Defoe in 1724 saw the same vast numbers of sheep there had always been on the downs between Winchester and Salisbury, and on to Shaftesbury and Dorchester; the difference was that everywhere there were new hedges to keep the sheep in. But in the wars of the beginning of the century, as in the wars of the end of it, corn was immensely profitable, and most enclosure was for new arable.

Arthur Young insisted – Tory as he was – that the dispossessed cottagers must be compensated with allotments so that they could grow their basic food. This was not done. The result was beggardom. The Revd Richard Warner, touring the Western counties, said, 'Time was when these commons enabled the poor man to support his family, and bring up his children. Here he could turn out his cow and pony, feed his flock of geese, and keep his pig. But the enclosures have deprived him of these advantages.' Lord Torrington, touring everywhere, remarked on the poverty and apathy of the labouring classes, and the absence of adequate relief: 'Time was, when an abundant yeomanry, with cottage rights well maintained, could support the numerous poor; but, now, debauched, impoverished, and oppressed, they think only of the present day.'

About half of agricultural England was seriously affected: the East Riding of Yorkshire, almost entirely arable; Leicestershire and Northamptonshire, almost entirely grazing; Huntingdonshire, mixed but mostly arable; Cambridgeshire, malting barley; Lincolnshire and Norfolk, wheat and turnips; Suffolk, dairy products, geese and turkeys; Bedfordshire, Oxfordshire, Wiltshire, mostly grazing. The Kentish fruit-orchards and hop-fields were not affected, or much of Sussex and Essex, because they were enclosed already. Empty wold was not affected because, until the invention of wire, there was no way to fence it: but in the West Wiltshire and Gloucestershire uplands, where the ground was littered with stones, new enclosures were quite cheaply walled.

(v) The Man-Eating Machines

Of enclosures early in the 18th century, the miserable effects were softened by the continued prosperity of village and cottage industry: of which by far the most important was still weaving. But in the first quarter of the century machines were beginning to take work away from the cottages. 'Priz'd Knit Stockings' had been made at Stourbridge and in all the countryside round: 'but that Trade', said Defoe in 1724, 'is much decay'd by the encrease of the Knitting-Stocking Engine, or Frame, which has destroyed the Hand-Knitting Trades for fine stockings through the whole Kingdom.' The Industrial Revolution was already bringing poverty to the countryside. The effect of machines was joined to that of enclosures, of the huge growth of trade with America and the Baltic, of ever more intensive mining for coal, iron, lead and copper, of the prodigious growth of cotton-spinning as soon as cotton became the major product of the American Deep South; the result of all these together was the movement from country to town. Liverpool and Bristol quadrupled in size between 1680 and 1720 on trade; Manchester grew at least as fast purely on manufacture: its 50,000 people in 1725 made it 'the greatest meer Village in England' – simply a mass of people, with no Corporation or Member of Parliament. Wigan and Bolton grew round their mines. There was an equivalent movement of people towards Doncaster and Halifax: but wool was still a far less centralised industry than cotton, and South Yorkshire had great prosperity and a vast number of close-together cottages rather than the proto-slums of Lancashire.

The change remained gradual: but not for long. In the lifetime of George IV England changed from an agricultural to an industrial country, the majority of its people urban, the majority of its wealth mineral, the majority of its poor in the depths of brutish misery. The villager had lost his common – and often his dwelling and garden – and his cottage industries were all quite dead. There was a greater gulf than ever before between rich and poor, made greater because many of the rich found coal on their estates, such as the Lowthers, Pettys and Russells. Ironmasters, brewers, bankers, lawyers and a few nabobs from India bought estates on an ever larger scale – seeing which the radical Cobbett became a romantic High Tory, reacting exactly as did 'Dornford Yates' observing the same phenomenon a century later. The industrial profits of great landowners, and the accelerated movement of the new rich from town to country, did not have the unifying effect so noticeable in Tudor and Stewart times: on the contrary: the late 18th century saw for the first time a bitterness between town and country which became a national disease in Victorian England.

The origin of this bitterness was logical, on both sides. The country-side hated being taken over by jobbers and attorneys, brickmakers and bankers 'foreign in their manners, distant and haughty in their be-haviour, looking to the soil only for its rents'; it resented the profiteering of turnpike companies or their dishonest agents; it felt cheated first by machines which took away part of its livelihood, then by low prices which took away much of the rest. The town was enraged by the high price of corn, in 1710 and in 1810, which resulted from war and export: but above all because its thousands of solid merchants sent no member to Parliament, while a private squire who owned a borough of two dozen voters – all completely under his control – sent two.

(vi) M.P. and J.P.

The countryside itself continued to be violently partisan; Defoe des-cribes local acrimonies in terms very like Addison's. The differences in the early 18th century were often religious, especially when urban dis-senters did at last move out to the country, or make country converts: or when, as in parts of Devon, dissenting yeomen became rich and influential. In boroughs with a somewhat larger electoral roll, elections were fought with great bitterness and with bribes of scarcely credible size. Colonel Draper, a local gentleman, contested Winchelsea against Sir John Banks, spent an alleged £11,000, and lost: this was £1,000 *more* than the insanely extravagant Jack Mytton of Halston spent in trying (unsuccessfully) to get re-elected for Shrewsbury a century later.

In the late years of George III's reign the issues settled more and more clearly into the single matter of the Reform of the parliamentary franchise. This was Whig against Tory, town against country, dissent against establishment: but not simply or tidily; the radical Cobbett hated townsmen, and was pro-Catholic and virulently anti-Quaker and -Jew. There were Whig and even radical foxhunting squires, whom their Tory neighbours ignored in the hunting field and cut at the races.

The squire continued to be the Justice of the Peace, administering laws made by his neighbours and himself. With the coming of William and Mary, the tendency was for the central government to delegate more responsibility to the unpaid local magistrate. Throughout the 18th century the squire was therefore more powerful than ever before, administering the Poor Law, in particular, according to local custom or personal whim, unregulated by the Privy Council. Most J.P.s were probably well-meaning and few seriously corrupt, but many were ignorant, prejudiced and wilful. The effect was apt to be energetic enforcement of the Game Laws and niggardly doles to the hungry. But the real cruelty of the bench to the humble followed the anti-Jacobin backlash of the French Revolution.

(vii) House and Garden

Hundreds of small manor-houses fell down, as the poorest gentry found their estates unable to support their state; often, Cobbett remarked, only the dovecote remained standing to declare what the ruin had once been. Hundreds more were occupied by yeomen. The gardens disappeared under the midden and the stables became byres or pigsties, until aspiring Victorians (like Trollope's Lawrence Twentyman in *The American Senator*) turned yeoman into 'gentleman farmer' and the Manor Farm back into the manor. When the manor was deserted, or degraded into a farmhouse, the village was without a squire; the parson then became the Justice, which to Cobbett was always a calamity.

Of the manor-houses that remained – those of the richer or cleverer gentry – the great majority were rebuilt between 1688 and the Napoleonic Wars. A Dutch style arrived with William of Orange; a classical style was learned from Italy; the elegant proportions of the latter disciplined the practical comfort of the former into the most excellent domestic architecture of any country at any time. Very often the new house was built well away from the old, resited in order to get a view : such was Sir Edward Blacket's, designed by Wren, on the bank of the Ure a mile from Ripon. (While Defoe was admiring it, Castle Howard was being rebuilt for Lord Carlisle.)

Indoors the rooms were higher and lighter, plate glass in sash windows replacing latticed casements. Panelling was very usual until the vogue for paper. Pictures were far more numerous – and far better – than in the country houses of the Restoration : but the naive bought a good many duds: in 1724, 'It is incredible what Collections have been made by *English* Gentlemen since that Time [1688] . . . we begin to be glutted with the Copies and Frauds of the *Dutch* and *Flemish* painters.' Wilton had the very finest collection of paintings in England, Burleigh the next best; both houses and both collections were new. A major innovation in interior decoration, introduced by Queen Mary, was the display of china. The best porcelain was imported by way of India, but as the century advanced there was much domestic ware on the shelves of manor-houses.

The growing taste for European travel transformed the contents of many houses directly and immediately, all others indirectly and eventually. Italian pictures and French furniture came back in wagonloads from the eldest son's grand tour. These in turn contributed to a great flowering of English painting and cabinet-making – domestic rather than grand, fit for the manor rather than the palace; a lot of Englishmen preferred, without sour grapes, Reynolds and Chippendale to the more declamatory and florid products of the Continent.

Early in the century the Dutch formal garden was usual, and trees were planted in precise avenues extending the eyelines of the walks between the parterres. There was no taste for the picturesque, the wild, the natural (Defoe detested mountains). But increasingly the formal garden was abolished; the landscaped deer-park swept right to the house, with trees planted in 'curious order'. In 1749 Richard Sykes planted 20,000 trees – beech, sycamore, wych elm and chestnut – in the 120-acre park at Sledmere; the garden he loved so much (and in which he grew successful pineapples) was walled and away from the house. A few years later Horace Walpole's Gothick – literary and architectural – began to show itself in grottos and follies: but the widespread imitation of wild nature in tamed parks waited until the Romantic Revival and the novels of Walter Scott.

(viii) Manners and Education

'Freedom' of manners remained the English ideal: absence of foppishness and ceremony, naturalness, visible goodwill. This Shakespearean rule was restated in every generation: but not everyone in the 18th century was aware of it. At the beginning of the century Addison remarked that Worcestershire manners were stiffer and more formal than those of London: a polite squire was too polite: he never stopped bowing. In the next generation, Squire Western in Somerset could hardly bear to bend his back in a salute. There is here a clear and growing difference between the fashionable town and the uncouth country, and between the countryman rich enough to be at home in London and his poorer and more deeply rural neighbour. The difference increased with easier internal travel, which encouraged squires and their women to become acquainted with the ways of London and Bath: and with the vogue for foreign travel, which infected the rich with the airs of continental *salons*. The supreme spokesman for manners of this new-learned sort was Lord Chesterfield; their best known arbiter Beau Nash at Bath, whose notions were so far removed from those of the country gentleman that he even forbade riding-boots at dinner.

If the sophisticated squire became more polished in his manners, the ignorant, perhaps reacting, became grosser in his. Defoe noticed (as a matter of manners, not morals) 'the sharping tricking Temper, which is too much crept in among the Gameing and Horse-Racing Gentry in some parts of England'. The effects of hunting were worse. In 1728:

> To me an untaught unpolished Gentleman is one of the most deplorable Objects in the world . . . Because of a voluntary and affected Stupidity and Ignorance, which they adhere to as obstinately as Muscovites. No Russian Stupidity was ever more gross in its Nature

or half so pernicious in its Consequences . . . Their Business is to hunt the Stag and the Fox with their own Hounds and among their own Woods. Their Fame is on the Field of Pleasure, not on the Field of Battle.

'Their mornings', wrote Lady Mary Wortley Montagu, 'are spent among the hounds, and their nights with as beastly companions – with what liquor they can get.' This is certainly Fielding's picture, and Goldsmith's: the squire has become a bumpkin, a Tony Lumpkin, a red-faced buffoon in riding boots, boorish, derided, miserable in the company of the polite.

There were clearly thousands of squires of this kind – Westerns who lived in kennel and cow-house, drank to the King over the Water, spoke in broad regional accents of 'Hanover rats', never opened a book or went to London. But William Somerville, himself a hunting Warwickshire squire, thus paints an elderly backwoods squire in 1730:

> A rural squire, to crowds and courts unknown,
> In his own cell retired, but not alone;
> For round him view each Greek and Roman sage,
> Polite companions of his riper age.

Drink they certainly did, both simple squires and fine gentlemen: not gin, which never infected the countryside, but October ale and a good deal of expensive imported wine, and from about the middle of the century a good deal of port as well. (They also drank both tea and coffee.) They gambled, at the table and on the racecourse, but not on the scale of the urban and fashionable; between the Restoration and the Regency few squires lost their fortunes in wagers. They entertained, keeping open house to their neighbours and having more distant friends to stay for weeks or months. The gentry were allowed to wear swords, but few did in the country and very few fought duels. They smoked long clay pipes – many country houses had 'smoking parlours' – until late in the century. Among gentlemen, 'smoking has gone out', said Doctor Johnson, touring the Hebrides in 1773; snuff, long known, had become the only polite way of taking tobacco.

Only two generations divided Peter Beckford, most learned of fox-hunting gentlemen, from Squire Western. Neither can be accepted as typical. But Beckford is certainly a fairer representative of his time (the first edition of *Thoughts on Hunting* was published in 1781) than any half-literate squire of the Western stamp. Education was one of the main reasons for this change. Of 'Eaton' in 1725 Defoe said: 'Besides the seventy Scholars upon the Foundation, there are always abundance of Children, generally speaking, of the best Families, and of Persons of Distinction, who are boarded in the Houses of the Masters, and within the College. The number of Scholars instructed here is from 400 to 550.' (Winchester and the Royal Free Schools of Westminster and Shrewsbury had equal scholastic reputations, but did not yet attract the equivalent of Etonian oppidans.) It was normal for school to be followed by university, and, among the rich, university by tour. The result was a gentry to whom ownership of a fine library was normal, and who had read some of the books in it.

The squire's nearest educated neighbour was almost always the parson, but early in the century the latter's influence on the manor family did not tend to piety or refinement. In Crabbe's well known picture:

> The reverend wig, in sideway order placed,
> The reverend band by rubric stains disgraced,
> The leering eye in wayward circles rolled,
> Mark him the pastor of a jovial fold,
> Whose various texts excite a loud applause,
> Favouring the bottle and the good old cause.

But during George III's reign several factors lifted the parson socially almost to the level of his patron; the pious respectability of the royal household had a gradual but considerable influence; the Church itself reformed itself; and the value of tithes and improved glebe land made many a country living an adequate basis for a gentlemanly way of life. It became typical, when the living was in the squire's gift, for a younger son or son-in-law to occupy the parsonage.

(ix) Resorts and Routs

Members of Parliament went to London; a rich minority of other squires with marriageable daughters did so during the season, which ended in June. Others went to Bath. As early as 1725:

Now we may say it is the Resort of the Sound, rather than the Sick; the Bathing is made more a Sport and Diversion, than a Physical

Prescription for Health; and the Town is taken up in Raffling, Game-ing, Visiting, and in a Word, all sorts of Gallantry and Levity.

Ladies – by which is specifically meant the wives of the country gentry – bathed in their shifts, ogling and being ogled by half-dressed, half-immersed gentlemen. On wooden dishes they floated their snuff boxes and patches: but the latter often failed to stick owing to perspiration. Balls were given twice a week in the season. Tunbridge Wells attracted a similar clientèle: country gentry from all over England:

> The coming to the wells to drink the Water is a meer matter of cus-tom; some drink, more do not, and few drink Physically: But Com-pany and Diversion is in short the main business of the place . . . As for Gameing, Sharping, Intrieguing; as also Fops, Fools, Beaus, and the like, *Tunbridge* is as full of these, as can be desired.

Epsom and Hampstead were worse because malicious gossip ruined reputations: but they were patronised by Londoners rather than gentry. Buxton and Matlock were medicinally celebrated, but never achieved the same fashionable status. Scarborough did: and it was there that therapeutic sea bathing was perhaps invented (it is shown in a picture of 1735). Margate had bathing machines by 1750. The change in the atmosphere of the watering places shows, as dramatically as anything, how the gentry became respectable during the reign of George III: Jane Austen's visitors to Bath (in *Northanger Abbey* and *Persuasion*) did not sit flirting in their shifts.

Throughout the century the social life of the squire's family, during most of the year, depended on the nearest considerable town. (Assizes and an important market were the things which made a town the centre of the countryside.) Assemblies were frequent in towns all over England from the 1720s: the local marriage market, the source of local scandal. When almost every town had a racecourse, the race week attracted all the gentry, and the balls and assemblies were the social high time of the year. At Lichfield, Staffordshire, in 1776 (according to the *Morning Chronicle*), 'The town was very full of company, who testified their ut-most approbation at the entertainment they had each day on the course, and the brilliancy of the balls.' A generation later Hunt Balls were also beginning.

Increasingly the squire's ladies had to be entertained because, increasingly, they had nothing to do. With respectability came refinement, with refinement idleness. This is horribly clear in Jane Austen. But a century earlier Farquhar's Belinda had been able to say, 'I can gallop all the morning after the hunting horn and all the evening after a fiddle. In short I can do everything with my father but drink and shoot flying.' Addison described a 'rural Andromache' who 'is one of the greatest fox-hunters in the country; she talks of hounds and horses, and makes nothing of leaping over a six-bar gate.' But as the parson took his place among the gentry at the covert side, the lady withdrew to her embroidery and megrims. By the action of a curious seesaw, the re-appearance of Victorian women in active sport coincided with the disappearance of parsons from it.

(x) Foxhunting of the Early 18th Century

If the great contribution of late Stewart England to sporting history was the invention of the thoroughbred, that of Hanoverian England was the invention of modern foxhunting. The latter was, like the former, the work of squires as well as of magnates: but with few exceptions they are even less remembered.

In 1700 Mr William Roper had the Charlton country in Sussex (in succession to the Duke of Monmouth); his was the one really fashionable foxhunting establishment in England, and he was followed by the Dukes of Bolton and Richmond. At the other extreme, the Duke of Buckingham had been succeeded in the North Riding by the yeomen of Bilsdale and Sinnington. Between these extremes were squires: Mr Richard Mason of Necton, Norfolk (followed in 1702 by England's first Prime Minister Sir Robert Walpole of Houghton), Messrs Boothby, Pelham, Monson, Orlebar. A number of writers make it evident (Shadwell, Addison, de Mandeville) that these remembered names are the tip of an iceberg: but how large, and where sited, is anybody's guess.

It is certain that the packs mentioned, as well as others forgotten, were bred for foxhunting and entered solely to fox. It is not certain how they went about hunting it. There were two traditional methods. One was medieval and Tudor, and well known to the Restoration: hounds unkennelled the fox and pushed him out of covert; greyhounds then coursed him. This was the method of the Russians for wolf-, fox-, and harehunting in the early 19th century (described in abundant detail by Tolstoy in *War and Peace*), and of the Americans of the Midwest and West for two generations more; it remained popular in England in all the many areas where Northern hounds or fox-beagles were unknown – the other scenting hounds were too slow to catch a fox above ground. It was abandoned in all foxhunting countries as soon as they could be so described, but it probably continued elsewhere until greyhounds were used for match-coursing.

The other long-established method was to unkennel the fox with one or a couple of old hounds, and to uncouple the pack 'as the scent mended'. This was the tufting method derived from deerhunting. It seems certain that the Duke of Buckingham and his successors abandoned it on the dales: his covert was the whole hillside, which could not be drawn by a couple or two or by a pack in couples. But in the coverts of Sussex and Wiltshire, with young hounds of uncertain steadiness, it was probably a usual method, and remained so for cubhunting until late in the century. Even when the whole pack was thrown into covert, it is quite uncertain when it came out uncoupled at the huntsman's stirrup.

Foxhunting recruited slowly but steadily, all over England, during the first half of the 18th century; the recruits included such great nobles

as the Dukes of Rutland, Richmond and Grafton, and the Earls of Craven, Gainsborough, Cardigan, Coventry, Scarborough and Carlisle and Earls Spencer and Fitzwilliam; they included rich squires like Mr Thomas Noel in Leicestershire and Rutland, Mr Evelyn in Hampshire, Mr Chaworth in South Notts, Mr Selby in Northamptonshire, Mr Calvert in Hertfordshire, Mr Thomas Fownes in Dorset, and in Yorkshire such as Sir Henry Slingsby, Mr Henry Brewster Darley, Mr James Fox Lane and Mr Thomas Bright. There were poorer squires foxhunting too, like Mr William Draper in Holderness, getting some kind of support or subscription. And in many places – most notably Devon – there were private packs of harriers killing foxes when they could.

A cry of hounds (often small and bobbery) had been an almost invariable part of a gentleman's establishment. A few couple of harehounds and a brace or two of greyhounds remained so. But foxhunting could not be undertaken without a good sized pack of foxhounds, more servants, better horses, and other expenses. The outlay was analysed, for the benefit of aspiring masters, by Mr Henry Brewster Darley of Aldby (East Riding) who kept foxhounds from 1733 to 1765:

A Yearly Calculation of the Expenses of 30 Couple
   of Hounds, 3 Coup. of Terriers, Nine Horses,
     Four Servants and Earth Stoping.

Twelve Quarters of Oats made into common Dog Meal
   will feed Thirty Couple of Hounds very sufficiently
   & also two Couples of Terriers – for one Month. If
   you have Carrion Flesh, so much the better, and less
   Oatmeal will be wanted. The Quantity of good Oats
   wanted for one year will be 156 Qrs., which at twelve
   shillings p. Qr. amounts to £93 12 0

Nine Horses at 11 pecks of Oats p. week for 40 weeks
   each horse 135 Qrs. 80 10 0

                                     Tol.   174 2 0

Excepting the Carrion, Hay, Straw, & Shoeing, and the
   Horses Grass.

Servants Wages & Cloaths 50 0 0

Earth Stoping 21 11 0

                                       Tol.   £245 13 0

N.B.   Four Servants, Huntsman, Groom, Whipper-In, & Dog Keeper.

The huntsman, Moses Wing, had 'Ten Pounds a year, half the Vales of the Stables & the Livery'; the whipper-in, James Wright, had 'Five Pounds a year, a Velvet Cap, Coat, Waistcoat, and Breeches'; the groom had ten pounds and half the vails of the stable. (These vails or perquisites can only have been tips from visitors, which suggests either stabling and care of visitors' horses, or, surprisingly, that with only nine hunt horses Mr Darley mounted his guests.)

These figures have been compared (by C. M. Prior) with other contemporary household accounts, and they are pretty typical. What emerges is the high cost. £245 was the *total* annual income of the great numerical majority of the smaller gentry; to spend such a sum on foxhunting alone argues a large rent roll indeed. And Mr Darley makes no mention of building kennels, nor of the purchase of horses or hounds. A good hunter in 1760 cost at least £150, and Mr Darley sold his pack to Lord Spencer in 1765 for 500 guineas.

Mr Darley's hounds travelled 150 miles to their new home. Such journeys were and had long been normal: Mr Fownes's Dorset pack went to Mr Bowes of Streatlam Castle in the North Riding in 1745: and the Duke of Richmond's kennel books from the 1730s show the use of stallions from all over England, including Mr Bright's Badsworth Luther. This indicates the trouble people took with hound breeding, the continual correspondence between them, the money they spent, and the sophistication they brought to what they were doing. The foxhunting squire had moved a long way from Squire Western.

(xi) Meynell and Beckford

Two individual squires – both hugely influential, but in different ways – illustrate the change: Mr Hugo Meynell and Mr Peter Beckford.

Meynell, already very rich, transplanted himself from his ancestral Derbyshire to Leicestershire in 1752 or '3, at the age of eighteen. He became the squire of Quorndon Hall, where he lived elegantly and hospitably for half a century.

Mr Meynell [said 'Nimrod's' Somerby, represented as speaking in 1788] is of the middle height, of a compact and well-proportioned form; with a highly expressive countenance, and a very intellectual eye. His manners and general deportment are those of a man of the highest fashion, and he combines zeal with talent, which would render him distinguished in any pursuit that might be congenial to his inclination and taste. Fortunately for fox-hunting, he made that his election.

He was indeed a man of the highest fashion, the best manners, and conversation on the widest variety of polite topics. This enabled him to negotiate smoothly with every covert-owner in his country, from prickly nobility to oafish graziers (and from prickly graziers to oafish nobility) and so to form a foxhunting country on the basis of an almost contractual consent. This has been called the most valuable contribution he made to the sport; certainly his precedent has provided the necessary basis for all foxhunting ever since.

He was intelligent enough to learn. He developed a clear idea of where he wanted to go, and had the patience to get there gradually. As a boy at home he had been notably unsuccessful with his harriers, owing to wildness and impatience, and things at first went quite as badly in Leicestershire. He first raised his pack and method to at least the general standard (by about 1765) and then, innovating, raised both to unquestioned pre-eminence. He went about catching foxes in a new way. All his predecessors had started early, hunted the drag up to the kennel, then hunted the fox slowly and methodically from covert to covert. The early start meant better scent, and above a fox still torpid from his undigested dinner. Meynell started drawing in the middle of the morning, and so unkennelled a fox fit to run.

This meant a new kind of foxhound (*below, right*), marked above all by drive. Many late-18th-century breeders were working in the same

The Old English Hound (Bewicke, 1790).

The Meynellian Foxhound.

direction (which enabled Meynell to use such valuable outcrosses as
Cheshire, Brocklesby and Burton) but it was his lead they followed.

His personality, the reputation of his science and his pack, and the
mature grassland he hunted, brought sporting pilgrims from everywhere. Squires with their own packs, like William Childe of Kinlet,
or with the strongest local foxhunting traditions, like Cecil Forester of
Willey, uprooted themselves to hunt with Meynell. Quorndon, Harborough, and then and supremely Melton, became the sporting headquarters of England. From this grew the special character of the Shires,
their special *déraciné* society, the special contempt of the 'flying countries'
for the 'Provincials'. From it grew also the 'Leicestershire style' (*above*)
of galloping right up to hounds, and from this the riding of blood horses
in the hunting field (*below, right*).

Strong hunter.   Blood hunter.

There was a potential awfulness in some of these consequences of his mastership. As though to compensate, Meynell was – to name a fifth contribution he made of the utmost importance – infinitely considerate to his farmers. He not only caused gates to be closed and fences mended, but also waited for farmers before the first draw if he saw empty saddles on a market-day. His flamboyant successors at Quorndon – Lords Sefton and Foley – followed him as faithfully in this as in all else.

Most of what Meynell achieved depended on his being a very rich man, above all his hound breeding. This was a point made firmly by Peter Beckford, who started with the same unfair advantage. He was in some ways a typical rich squire of the late 18th century, being the son of a merchant who had bought into the country, and being highly educated and widely travelled. His father Julines Beckford used his Jamaican sugar fortune to buy Mr Thomas Fownes's house at Stepleton, near Blandford, in 1745. Peter divided his youth between Westminster and Oxford on the one hand (followed, typically, by the Tour) and his own harriers on the other. He bought foxhounds in 1766, assembling a pack, and drafting to it over the years, from a very wide variety of sources. As a hound breeder he was probably too experimental, but he had the problem of a heavily overwooded country.

Recovering from a fall in 1779, Beckford did what scarcely anyone had attempted, in English, since the days of Gervase Markham: he wrote a hunting treatise. (The exceptions were Arthur Stringer, whose *Experienc'd Huntsman* was hopelessly out of date when it was published in 1714, and Nicholas Coxe, whose *Gentleman's Recreation* and *The Huntsman* of 1674 and 1680 are so plagiaristic as to raise doubts about whether he had any practical experience at all.)

Beckford combined hard and copious experience as a practical M.F.H. and hound breeder with a wide acquaintance among contemporary pack owners, and these with elegance and erudition. His book was popular and influential in his own time, and has remained so ever since: and it is a comprehensive, reliable and almost unique account of late-18th-century foxhunting.

On hounds and hound breeding: Beckford described a good hound as would a modern judge at Peterborough (and as did Meynell, quoted by his hagiographer John Hawkes). He looked for straight forelegs, broad breast, deep chest, small head, clean neck, cat feet. He had no superstitions: 'A good dog cannot be of a bad colour.' The pack 'should be nearly all of a size; and I even think they should all look of the same family . . . I most approve of hounds of the middle size', but country and obstacles must be considered. The pace at which the whole pack can hunt for ten miles is far more important than the speed of any individual hound; they should hunt 'all a-breast' – in the later phrase, carry a good head. In temperament: 'It is the dash of the fox-hound which distinguishes *him*. . . The fox-hound, full of life and spirit, is always dashing and trying forward.' A marvellous phrase of Will Crane is quoted with approval: a good pack 'never come to a fault but they spread like a sky-rocket.' (Crane was the drunken genius who trained Mr Smith Barry's hounds for the famous Newmarket match of 1763, in which they beat Mr Meynell's couple out of sight; he was then huntsman to Colonel Bullock of Falkborne Hall, Essex.) This is one of many indications that Beckford was by no means a lone original far ahead of his time, but expressed its best general opinion.

The same is clear in most of his remarks about breeding and entering hounds. (The exceptions are some of his suggestions about outcrossing to completely different breeds.) 'It is the judicious cross that makes the pack complete. . . Send your best bitches to the best dogs, be they where they may.' Many people said that some packs of foxhounds were 'too high bred' to own a cold line; to Beckford as to Meynell this was nonsense: true high breeding gave a hound cold-scenting powers as well as drive: hunt as well as chase.

Beckford's hounds, like Meynell's, were walked all summer among riot to get them steady, especially to sheep. (Farmers were friends as necessary in Dorset as in Leicestershire.) Unlike Meynell in his youth, Beckford entered his hounds in woodland cubhunting (*above*) and only to fox; he was sure that entering to hare led to incurable wildness. A train-scent (drag) was a bad idea. A bag-fox might be necessary for blooding the young entry if wild foxes were scarce, but bagmen should only be hunted occasionally and for this one purpose. Beckford sometimes kept his young entry coupled at the covert side before cubbing; some people actually let them hunt in couples, but Beckford never in case they hanged themselves.

On hunt servants: 'the huntsman generally speaking, is an illiterate fellow, who seldom can either read or write.' What he should have is 'a clear head, nice observation, quick apprehension, undaunted courage, strength of constitution, activity of body, a good ear, and a good voice. . . He should let his hounds alone whilst they *can hunt*, and he should have genius to assist them *when they cannot*.' If they are lifted too soon, 'not a hound will stoop again'. But they must be lifted and cast in a cold-scenting country.

Of the way the fox is unkennelled: 'I look upon a fox well-found to be half-killed.' Hounds should get away close to his brush, and the chase should be '*short, sharp,* and decisive' – what Leicestershire called 'a pretty thing'. The kill is the purpose: 'I always return home better pleased with but an indifferent chase, with death at the end of it, than with the best chase possible, if it end with the loss of the fox.' One of the few archaic touches is Beckford's refusal to draw for an afternoon fox, which has often, in the intervening centuries, given a much better run.

As in the Quorn and Pytchley countries, 'if you can keep your brother-sportsmen in order, and put any discretion into them, you are in luck.' People who rode too close to hounds enraged Beckford: such men would do better riding to a train-scent.

Many contemporaries used no horn, but only the voice. Others still used the melodious French horn, and pictures show bugles twirled into various shapes. Beckford recommended the little straight English horn, unmusical as it was, especially in large coverts.

(xii) Other Squires and their Hounds; George Forester of Willey

Beckford's hounds were followed by guests staying in his house, and a few neighbours. Meynell's were followed by men of fashion from all over Britain (and some from Ireland) who stayed locally for the season, took houses, or formed residential clubs. But most packs – and there were very many new ones during Beckford's and Meynell's careers – were followed entirely by local gentry and farmers who could not afford fox-hounds of their own, and lived, in any case, within established fox-hunting countries which now had recognized frontiers. The vast majority of foxhunting squires in the late 18th century rode, in fact, to someone else's hounds; the most they contributed was a fox-holding covert and an occasional hunt breakfast. Coverts were properly looked after most exceptionally until well into the next century; but the merit of gorse was well known – 'furze-covers cannot be too much encouraged,' said Beckford – and a small amount was planted, in the Shires and East Anglia, by both owners of packs and the gentry who followed them. A few artificial earths were made in countries like the Roodings (Essex) where most foxes were stump-bred.

Mr Meynell was probably the first country gentleman who physically transplanted himself in order to hunt the fox with his own hounds in better country. Most stayed at home – Mr John Musters and Mr Francis Foljambe in Nottinghamshire; the Smith Barrys and Mr Leche of Carden in Cheshire; Mr Forester in Shropshire; Mr Ridge and Mr

Mr Tom Rounding M.F.H., of Woodford Wells, Essex.

Chute in Hampshire, with Mr Gilbert in the New Forest; Mr Grove, following Beckford, in Dorset; Mr Humble in County Durham; in Yorkshire Sir Charles Turner, Mr William Challoner, Mr William Bethell, Sir Thomas Gascoigne, Sir Walter Vavasour, Sir Rowland Winn; the Revd John Loder in Berkshire; in East Anglia Mr James Panton, Mr Coke, Mr William Mason, Mr Henley of Sandringham.

Of several of these gentlemen in the hunting field there is some record, usually of eccentricity: Mr Leche was so good-natured that his hounds and field were utterly out of control, and although rich and well educated he had allowed himself to slip into the broad accents of his farmer friends; Mr Chute of the Vyne 'looked like anything except a foxhunter', and crossed the country with a flying pigtail long after every other squire had chopped such a thing off; Mr Loder set his face against the marriage of his daughter to the Revd Robert Symonds (another clerical pack owner) until won over by the gift of a stallion hound; Mr Coke of Holkham was one of the greatest agriculturalists of any age.

Squire Forester of Willey.

Of this generation of local squires hunting the fox locally with their own hounds we focus, for a representative account, only on Mr George Forester of Willey, Shropshire (*above*). His ancestors were officials in the royal forest of the Wrekin in Henry I's time, from which hereditary appointment their name derived. The Weld family held Willey Hall (often Wylie or Wiley) named, it was said, from the osiers which grew profusely on the banks of the Severn (basket-making was an important local cottage industry). The families were united by marriage; George, born in 1739, was the son of that union and inherited as Squire of Willey, a title by which he was invariably addressed.

'Gone to Earth': burial of Tom Moody in Barrow Churchyard, near Wenlock, 19 November 1796.

About 1770 he established the first pack of foxhounds in those parts, his very large country being the modern Wheatland and a good deal of the North Shropshire on the other side of the Severn (the Wrekin) for which he had separate kennels. His hounds were steady line-hunters because of the extensive woodlands, big and powerful because of the severity of the country: they came from his childhood friend the Duke of Grafton, and from Mr Tom Noel of Cottesmore, Mr Pelham of Brocklesby and Mr John Corbet of Sundorne, then hunting the country to his north and east. 'Four o'clock on a hunting morning usually found him preparing the inner man with a breakfast of underdone beef, with eggs beaten up in brandy to fill the interstices; and thus fortified he was ready for a fifty-mile run.' His famous whipper-in was Tom Moody, who liked hunting, grog and women, never washed or removed his boots on a weekday, spent the summer catching eels, and earned the utmost affection and respect. His death was celebrated in a poem by Charles Dibdin, which was set to music and sung by Charles Incledon at the Theatre Royal: 'It just suited', said Pierce Egan, 'his melodious expressive voice, and he gave it such a superior style of manly excellence that we do not expect to hear anything like the execution of it again.'

Mr George Forester's hounds at Hangster's Gate in the Willey Woods, a favourite meet in his time. The ghost of Tom Moody is one of the figures visible in the distance.

Like Beckford's, the Willey hounds were followed by country neighbours and tenant farmers, and by the guests who came to stay in large numbers and for a long time. They dined immediately after hunting at four in the afternoon (evidently Mr Forester, like Beckford, did not draw for an afternoon fox), and often went straight from the dinner-table to the courtyard, the following morning, to mount their hunters again. Among regular guests were Mr Hugo Meynell of Quorndon, Mr William 'Flying' Childe of Kinlet (who had himself hunted the Ludlow country before being seduced by Leicestershire), and Mr Orlando Stubbs, who hunted part of Warwickshire.

Another notable follower was the 'fair but frail' Phoebe Higgs. Mr Forester was disappointed in love in his youth, and so never married, but never lost a partiality for women at least as strong as his whipper-in's. He assembled over the years a kind of harem of country girls, installing them on his land: 'he spent much of his time in the rural little cottages which he dotted over the estate at no great distance from the Hall.' The women were violently jealous of each other – mostly about money – and the squire had a large number of children and grand-children, all of whom he educated. More than one rode to hounds, but none as dashingly as Phoebe, who leapt the most daunting obstacles, and often showed Master and field the way across the formidable country. The squire issued a general challenge, for a heavy wager, that she would outjump any woman in England.

This all suggests a life uncouthly devoted to sport, port and passion: but falsely. Regular guests at Willey included parsons (some gentle and learned), lawyers and politicians, inventors, and local ironmasters and industrialists, many of whom were no less esteemed by the squire for not being sportsmen at all. Although he hated London and London manners, he was Member of Parliament from 1757 to 1790, latterly a strong follower of Pitt and his anti-Jacobin policy; he was succeeded in the seat by his cousin and heir Cecil (1st Lord Forester) another cele-brated follower of Meynell's hounds. The squire was also Chief Magis-trate and Justice for the Wrekin, and at the beginning of the French War raised and was Major of the Wenlock Loyal Volunteers. Though a Pittite Tory he was a man of great humanity. When there was severe poverty and suffering among the colliers and workpeople, he faced the threat of violent handling with extreme personal courage: and then bought the entire local stock of both food and coal and distributed it to the poor. He died in 1811.

(xiii) Mobile Masters: John Corbet and John Warde

Towards the end of the century Meynell's precedent (yet another of his precedents) was several times followed: and on the mobile or itinerant pack owner much foxhunting depended for generations. The outstanding 18th-century examples were Mr John Corbet of Sundorne Castle, Shropshire, and Mr John Warde of Squerries, Kent.

Mr Corbet first had hounds in his home territory, the Shifnal country (straddling modern North Shropshire and Albrighton); they were hunted by Stephen Goodall – ancestor of two of the greatest huntsmen in history, Belvoir Will and his son White-Collar Will of the Pytchley – who had descended on the social ladder owing to financial misfortune. Though not yet as immensely fat as he became, when he hunted the hounds of Lord Sefton at Quorn and Sir Thomas Mostyn at Bicester, he already needed a thoroughbred weight-carrier called Curricle, which afterwards went to the Prince of Wales, a horseman of similar build.

In 1778 Mr Corbet began spending part of each season in North Warwickshire, 'a fine, wild, fox-hunting-looking country' with only one ploughed field in a 12-mile run. In 1791 he took over the whole of Warwickshire, until 1811, hunting this large area four or five days a week, entirely at his own expense, with kennels at Meriden and Stratford. 'A more popular master of hounds never hunted,' said 'The Druid'. 'Warwickshire never before, nor since, witnessed such glorious days,' said 'Nimrod'; Mr Corbet had 'the manners and deportment of a highly-finished gentleman, although of a school of a somewhat earlier date'. He had 'a great dislike of fences', but contrived to stay close to his hounds because he knew the country and rode very fast Shropshire-bred horses.

Mr Corbet and his principal followers (such as the Canning brothers, rich Catholic squires who both rode 17 stone) started the Stratford Hunt Club. Limited to strictly elected members, like the Tarporley Club in Cheshire, it dined, in uniform, at the Tempest Inn. Low whist was the only gambling allowed, and drinking was more moderate than in Cheshire. Mr Corbet came every Thursday. 'One of the bright features in this hunt is a ball and supper, given annually.' These were said to be the best parties outside London, and were probably the first regular hunt balls.

Mr Corbet's daughter married Mr (later Sir) Richard Puleston of Emral, Flintshire; like his father-in-law, he divided his hunting career between his home country and a distant one, the latter (from 1799) being the Enville, once Lord Stamford's, neighbouring the Shifnal. Sir Richard was the first well known Master to hunt his own hounds.

If any sportsman in England was more popular than Mr Corbet it

Mr John Warde M.F.H.: J. Webb after Barraud, *The New Sporting Magazine*, May 1831.

was John Warde (*above*). Like most others of his time, he began hunting the fox from his home in West Kent, and was probably the only person to do so in that unpromising area until Sir John Dyke established his family's West Kent hounds in 1793. About 1776 Mr Warde went looking for a better country, and found it at Yattendon, Berkshire; from there he hunted part of the modern Garth and South Berks country and, from another kennel, part of the Bicester. In 1780 he moved to Bicester itself, making an immense reputation: by the time he moved his hounds to Pytchley (probably 1797) they were known as the most effective as well as the largest in England, and he as the happiest and most sunny-tempered Master. He had not the polish of a Meynell or Corbet: 'Rough as was his exterior,' said 'Nimrod' (who preferred very smooth exteriors), 'Mr Warde was accomplished and well informed, and capable of adapting his conversation to any society into which he might be thrown.' He had 'gaiety of heart and lightness of spirit', invariably communicated to everyone round him. He made a number of aphoristic pronouncements about hound-breeding, feeding and hunting, and one about the more general conduct of life which shows that his merriment had a basis of sound sense: 'Never keep a drinking man,' he said, 'nor a very pretty maid-servant.'

The 'rough exterior' remained, even in the Shires, and spread from Master to establishment: 'the turn-out was not equal to Mr. Corbet's. There was something like an affected disregard of appearances in the costume of the men, and the horses were of a coarser description.' But the hunting went superbly, and the Pytchley Club was as festive as Stratford or Melton itself.

In 1808 Mr Warde sold most of his pack to Lord Althorp (son of Earl Spencer and in contemporary terminology his Field Master), and went with a breeding nucleus to the dramatically different New Forest country. 'I never knew the nature of a bog', he said, 'till I went to Hampshire. I saw a good hat on top of one, and there was a head in it, and the head said, I don't care for myself, but do help to get my horse up, he's in a bog below.' The hounds were as successful in these unfamiliar conditions as on the Northamptonshire grass, and their Master as popular. 'Aesop', Hampshire's indefatigable sporting historian, said, 'Mr Warde revelled in jokes and jests, and, being always cheery himself, had the happy knack of making everybody about him cheerful.'

In 1814 he moved yet again, to Lord Craven's country in Berkshire and Wiltshire (the 5th Earl having recently retired), creating yet another pack from a few hounds saved from an attack of rabies. He retired in 1826, having been a Master of Hounds almost continuously, in six counties, for about fifty-five years: of which he only spent the first three or four at his own home.

(xiv) Somerville and the Hare

Wild deer were hunted until about the middle of the century in a few areas: notably the Dukeries (North Notts) and Gloucestershire. But in the former the Duke of Portland and Lord Scarborough turned to foxhunting in the Grove and Rufford, and in the latter the Duke of Beaufort was converted at Badminton. By 1800 wild red deer were hunted only by the Devon and Somerset Staghounds, owned successively by Sir Thomas Acland, Colonel Basset and Lord Fortescue. The hunting of carted deer was, instead, just beginning to become popular with packs additional to the Royal Buckhounds: but establishments such as the Common Hunt of the City of London, enlarging its deer in Epping Forest, and Bill Bean's suburban staghounds attracted fields of cockney grocers. Squires no longer had wild deer to hunt; the tame ones in their parks were not longer hunted or coursed, but culled for the pot with guns.

In most places there was a large gap in time – in some two or three centuries – between the disappearance of the wild deer and the arrival of organized foxhunting. What gentlemen chased was the hare.

The harehunting of the 1730s is, by Somerville, almost as vividly described as the foxhunting of fifty years later by Beckford. William Somerville was a Warwickshire squire who had his own harriers for about forty years. His poem *The Chace* (1735) put the knowledge of an expert into elegant blank verse, and we picture the cheerful, informal sport of Sir Roger de Coverley a generation earlier:

> Delightful scene!
> Where all around is gay, men, horses, dogs,
> And in each smiling countenance appears
> Fresh-blooming health, and universal joy.
> Huntsman, lead on!

A major difference was that Somerville had much faster and more purposeful hounds (*below*) than Sir Roger's 'stop-hounds'. His pack was described by an anonymous contemporary as 'about twelve couple of beagles, bred chiefly between the small Cotswold harrier and the Southern hound'. ('Beagle', of course, conveys no implication at this date that the hounds were followed on foot.) This kind of cross was normal for energetic harehunting, which, like Somerville's, included some galloping and some jumping; such hounds fell on Parson Adams's wig (in *Joseph Andrews*) when he lay asleep under a hedge. One of these was 'Ringwood, the best hound that ever pursued a hare, who never threw his tongue but where the scent was undoubtedly true; good at trailing, and sure in a highway; no babbler, no overrunner, respected by the whole pack, who, whenever he opened, knew the game was at hand.' Ringwood had all the virtues of the Southern hound, but he hunted to kill, and tore his hare in pieces; this proves him a crossbred hound like Somerville's.

Somerville's hounds drew a covert like foxhounds:

> see, where they spread
> And range around, and dash the glitt'ring dew.
> If some staunch hound, with his authentic voice,
> Avow the recent trail, the jostling tribe
> Attend his call, then with one mutual cry
> The welcome news confirm, and echoing hills
> Repeat the pleasing tale.

Harrier of Mr Somerville's fast sort.

(xv) Conversion of Harehunters to Foxhunting

With other harriers than Somerville's it was still normal to 'thistle-whip' the covert, doing the hounds' work for them. When Mr Fownes sold his foxhounds to Yorkshire in 1745, the sportsmen there were educated only in this method: 'When the huntsman came with his hounds in the morning, he discovered a great number of sportsmen who were riding in the cover, and whipping the furzes as for a hare.' After a spanking run their conversion to foxhunting was joyful and immediate.

Another conversion recorded is that of the gentlemen of Cheshire. On 7 November 1762, a number of owners of harriers formed the Tarporley Hunt Club. The ten founder members included Mr John Crewe, Beckford's friend Mr Booth Grey, and Sir Harry Mainwaring; the first president was the Revd Obadiah Lane and the Lady Patroness Miss Townshend. The proceedings of the club are packed with information about the ways of the leading gentlemen of a remote provincial country.

The first rules stipulated two meetings a year, one for hunting. This, at the Swan, Tarporley, started on the second Monday in November: 'each meeting to last seven days. The harriers never to wait for any member after eight o'clock in the morning. Every member must have a blue frock, with plain yellow metal buttons, scarlet velvet cape, double-breasted scarlet flannel waistcoat. The coat sleeve to be cut and turned up.'

The next year it was voted that: 'the metal buttons be changed for basket mohair ones; and that every member provides himself with a scarlet saddle-cloth, bound with blue'; and in 1764: 'if any member does not appear in the strict uniform of the hunt (as before described), he shall forfeit one guinea for each such offense.'

The 16th rule said: 'If any member of the Society should marry, he is to present each member of the Hunt with a pair of buckskin breeches'; in 1766, 'any member of the Hunt that marries a second time shall give two pairs of leather breeches to each member of the Hunt.'

These rules were enforced. In 1766:

Mr. Crewe was fined for having his bridle lapt with red and blue; Mr. Barry for not taking the binding off the button-holes of his coat; Mr. Whitworth for having his saddle-cloth bound with purple; Lord

Grosvenor for riding to covert with a white saddle-cloth, and likewise for having his bridle lapt with white; also for having quitted the
Hunt without leave on Tuesday, he was fined five guineas.

The last could afford his fine; he was the richest man in England and
one of the kings of its turf.

The fines were used to buy claret, of which, by the rules of the club,
Homeric quantities were drunk after dinner and further quantities
after supper.

In 1769 there was a change in the direction of sobriety, and (not
necessarily connected) a change from hare to foxhunting. It was agreed
that, 'Instead of three collar glasses, only one shall be drunk after dinner,

except a fox is killed above ground.' (Such a death was rare in a wild country full of unstoppable earths.) In 1770 it was voted: 'that the Hunt should change their uniform to a red coat unbound, with a small frock sleeve, a grass-green velvet cape, and green waistcoat, and that the sleeve has no buttons, the red saddle-cloth to be bound with green instead of blue, the points of bridles same as before'. The green cape, which became a collar, was an acknowledgement that the members had been harehunters. It remained (and remains) a badge worn only by invitation of the Tarporley Club, although the members now rode to Mr Smith Barry's foxhounds.

Many gentlemen refused to turn to foxhunting, although they lived in foxhunting countries. 'Nimrod's' Andrew Raby, for example, kept on his harriers in Lincolnshire, in spite of his son's contemptuous boredom. His pack was exceptionally good and his establishment exceptionally big: forty couple of dwarf foxhounds, carefully bred over fifty years, and ten excellent hunt horses. Mr Raby kept his harriers because it was family tradition to do so; because he doubted his own nerve for crossing a country after foxhounds; because he was too busy with his estate and duties as a magistrate to give enough time to a private foxhound pack; and because, with a disposable income of £7,000 a year after all major expenses had been met, he was not really rich enough. This last factor was the crucial one all over England except in parts of the North and in Devon and Cornwall.

Although so many of the smaller gentry disappeared during the 18th century, there were still some too poor (owing to large families, or to racing) to keep even the smallest pack of harehounds. Loving hounds and hunting, they made do with the otter. One of the Rabys' neighbours, 'so poor that he could scarcely keep himself and his family', kept three couple of otterhounds and one crossbred bull terrier. The sport was conducted exactly as Somerville described it about sixty years earlier: very interesting houndwork but a gory finish with the spear. Somerville himself had five couple of otterhounds, which joined his six couple of foxhounds – 'rather rough and wire haired' – in the winter.

A few people towards the end of the 18th century began to be aware that the badger was not destructive vermin, but principally a nut eater: and that it had great value in a foxhunting country as a maker of earths. But superstition to the contrary survived, and the tremendous fight the badger put up was thought great sport in itself, as well as excellent blooding for fox terriers. This was one of the sports – like dog-fighting, cocking and boxing – against which moral disapproval was beginning to be voiced well before 1800.

(xvi) The Coursing Greyhound

Coursing wild hares informally, for sport and pot, remained extremely popular, but more among farmers than gentry: William Cobbett had as many days with greyhounds as with harriers during his rides as late as the 1820s. Gentlemen like Lord Craven coursed hares as a change from hunting foxes, although they had long given up their harriers. One of Lord Craven's neighbours was Miss Ann Richards, of Compton Beauchamp (*below*), a rare 18th-century example of the sporting female squire. This determined spinster often went twenty-five miles on foot with her greyhounds, on the Berkshire downs. According to the epitaph which she wrote for herself (quoted in Thacker's *Courser's Companion*):

> But Ann at length was spied by Death,
> Who coursed, and ran her out of Breath.

Miss Ann Richards with two brace of greyhounds.

Foxes were also coursed in countries not drawn by recognized fox-hounds, but decreasingly. The warning given by *The Master of Game* was still repeated: 'If grey-hounds course him on a plain, his last refuge is to piss on his tail, and flap it in their faces as they come near him; and sometimes squirting his thicker excrements upon them, to make them give over the course or pursuit.'

Coursing at Swaffham: from *The Sporting Magazine*, 1793.

What most country gentlemen did was to enter their greyhounds in organized match coursing, a sport regularised at just the time when modern foxhunting was being developed. Lord Orford founded the Swaffham Coursing Society in Norfolk in 1776, which held the first proper meetings (*above*) and laid down the first rules. An early devotee was that most eminent of Suffolk squires, Sir Charles Bunbury of Mildenhall, winner of the first Derby and for nearly forty years benevolent dictator of Newmarket racing. Prizes and wagers were considerable; breeding and training therefore became as scientific as those of the racehorse. But not at once. Lord Orford himself tried as many different crosses with his greyhounds as Beckford with his foxhounds; and on a coursing day the greyhound was given only buttered toast in the morning, and after its course its feet were washed with butter and beer. (The latter treatment caused the dogs to lick their feet clean, their own saliva being credited with unrivalled medicinal powers; some Masters of Hounds walked their hounds after hunting through troughs of broth, for the same reason.)

The new sport had extraordinary growth, and within twenty-five years there were organized coursing meetings all over England. 'Nimrod' has Frank Raby turning against it about 1800 owing to the bewildering complexity into which the rules had developed, the extreme difficulty facing the tryer (judge), and the intensity of feeling to which matches gave rise. ('Nimrod' gives the impression that gentlemen who went coursing were bad losers.) The breeding and training of a kennel of greyhounds became scientific to the point that it took all a man's time: it was scarcely possible to be a courser as well as a foxhunter.

Match coursing: Lord Orford's Czarina (black) and Maria; from the Revd William Daniel's *Rural Sports*, 1801.

(xvii) Gentlemen on the Turf

Canals and navigable rivers increasingly carried heavy commodities, and a few, but only a few, passengers. Ox-carts were common in one or two areas, but infrequent or unknown in most of the country. All travel and almost all draught relied on the horse.

Horses were bred for six functions during the 18th century: racing, hunting, the saddle, pack, harness and draught. Horses for all these purposes continued to benefit from importation and selective breeding, and in all categories a minority of the country gentry made an immense contribution, directly, as breeders: and all the rest an equal contribution, indirectly, as purchasers.

The thoroughbred racehorse (so called from about 1710) was the first to assemble all its modern genetic ingredients. The importation of Arabians – largely by private gentlemen; wholly by them after the accession of George I – continued to enrich and refine the breed. The last important stallion to arrive was the Godolphin Arabian (*below*) (foaled 1724); although many more were brought over after him, they made no mark on thoroughbred pedigrees. The racehorse continued to change, however. Defoe noted, between the Godolphin Arabian's birth and his arrival in England, that Yorkshire-bred racers were substantially taller than Barbs, with much more bone; racehorses continued to grow for another century and a quarter, at a rate calculated by Admiral Rous (in 1850) at an inch every twenty-five years. Feeding accounted for much of this growth in the first generation or two; selective breeding was the cause thereafter. Other important changes – or aspects of the same change – took place very slowly between 1725 and 1775 and very rapidly for the twenty-five years following: horses matured younger and ran faster. The immortal Eclipse ran his first race as a five-year-old; he ran, between 1769 and 1771, the kind of race that had been devised in Charles II's reign – four four-mile heats and a final; two of his sons won the Derby, a 1½-mile 'dash' (originally only one mile).

The Godolphin 'Barb': actually a desert Arab from the Yemen.

To an extent, perhaps, the change in races was consequent on a change in the thoroughbred, but to a much larger extent the reverse was true. People bred horses which ran faster over shorter distances so that they could have more races in an afternoon, and so more opportunities to bet; they bred horses which could run younger so they got a return earlier. The motives were financial. Betting on horses in the Restoration period had sometimes been heavy but seldom ruinous, but its scale grew sharply, at least at Newmarket, in William III's reign; that solemn king was himself a deep plunger on horses (and on gamecocks), and still deeper plunged his racing manager, a transplanted Dorset squire called Tregonwell Frampton (*below*). In 1709 Sir William Strickland brought from York to Newmarket a horse called Merlin, belonging to another Yorkshire landowner Sir Matthew Pierson, and with it made a match with an unnamed horse of Frampton's. Yorkshire's victory (adroit, if not absolutely fraudulent) caused unprecedented losses, and is said to have been the reason for the legislation (9 Anne ch. 14) which made illegal the recovery of any bet of over £10: which remained on the statute book for 200 years, and which was one of the least enforced laws in British legal history.

Mr Tregonwell Frampton, of Moreton, Dorset and Newmarket;
turfite, courser cocker.

The Merlin match was arranged by gentlemen; gentlemen were the winners and losers. Gentlemen were the subjects of D'Urfey's squib (from *Pills to Purge Melancholy*, 4th edition 1719):

> Let cullies that lose at a race
> Go venture at hazard to win,
> Or he that is bubbled at dice
> Recover at cocking again;
> Let jades that are founder'd be bought,
> Let jockeys play crimp to make sport . . .
> Another makes racing a trade,
> And dreams of his projects to come;
> And many a crimp match is made,
> By bubbling another man's groom.

Gentlemen also were observed by Defoe a few years later:

> Being come to *Newmarket* in the month of *October*, I had the opportunity to see the Horse-Races; and a great Concourse of the Nobility and Gentry, as well from London as from all Parts of *England*; but they were all so intent, so eager, so busy upon the sharping Part of the Sport, their Wagers and Bets, that to me they seem'd just so many Horse-coursers in *Smithfield*, descending (the greatest of them) from their high Dignity and Quality, to picking one another's pockets, and Biting one another as much as possible, and that with such eagerness, as that it might be said they acted without respect to Faith, Honour, or good Manners.

A notable example, according to gossip, was Sir Robert Fagg, a Sussex gentleman: 'his Horses, they said, were all Cheats'.

John Toland's *Letters to Eudoxa*, of about six years later again, report:

> However, there be sharpers at this, as well as at other diversions of England; a groom's riding on the wrong side of the post; or his riding *crimp*, or people's crossing the horse's way in his course, makes a stranger risk deep when he lays his money, except he be let into the *secret*, which you can scarce believe he ever is.

(A 'crimp' match was fixed beforehand: Mr Frampton thought he was doing it to Sir William Strickland, when Sir William was actually doing it to him.) It all led to great unpleasantness: in 1732 John Cheny of Arundel noted in the preface to his annual *Historical List of all Horse-Matches Run* (earliest ancestor of Messrs Weatherbys' official *Calendar*):

The Diversion of Horse-Racing is advanced to such an Hight as to render the Practice of it Intimate and Familiar to almost every part of the Kingdom: notwithstanding which, the Accidents incident to these Affairs are so numerous; the Conditions of Running so various and different; the Articles, or Advertisement, or both, so often capable of counter Constructions; the Methods of deciding Bets in particular Cases, known to so few, and with such Reluctancy (through Byass of Interest) submitted to by many, who are well acquainted with them, that those Affairs are frequently attended with Disputes and Contentions, too many of which, proceed to expensive Law Suits, that terminate not, but with the additional Evil, of leaving behind them Impressions of Resentment, between the Persons concern'd.

At this date the persons were, almost without exception, country gentlemen.

As Cheny said, the problem was nation wide. Nottingham has never been regarded as an important racing centre, but in 1727, 'here is such as Assembly of Gentlemen of Quality, that not *Bansted Down* [Epsom], or *New Market* Heath, produces better Company, better Horses, or shews the *Horse* and *Master's* skill better'. Nottingham races were attended by 'an infinite throng of Gentlemen from all the Countries round'. Drake's *Eboracum* (1736) notes, 'It is surprising to think what a height this spirit of horse-racing is now arrived at, in this kingdom, where there is scarce a village so mean that has not a bit of plate raised once a year for the purpose.'

Everywhere, in every aspect, the country gentry were central. They often financed the prizes, they always provided the horses. At York's inaugural meeting in 1709 all the runners belonged to Yorkshire squires: not necessarily local, but including Colonel Childers of Doncaster and Mr Scrope of Danby (Wensleydale), as well as nearer gentlemen like Sir William Strickland; they nearly all rode their own horses, although this became exceptional within a very few years – horses were 'generally ridden by Grooms and Boys, chiefly for Lightness', which permitted one gentleman, with a bribe, to stop another's winning. Their predominance enabled the local gentry to make their own rules, and interpret them to suit their own wagers, as much at Nottingham, Chester or Hambledon as in their own parks or on their own village commons.

This was, no doubt, the golden age of racing from the point of view of the local gentleman; it could not be and was not allowed to continue. In 1740 there was *An Act* (13 George II ch. 19) *To restrain and prevent the excessive Increase of Horse Races*, which forbade any race with a prize worth less than £50. In 1751 there was mention in Pond's *Kalendar* (another forerunner of Weatherby's) of the Jockey Club, which the next year established itself at Newmarket (*below*). Initially ruler only of Newmarket, the Jockey Club grew within a generation to accepted, if incomplete, control over all British horse racing. It was an association of royal dukes and great nobles rather than of private gentlemen: yet its first really important member, in terms of real personal authority, was a local squire, Sir Charles Bunbury of Mildenhall.

The Betting-Room at Newmarket.

The gentry did not thereafter give up racing: but their local control over it was – to the benefit of all gullible visitors – increasingly qualified by Jockey Club rules.

What the gentry did was initiate the several new kinds of race of the period.

(xviii) New Kinds of Races

The earliest novelty was the give-and-take race, in which horses were weighted according to size:

On the 9th of October next [1711] will be run for on Coleshill Heath, in Warwickshire, a plate of six guineas value, three heats, by any horse, mare or gelding, that hath not won above the value of five pounds, the winning horse to be sold for 10 pounds, to carry 10 stone weight if 14 hands high: if above, or under, to carry or be allowed weight for inches, and to be entered on Friday the fifth, at the Swan, in Cole- shill, by six in the evening. Also a plate of less value, to be run for by asses.

For many years even the sharpest gentlemen were unable to cheat in give-and-take conditions, but a technique was devised at last. Charles ('Louse') Piggott's scurrilous *The Jockey Club* of 1792 reports of a mem- ber: 'he passes for what is called a *knowing one*, and is thought to have acquired a particular and curious method of making a horse sink, while measuring for a *give-and-take Plate*. This kind of exotic fame gratifies every feeling of Sir F—k, and is the only ambition to which he aspires.' The knowing one thus libelled was Sir Frederick Evelyn, who in 1773 had beaten Sir Charles Bunbury in a sweepstakes of 100 guineas and a hogshead of Ringwood. Ringwood, brewed at the Hampshire town, was 'the most orthodox ale in the Kingdom', and Sir Frederick won sixty-three gallons.

The sweepstakes principle had been invented about the middle of the century: the prize consisted of the sum of the entry money paid by all the entrants. The sweepstakes eventually became far more popular with owners than the two horse match, because the winner had provided a fraction of his prize instead of half of it, and because a field of horses is a more interesting betting proposition.

Weight for age (and sex) was added to weight for size a few years after this; the Chester City Plate of 1780 was 'for five, six-year-olds, and aged horses; five-year-olds to carry 8st. 2lb., six-year-olds 8st. 11lb., and aged horses 9st. 5lb.; mares to be allowed 3lb'.

The first three-year-old race apparently took place in 1731; it was very little imitated for the next forty-five years, pending the appearance of horses capable of running so young. In 1776 a group of Yorkshire gentlemen held a three-year-old sweepstakes at Doncaster, which became annual; in 1778 it was called, after one of the gentlemen, the St Leger (he was General Anthony St Leger of Park Hill, an extremely popular man almost entirely forgotten by history except in this one rôle). The Epsom equivalents (Oaks and Derby) followed in 1779 and 1780: the difference was that the gentlemen involved were not local, but visitors. A two-year-old ran at Newmarket in 1769; by

1780 two-year-old racing was established there and at Hambledon.

Handicap matches had been made between gentlemen in Charles II's reign; the advantages of a field of horses brought together in merit by variation of weights – spectacle, betting opportunities – must have been obvious. But for a long time such a race was not attempted, owing, almost certainly, to the impossibility of finding a handicapper trusted by all parties. The first public handicap for more than two horses was not run until the Ascot meeting of 1791. Handicaps were at once, and remained, subject to more fraud than all other sorts of races put together.

(xix) Breeders and Racegoers

Although many gentlemen ran racehorses, a minority bred them; these few were limited in the early 18th century largely to Yorkshire and the North. The greatest centre was Bedale; Defoe described it as full of breeders and jockeys (experts on horses in any capacity, of any rank). Horses were priced according to the reputation of their sires, but Defoe considered that pedigrees were not accurately kept; the evidence of surviving private studbooks suggests that he was quite wrong. Thorough-breds were bought and sold among Yorkshire gentlemen, and many were tried at Hambledon, a racecourse which existed entirely for this purpose; a great number were also sent south for sale. The greatest market was then a 'small but ancient Town call'd Penridge, vulgarly Panrage . . . an incredible Number of Gentlemen attended with their Grooms to buy Gallopers, or Race-Horses, for their *Newmarket* sport'. Richard Tattersall founded his sales at Hyde Park Corner in 1766; his famous premises became the leading exchange for thoroughbreds (as of hunters, coach-horses and hounds) and the focus of any visit to London of thousands of country gentlemen. Thoroughbred breeding had mean-while spread to most parts of the country, both those suitable (with calcium in the soil) and grossly unsuitable.

Even gentlemen who never owned a racehorse normally attended their local races, often persuaded thereto by their wives and daughters. 'On the Publick Race Days [Banstead Downs in 1724] are cover'd with Coaches and Ladies, and an innumerable Company of Horsemen, as well Gentlemen as Citizens, attending the Sport.' At country meetings, the ladies stayed in the town, throughout the meeting, for the balls and assemblies. But not at Newmarket; the only ladies there were the wives of local gentlemen, who went home immediately after the racing, owing to the migration of all visiting gentlemen to coffee-houses, gaming-rooms and cockpits.

Gimcrack, bred 1760 by Mr Gideon Elliot of Hampshire, one of the most gallant and popular horses in turf history; engraving after George Stubbs.

Towards the end of the century racing became, like hunting, rather a bachelor sport. 'It was', said 'Nimrod' of his youth, 'the custom for the public dinners, or "ordinaries" as they are termed, at race meetings, to be attended by the gentlemen of rank and wealth in the neighbourhood, as well as, occasionally, by a few whose situation in life, although respectable, did not allow of their being in such good company on any other occasion.' Dinner was at six o'clock; the yeomen present sometimes got above themselves, being over-excited, which was of itself enough for a gentleman of 1800 to keep his wife away. At Chester there were 'two o'clock ordinaries' where 'much mirth and good fellowship prevailed' among the Welsh and Cheshire squires, which the presence of ladies would have inhibited. Thus the growing refinement of society had the curious effect of coarsening the sports of the gentry.

A kind of bastard child of racing (out of foxhunting) was steeplechasing. This sport may be said to have descended from Tudor wild-goose chases and Stewart hunting-matches, but the immediate occasion for it was the jealous riding of very good hunters after very fast hounds in Leicestershire, followed by challenges after dinner. The genesis is well described in Dick Christian's 'lectures' to 'The Druid' during the famous rides in the gig. Steeplechase matches were practically confined to the Shires until well into the 19th century, and the contestants were visiting cracks rather than local gentlemen.

(xx) Halfbreds and Heavy Horses

The gentlemen who bred racehorses early in the 18th century invari-ably bred hunters and hacks too: Sir Edward Barnett at Ripon was as careful about his hunters as his racers in 1727, and bred them differ-ently. What was the same was the sire. The most celebrated imported Arabians – Captain Byerley's, General Honeywood's, Mr Darley's – covered very few high-class racemares, and got very few racehorses; even Lord Godolphin's Arabian, standing near Newmarket, only covered about 90 racemares in a very long stud career. There is no doubt that these stallions were used extensively to get half-bred hunters and hacks.

A number of gentlemen also made stallions of racing class – Arabians, and later thoroughbreds – available to their tenants and neighbours. Outstanding examples were the Pelhams of Brocklesby, Lincolnshire, who had an exceptionally prosperous and sporting tenantry. (It has often been noted that only hunting farmers breed good hunters.) Other places where the same kinds of landlords and tenants produced horses of comparable quality were Shropshire and the East Riding of York-shire.

Gentlemen who lived in such areas, or near them, could get their hunters direct from the farmers or, more usually, at local fairs; the most important of these was Horncastle, Lincolnshire. Early in the 18th century others would go to nationally famous fairs, such as Penridge: 'for Saddle-Horses, for the light Saddle, Hunters, Pads,' as well as racers, 'I believe the World cannot match this Fair.' Later in the century Mr Tattersall took the cream of the trade.

The hunter in most general esteem was out of a 'light cart mare', itself a product of the same period and the same kind of breeding: thoroughbred out of Friesland, the latter a fast trotter of moderate size

from the Netherlands. As early as 1727 Teesside was celebrated for a somewhat more substantial and powerful horse than the Yorkshire racer and hunter: the Tees is the northern boundary of the Cleveland country, and what contemporaries described came to be known as the Cleveland Bay (*above*). The Norfolk trotter was a rangier, faster, later product of a similar cross, more like (though not very like) the American Standardbred. These and similar breeds were the supreme light harness and pack horses; from quite early in the 18th century they were sometimes heavyweight hunters and very often the dams of crossbred hunters. Gentlemen bought all of them that could possibly be bred.

Hacks or pads (*above*) were particularly associated – as they had been since Tudor times – with Galloway in the Scottish lowlands and with Ireland. Galloway nags and Hobbies were at best of more specifically

Barb type – small, amenable, with limitless stamina, not very fast – and were very good for travel and for such sports as hawking, shooting from horseback, and match coursing. They were continually improved by infusions of thoroughbred blood throughout the 18th century. The same is true of ponies in the great pony breeding countries, especially Devon; there gentlemen went hunting on half-breds, with Exmoor or Dartmoor pony dams, far better suited to trappy country than the showier animals of the 'flying countries'.

Heavy draught horses were comparatively new to most of England, although there were small numbers imported from Flanders in the late 16th century and thereafter, mostly for gentlemen's coaches. The stock was dispersed during the 17th century. In the early 18th, the best draught horses were said to be bred in Leicestershire, Northamptonshire and Bedfordshire, and sent to Northampton fair. Almost everywhere heavy horses replaced oxen for plough, harrow and wagon: Gloucestershire was, Arthur Young found in 1769, one of the few places where oxen remain in normal use.

(xxi) The Gun and the Sitting Bird

Shooting developed towards modernity more slowly than hunting or racing. Hunting depended on the foxhound, racing on the thoroughbred, with both of which the gentry successfully busied themselves; both made earlier and larger advances than the gun, in regard to which the user was at the mercy of his tradesman.

The 18th century began and ended with a muzzle-loading piece in which the black powder was fired by flint and steel (*above*). Powder was poured in from the horn and covered with a wad, usually of cork or flannel; then came the shot, made by cutting up sheets of lead and rattling them into approximate roundness. It was entirely possible for the powder to ignite the moment it was poured in, owing to the heat of the metal from the previous shot; it was also possible for this premature explosion to be delayed until the ramrod too was fired out of the barrel.

An explosion in the powder flask (*below*) sometimes attended these disasters. Loading was not only hazardous but also slow and noisy.

Powder-Flask and Horn.

The best flints were knapped in Suffolk, but even with these a spark sometimes failed. When there was a spark it ignited the corner of the powder in the pan by the touch-hole, a factor which both delayed and weakened the explosion. Hangfires were as frequent as misfires, and still more dangerous. The powder itself was not only smoky in the air and greasy in the barrel, but also unpredictable as to power: calculations about how much powder to use were never better than approximate. The nature both of the shot and of the ignition imposed a normal minimum barrel length of forty inches, which was too long for balance and sent many shots low.

With pieces like these it is amazing that anyone shot flying. Fictional characters did so – two of Sir Roger de Coverley's neighbours in the first decade of the century – but very few flesh and blood birds, really perhaps hardly any, were killed off the ground or the branches of trees. Any birds shot flying were certainly going away, neither oncoming nor crossing. Driving and walking in the modern sense were beyond the possibilities of the gun. Birds were stalked and shot sitting.

Partridges were typically shot in long stubble immediately after the harvest (*opposite*); pheasants sometimes there, sometimes in the woods, a little (but only a little) later. The open was more genteel. Edie's *Treatise on English Shooting* (1773) remarks:

Partridge shooting, on account of the cleanness, little fatigue, and more certain diversion than any other, by their being found in coveys, and taking short flights, is generally esteemed the genteelest and best sport we have in England . . . Pheasants also afford very pretty shooting, though far more fatiguing and tiresome than partridge shooting, owing to the bushes, briars, and other disagreeable circumstances of the woods.

But the pleasure of the open country was much diminished when instead of stubble and grass there were fields of cabbages and especially turnips, which were multiplying immensely just as Edie wrote.

(xxii) Shooting Flying

The gun was in no way significantly improved until the 1780s, but there had already begun a change of taste to be ascribed, almost certainly, to the Grand Tour. The better shots (with better guns) of the continent reinspired the English with the idea that a gentleman shot flying: and in 1770 was published a book called *The Art of Shooting-Flying:*

And now, Sir, take the piece, carry it upon your left arm, with the thumb of your right hand upon the cock, and fixing your eye upon any particular object, present the gun in the manner before directed, and in the motion of bringing it up to cock it; do it pretty briskly, but in no hurry, so as to confuse yourself . . . Briskly draw the trigger as soon as you have got an exact sight of the object, and continue to keep your muzzle at it for some time after you have drawn the trigger lest you should hang fire.

(The follow-through has, in fact, other merits, especially with a 40-inch barrel.)

It became gentlemanly to shoot a flying bird, but your gun obliged you to pick the easiest one: a low bird started out of a hedgerow, taken close from directly behind. The birds were started by a small pack of spaniels, preferably mute, counted in couples like hounds. It is probably relevant to the growing popularity of this method that an immense number of new quickset hedges was established, especially in the best pheasant-shooting areas like Norfolk, during the third quarter of the century, as Arthur Young repeatedly notes.

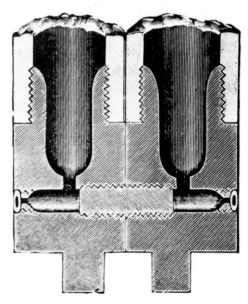

Two technical developments enabled shooting flying to spread. In 1782 William Watts, a Bristol plumber, discovered how to make drop shot; molten lead poured in a coarse spray from the top of a tower solidified into pretty good spheres during its cooling journey to the ground, which greatly increased both the regularity of the pattern and the penetration of the shot. In 1787 the London gunmaker Henry Nock invented his 'patent breech' (*opposite*). This had a hole through the block to the middle of the charge, instead of its edge; igniting from the middle outwards the explosion was faster and more powerful. These inventions together enabled the barrel to be reduced from an average of forty inches to an average of thirty; the weight saved was an infinite convenience, caused better accuracy because of better balance and less fatigue and 'muzzle drooping', and opened the way for the double-barrelled gun, which was not, however, in general use for some time. (The sagging muzzle actually remained a cause of very many misses because the left hand was kept well back: the reason for this was still the danger of the barrel exploding. Of course the gun sometimes exploded at the breech too. Joseph Manton – one of the greatest and most inventive gunmakers of his time – invented in 1806 the 'Elevating Rib' (*below*), which had some success in stopping people from shooting low.)

The Sportsmen's Directory of 1792 said, 'the art of shooting flying is arrived at tolerable perfection'. The Revd William Daniel's *Rural Sports* of 1807 said it was 'not exactly at present the *custom for Gentlemen* to shoot on the ground'. Daniel instructed his readers thus: 'Both eyes should be open and the object fired at the instant the muzzle of the gun is brought up, and fairly bears upon it. The sight becomes weakened by a protracted look along the barrels at a bird, and keeping the aim long fatigues the *eye*, and the *finger* does not obey the eye so readily as when employed at a first glance.' The head kept up and the shot got off quick became and remained the distinctive English style, for the first time respected and even copied by Frenchmen: 'L'enfant de la superbe Albion ne baisse jamais la tête, même devant le gibier qui fuit en ligne droit. Au départ, il fixe la pièce, la tête haute, de manière à la suivre dans tous ses movements.' The child of proud Albion was safer, too: Thornhill's *Shooting Directory* of 1804 instructs him, 'On the birds rising, you should coolly select a bird to take aim at, never cocking your piece until you have made the choice. I can assure every young beginner that all excellent shots never attempt to cock their pieces until the game rises.'

The principal problems continued to be misfires and the delay (reckoned at one-tenth of a second) between trigger and combustion. The first beginning of a real solution to both problems was the invention in 1807 of the detonator; this involved the use of 'fulminating powder', the virtue of which was ignition by a blow instead of a spark, which in turn instantaneously ignited the main charge. Ultimately the detonator entirely superseded flint and steel, but the early prejudice of conservatives against it was well founded in its unreliability. It is also probable that instantaneous ignition took experienced shots by surprise, with the result that they fired below dropping birds and in front of crossing ones.

Another innovation, following Watts's invention but not immediately, was the use of much smaller shot. *The Gentleman's Recreation* had urged, a century earlier, the use of large shot: with small shot 'the Fowl will fly away with it, as having neither strength nor weight to enter far to their Prejudice'. In 1780 number 2 or 3 (110 and 135 pellets to the ounce) was invariable, even for partridges. But Daniel in 1807 deprecated 3 and 4, recommending 5, 6, or even 7: 'Small shot go between the feathers like *pins* and *needles;* whilst the large shot as often *glance off* as penetrate them.' Correct advice, though for an absurd reason.

At the turn of the century the most celebrated exponent of shooting flying (as of much else) was Coke of Norfolk. At his manor of Warham, near Holkham, in October 1797, within the circumference of a mile, he shot forty brace in ninety-three shots in eight hours; each bird was shot singly. In January 1803 Mr Coke, Sir John Shelley and Mr Thomas Sheridan, at Houghton, shot fourteen brace of hares, sixteen couple of rabbits, twenty-four brace of pheasants, thirteen brace of partridges, and sixteen couple of woodcock. For the times, and even for the place, this was an immense bag. (In 1811, at Holkham itself, 'the bag of a certain royal duke was thus entered: 'killed, of game, o, wounded, 4; 1 footman slightly, 1 groom severely, 1 hat (on the head of a friend), 1 horse.')

Most bags continued extremely small. Colonel Peter Hawker in Hampshire was perhaps (he thought he was certainly) the best shot in England in succession to Mr Coke: in 1814 'my having this wild season bagged fourteen double shots successively (walking) is the best shooting that has been accomplished in England'. But his diaries show how pleased he was, day after exhausting day, with four or five brace, usually of mixed game. And he walked his pheasants very early in the morning, starting on 1 October, when they are at their easiest.

Big bags depended on preserving, which meant the elimination of vermin, and above all of foxes. Beckford says that this was beginning in his day (1780) to the furious despair of foxhunters, though not in his own Dorset country. The destruction of litters by gamekeepers was becoming a severe problem in Hampshire by 1800 and in Essex when Colonel John Cook was Master of Hounds (1808–13). A division began among country gentlemen which sometimes became quite as bitter as the political or sectarian feuds of the early 18th century. Colonel Cook (as he records in his *Observations on Fox-Hunting*) was 'a great advocate for a ball and supper. I have known it the means of saving many a fox from being trapped'. The logic of this was that a local squire's daughter wanted to dance in the assembly rooms; her father therefore had to welcome the foxhounds, and have a fox in his coverts, even if he preserved pheasants.

There were far more woodcock than later, rooted out of covert by spaniels, and in many places far more duck. The latter were of great commercial importance to professional wildfowlers and to the owners of decoy ponds; good sport was 'flapper shooting' on a lake, of young mallard and teal which had bred there, for which you needed two good retrievers.

(xxiii) The Shooting Dog

The first major technical improvement was not to the gun but to the dog. Previous ages in England had had, by and large, only retrievers, disciplined not to stir until after the shot. Officers returning from the continental wars at the beginning of the 18th century introduced the pointer, which transformed the sport. What the pointer did was not

NEWFOUNDLAND RETRIEVER

ENGLISH SETTER

SMALL WATER-SPANIEL

SPRINGER OR COCKER

(Bewicke, 1790).

only to find the birds on the ground and indicate their position, by the point, to the gun, but also effectively to hypnotise them. 'When hunted by a pointer the pheasant squats down and looks steadily on the dog, so that the sportsman may take his aim at leisure.' Likewise the partridge, green and golden plover, dotterel, bittern, wheatear and landrail among other species. Imported pointers were crossed with English dogs to give them stamina; they also retrieved. Every sporting squire had a kennel of pointers, usually liver and white, flecked or spotted, commonly home bred.

Pointers training; from the Revd William Daniel's *Rural Sports*, 1807.

The setter (setting-dog) followed the pointer in time and in importance. It was believed to have originated in a retriever-pointer cross itself crossed to foxhound, and with a dip of water-spaniel; in use it was identical to the pointer, having the advantage only of greater strength and stamina. The other significant 18th-century dog was the springer, by which was meant any kind of spaniel; its function was to spring game out of hedgerow or covert, and its importance grew late in the century with better guns and better shots.

English Pointer; English Setter: both after Reinagle, 1803.

The growth of shooting flying took away the emphasis from pointers and put it back on retrievers. Frank Raby's Lincolnshire kennel about 1800

he found quite to his satisfaction. It contained three brace of well-broken setters; three couples and a half of spaniels, all as mute as a gate-post; two capital Newfoundlanders, then just coming into fashion as retrievers of wounded game; and four brace of greyhounds of the best blood in the country, some of them having proved themselves such by the various prizes they had gained. But matters did not end here. Two brace of fine young setters had been sent off into Cheshire in the pairing season, to be broken on the down-charge system, by old Potts.

Springers or Cock-Flushers, with William Mansell, Keeper to the Duke of Newcastle. Engraved by Wm Nicholls, *The Sporting Magazine*, 1807.

Old Potts charged no less than £10 for breaking each dog, for which £25 each had been paid. The down-charge system meant simply that absolute obedience and stillness on which Gervase Markham had insisted two centuries earlier: the dog was trained to drop and lie motionless on command, on the simple raising of the shooter's hand, or on the game being flushed; this discipline became, of course, just as important for retrievers as for setters.

(xxiv) The Grouse

Frank Raby's down-charge setters were for grouse shooting. Grouse had been shot on the ground over pointers in Yorkshire, throughout the 18th century, by such local sportsmen as Mr Henry Darley of Aldby. Lockwood, narrator of *Wuthering Heights*, travelled to Yorkshire from London for the grouse shooting in 1802; he there found Heathcliff, living on the edge of the moors and shooting grouse with something as near enthusiasm as his miserable character allowed; he was extremely jealous to protect the breeding birds. Heathcliff had a kennel of pointers (the only other dog mentioned was Isabella Linton's pet springer) so it may be assumed he shot his birds on the ground. His gun burst, sending a splinter into his arm and causing profuse bleeding.

Sport in Scotland was potentially opened up for visiting Englishmen by the building of military roads after the '45 rebellion; hardly any took advantage of this before 1800 and very few before 1850. Mr Raby and two friends took a moor for £400 about 1800; their bag after a month was considered good: 'Black-grouse, seven and a half brace; red grouse, eighty-five brace; ptarmigan, three and a half brace; red deer, seven; and roe, thirteen.'

In Scotland grouse were less common than later (because the care of heather was not understood; perhaps because there were far more buzzards, eagles, martens and wildcats) but also less shy. Thomas's *Shooter's Guide* of 1816 recommended his pupil 'to take this diversion on horseback, which, of course, very much lessens the fatigue; and for this purpose Galloways or ponies are used, so trained that they will stand still with the bridle on their necks, while the sportsman takes aim and shoots.' A grouse walked up on horseback is not the bird familiar to later generations. Blackgame was commoner than now, but localised.

It can be assumed that the visitors shot their roe with guns (*below*); it is not clear what they shot their stags with.

(xxv) Snaring and Liming

The Gentleman's Recreation of 1680 has fifty pages on fowling, of which only four treat of 'The Birding or Fowling-Piece'. Netting, snaring and liming occupy, as the principal polite recreations, the remaining forty-six pages. During the next century and a half the proportionate emphasis was just about reversed: but very gradually.

Commercial (or gastronomic) motives impelled taking several sorts of birds too small to shoot. The most important was the wheatear, 'or *as we may call them*', said Defoe, 'the English *Ortolans*, the most delicious Taste for a Creature of one Mouthful'. They were netted in large numbers on the South Downs when they arrived exhausted after migration. Quail were another but less numerous crop.

This is perfectly explicable. What is astonishing is the instruction given in the fifth edition, as late as 1828, of John Mayer's *Sportsman's Directory or Park and Gamekeeper's Companion*: there are long and detailed sections on taking woodcock and partridge with nets and birdlime, using limed twigs for smaller birds, and intoxicating birds:

There is a way of intoxicating birds, so as to catch them with your hands – Take some lees of wine and some hemlock juice, and having tempered them together, steep a quantity of wheat therein for the space of one night; then throw the same into a place where the birds resort to feed, and when they have eaten thereof, they will drop down dead drunk. If too much hemlock be used, there will be danger of poisoning the birds, and of rendering them unwholesome food; or of poisoning game, or domestic poultry, which may accidentally eat the wheat.

It is impossible to doubt that this was done (the caution about hemlock rings an unmistakable note of practical experience), or to detect awareness of any moral or sporting disapproval.

(xxvi) Hawking and Colonel Thornton

Another principal method of taking birds had been hawking, decreasingly practised during the 17th century and virtually dead in the early 18th. Its survival (as into our own day) was the work of a very small number of devoted enthusiasts. Leader of these in the late 18th century was Lord Orford, of Houghton, Norfolk, that polymath sportsman who also established match coursing. He flew kites (known to but despised by 'Auceps'); he was involved successively with the Falconers' Society (1771), the Falconers' Club, and the High Ash Club. The last lived from about 1792 to the 1830s; its members included Lord Berners and Colonel Thomas Thornton of Falconer's Hall and Thorneville Royal.

Colonel Thornton is a notable figure in the history of hunting, racing, and sporting literature, as well as falconry; his eccentricities were financed by a large fortune and two fine estates near York. According to 'The Druid' he went out thus: 'Fourteen servants with hawks on their wrists, ten hunters, a pack of stag hounds and lap-dog beagles, and a brace of wolves formed the advance guard. Two brace of pointers, and thrice as many greyhounds in rich buff and blue sheets, with armorial bearings, followed in their train.' He was therefore equipped for encounters with any bird (pointers and hawks), hares and rabbits (hawks, beagles, greyhounds), and deer.

He also had an eminent pack of foxhounds, with which he hunted much of the modern York and Ainsty country from about 1780 to 1810.

In 1785 he received a piece of plate from Sir Harry Featherstone and Sir John Ramsden as 'a compromise to a bet in honour of a Hambledon Fox', as recorded in Pick's *Calendar* of the following year. The colonel had wagered that he would find a fox in Hunt's Whin to run for twenty miles. Five persons present on the appointed day signed a certificate that the fox had broken in view and was killed after a run of two hours and thirty-eight minutes without a check, only eight horsemen out of seventy being up at the death. The five gentlemen 'do believe the said Fox ran at least twenty-eight miles'. In 1795 the colonel made a general wager, his hound Merkin (*below*) against any other, five miles 'over Newmarket', the challenger to have a start of a furlong, for 10,000 guineas. There were no takers. Merkin was probably half greyhound, and capable of owning only the scent of an aniseed drag. But another hound, Lounger, was good enough to go to the Duke of Northumberland as a stallion (the 2nd Duke, one of the few Masters of Hounds who have eaten for dinner a fox they killed in the morning).

In the history of racing the colonel is remembered as the husband of that Alicia Thornton who rode a celebrated match at York in 1804. She was then only 22, 'very handsome, of a fair complexion, light hair, blue eyes, and very fascinating'. She was an accomplished horsewoman, something unusual at the time, and rode regularly to her husband's hounds, which was still more unusual. Her sister was married to a Captain William Flint, who lived in York and was a well known hunting man and turfite. One day early in the year Mrs Thornton and Captain Flint met out hunting. They argued about the merits of their horses, and ran an impromptu match. Mrs Thornton won. Captain Flint, chagrined, challenged her to ride a proper match for 1,000 guineas a side. She accepted, and terms were arranged. In the match, run before an unprecedented crowd which had bet unprecedented sums, Mrs Thornton's horse broke down and the captain cantered in.

Mrs Thornton on the Knavesmuire, York.

Vituperative exchanges in the *York Herald* were followed by an assault with a horsewhip, of the colonel by the captain, in the grandstand at York, consequent upon the colonel's refusal to pay his losses. A lawsuit followed. Captain Flint went to prison: but in 1815 published *A Treatise on the Breeding, Training and Management of Horses*. He died in penury in 1832, of an overdose of the prussic acid he took for his asthma.

Colonel Thornton had toured France during the Peace of Amiens, and published in 1806 his *Sporting Tour Through France* (a good book). He gave up his hounds and went to live in London, and immediately after Waterloo took up residence in Paris. He there, according to Pierce Egan, 'always dined in a scarlet straight-cut coat of the whipper-in style'. It had by this time emerged that Alicia was not Mrs Thornton at all, but a Miss Meynell, daughter of a Norwich clockmaker. The colonel's eccentricities would have seemed, to many of his contemporaries, no more than would be expected of a man who kept hawks.

(xxvii) Decoys

Whatever they did with their guns, gentlemen took an undiminished interest in their decoys. The most important area was the fens. 'In these Fennes', said Defoe, 'are abundance of those admirable Pieces of Art call'd Duckoys.' For one near Ely the landlord, Sir Thomas Hare, was paid £500 a year in rent. From one on the Ouse near St Ives (Huntingdonshire) 'they generally send up three Thousand Couple a Week' to the London markets. In the fens the decoy ducks were not pinioned or tied down, but were home bred and extremely tame. They flew as far as Holland, it was believed, and brought back immense flocks onto the water and into the decoy. Attempts had been made to drain the fens in the very early 18th century, quite successfully in some places owing to the new use of windmills, but total inundation still occurred; the wildfowlers and decoyers violently resisted more serious drainage undertaken later in the century by improving landowners.

The business was so profitable and so diverting that many new decoys were established, which involved artificial ponds and new plantations of trees. Defoe examined one near Corfe Castle on the Isle of Purbeck (South Dorset):

an open Peice of Ground where a Neighbouring Gentleman had at a great Expence laid out a proper peice of Land for a *Decoy*, or *Duck-coy*, as some call it; the Works were but newly done, the Planting young, the Ponds very large and well made; but the proper Places for shelter of the Fowls not cover'd, the Trees not being grown, and Men were still at Work improving, and enlarging and planting on the adjoining Heath, or Common: Near the Decoy Keeper's House, were some Places where young Decoy-Ducks were hatch'd, or otherwise kept to fit them for their Work; To preserve them from Vermin, Polecats, Kites and such like, they had set Traps, as is usual in such Cases, and a Gibbet by it, where adundance of such Creatures as were taken were hang'd up for Show.

One of the creatures displayed in this early 'gamekeeper's larder' was an eagle. The squire was extremely angry at the destruction of this astonishing visitor, a reaction as creditable as it is, for the time, unexpected.

About 1800 there were 200 decoys in England, all on still water enjoying the protection of trees. Two changes had taken place: instead of large lakes, small ones of about two acres had been found most effective; and the pipes were so placed that the duck came into their mouths regardless of the direction of the wind. The pipe was at this date about 70 yards long, the mouth 20 feet wide and high. The pipe tapered to its final net over increasingly shallow water. The tame ducks were called in by whistles and food; the wild followed, and were then chased up the pipe by man and dog. It was still extremely big business.

(xxviii) The Unadventurous Anglers

The fishing of the 18th-century gentleman is the major sport about which least can be said; there were many improvements, but there was very little literature that was not derived from the extensive library of the previous century.

Giles Jacob's *The Complete Sportsman* of 1718 is typical in adding almost nothing to earlier writers; he does, however, describe in detail the execrable practice of cross-lining for trout, which was unique to Hampshire and especially a diversion on the Test. The essence was a line stretched from bank to bank, frequently left there all night; it was sometimes armed with as many hooks as possible – a sort of nightmare paternoster – baited with worms.

A worthier innovation was silkworm gut, known to James Saunders (*The Compleat Fisherman*, 1724) but not in general use for a long time.

Charles Bowlker's *The Art of Angling* of 1747 is the one major original book of the century. What he shows is a considerable advance in entomology and fly-dressing; he fished his exact imitations upstream, as had Venables and Worlidge a century earlier. But it is clear from later writers that this common-sense practice did not, bizarrely enough, reach the Hampshire chalk streams for another century. (All that Defoe could find to say about that great Berkshire river the Kennet in 1724 was, 'This River is famous for Craw-fish, which they help Travellers to at *Newbery;* but they seldom want for Price.') Bowlker's coarse fishing relied more heavily on the 17th century; he subscribed to what he said was a general faith in kitten or puppy flesh, from the 'tenderest part of the leg', as an ingredient in paste. Thomas Best (*The Art of Angling*, 1787) likewise recalls Walton and his contemporaries in recommendations for various aromatic (and sometimes ghoulish) constituents for paste, and for mixtures to improve the attractiveness of worms.

The reel at last came into general use for trout fishing. The trout rod considerably shortened, and good rods were made of foreign woods such as hickory, greenheart and lancewood. Split cane is first mentioned in Snart's *Practical Observations on Angling in the River Trent* of 1801; there were four sections whipped and lashed together, the six-section construction being an American development of about 1850.

Although gut was known, it was either not trusted by or not available to most anglers. The anonymous author of *The North Country Angler* of 1786 urges most careful choice of horsehairs; he used three hairs, each singly, of diminishing stoutness. Grey was best. He tied the two knots so that one end stuck out at right angles for the dropper. This fisherman was pretty typical by now in trying to achieve an exact imitation for trout; he was also typical, though quite misguided, in making the same attempt with his salmon flies. He records the strict and often violent keepering of northern rivers and the ferocity (anticipating affairs 30 years later) with which J.P.s pursued poachers: the only poachers who habitually got away with large numbers of illicit trout and salmon were millers, who netted their mill-pools.

The reason for protection was still far less sport than finance. Tay, Derwent and Trent were salmon fisheries of enormous value; in the south the most rewarding were the Tamar and Severn. In Defoe's time the country people did extremely well out of the salmon they caught and sold, but fisheries, like so much else, were taken into gentlemen's hands. The fens sent tench and pike to London in numbers which made them, in some seasons, almost as profitable as the duck; they went alive, in casks of water on carts.

A sport very popular in the late 18th century (and perhaps worthy of a modern trial) was the use of the casting-net. Many gentlemen tried to master its considerable difficulties, and some became wonderfully skilful. The casting-net was mostly used to catch gudgeon for pike-bait, or small perch for stocking a pond; sometimes bigger fish were caught: sometimes even pike.

Pike fishing itself was as popular a sport as ever, and in no way changed except that artificial minnows were more widely trolled than live frogs. It is recorded that as early as 1790 a feeling was growing against live bait, which a generation later extended itself to the prevention of cruelty to worms; this cause was passionately but not widely espoused. Parson Woodforde in Norfolk escaped the campaign: his diary records two trout, each of $1\frac{1}{4}$ lb., caught in 1786 on grasshoppers.

Real ponds were still stocked and artificial ones still made; Mr Henry Darley built enormous dams across the Hutton Beck to make fishponds about 1745. Many artificial ponds doubled as stews and decoys.

(xxix) Cockpit and Prize-Ring

The importance of cockfighting as part of the polite sporting scene is shown by the inclusion of its records in all racing calendars. This practice began – or was at least planned – by Mr John Nelson as early as 1679: he announced in the *London Gazette* in February 'a Register at the Groom Porter's office in *Newmarket*, of all such Horse-matches, Foot-matches, Cock-matches, or Bets relating to the premises, as any person therein concerned hath or shall desire him to Register'. Mr Nelson's record was probably only in MS, and does not survive. John Cheny's first printed *Calendar* of 1727 records all horse matches of over £10 value, 'With a LIST of all the Principal COCK-MATCHES of the kingdom in the Year above, and who were the Winners and Losers of them'; his precedent was followed until 1840.

There were cockpits in every town, but most particularly in towns whose racecourses attracted the gentry in numbers. The mains (matches) were a part of the race week scarcely less popular than the racing itself. The York racecards always included a note that 'A Pair of Cocks will be on Sod at the Cock-Pit, Coffee Yard, every Day, during the Races, precisely at eleven o'clock.'

Cheny records notable matches in 1731:

At Grimsthorp very early in the Spring, her Grace the Duchess of Ancaster fought Mr. Banks, showing 31 cocks aside, for 20 guineas and 200, in which Match were 20 Battles, 11 of which were won by her Grace and 9 by Mr. Banks. Her Grace also fought Mr. Banks of Horncastle in the middle of July, showing the same number, for the same sums. In this Match was 24 Battles, 14 of which were won by her Grace and 10 by Mr. Banks. . . . In the last week in *July* a great Cock-match was fought at the city of Carlisle between Mr. Philipson and Mr. Warwick, showing thirty-one cocks aside, for ten guineas a battle, and a hundred guineas the odd battle; in which Match was 25 Battles, 13 of which were won by Mr. Philipson and 12 by Mr. Warwick. This was a remarkably hard-foughten Main, for it came to 12 and 12, and the 25th Battle was long and strenuously contested on both sides, but Mr. Warwick's Cock at last gave it up, by actually running away.

As in the closely associated sport of racing, there was tradition and usage about rules, but no official statement of them and no guarantee that local influence would not make adjustments. And as in racing, standard rules were important because of the large sums of money involved (not the principal wagers, which were modest, but the side bets). Cheny therefore in 1743 included in his *Calendar* a full schedule of

Gamecock.

Cock in Fighting Trim.

RULES and ORDERS for COCKING, so revealing and unfamiliar that it is worth setting out in full:

> *Imprimis.* IT is agreed, That every Man having Cocks to fight, shew and put them into the Pit with a fair Hackle, not too near shorn or cut, or any other Fraud, under pain of forfeiting, for every time so offending, Three Shillings and Four Pence; and his Cock to be *put by* from fighting that Year.
>
> II. *Item,* That every Cock match'd, shall fight as he is first shew'd in the Pit, without *sheering* or *cutting* any Feathers afterwards to a Disadvantage, without the Consent of both Parties that made the Match, upon pain of forfeiting, for every time so offending, ten Shillings.
>
> III. *Item,* That when two Cocks are set down to fight, *and one of them run away* before they have struck *three Mouthing Blows,* it is adjudged *no Battle to the Betters.*
>
> IV. *Item,* That in all Matches, none shall presume to set too, but those that are appointed by the *Masters of the Match.*
>
> V. *Item,* When a *Battle* shall come to setting too, and both Cocks refuse to fight ten times, according to the Law, then a *fresh Cock* to be hovell'd, and set to each Cock; and if one fight and the other refuse, then the fighting Cock to *win the Battle;* but if both fight, or both refuse, then it to be *a drawn Battle: Item,* That the Crowing of a Cock, or Mantling in his *Battle,* shall be adjudged no Fight; and if both be blind, although they peck and fight, yet they shall be set too, telling the *Law* betwixt every time.
>
> VI. *Item,* That when Cocks are far spent, and come to setting together, it is ordered, That they shall be set too as followeth (that is to say) *Bill to Bill, if they both see;* but if either be blind, then the *blind Cock to touch;* if either be drawn neck'd, then his *Head to be held fair,* and even with the other Cock, so that the Party do his best in setting too, to make his Cock fight; *Provided,* That after they come to be set thus, as aforesaid, between every setting too they shall stay till one tell *Twenty* before they set too again, until the *Law* of two times are forth, and then to tell *Ten* but ten times.
>
> VII. *Item,* It is ordered, That when a Cock is so hurt that any of the Pit shall lay ten Pounds to Five Shillings, that after the Cocks fighting shall be told twice Twenty, and if then no Man will take that Lay, then *the Battle* to be adjudged won on that Cock's side the Odds is on.

VIII. *Item*, That no Man shall make any Cavil or Speech about Matching of Cocks, either to the Matchers or the Owners of the Cocks, after the Cocks be once put together; upon pain of forfeiting Five Shillings for every time so offending.

IX. *Item*, That all Losses in the Cockpit be presently paid down at the End of every Battle, before any other be fought; or else, that the Party winning be satisfied before the Party losing go out of Doors; and also, That every Man pay good current Money.

X. *Item*, Whosoever they be which shall put any Lay or *Bett* to Judgment, being in variance, they shall both stake down the Money laid on either side, and Six-pence a-piece over; and the Party that is adjudged to be in the wrong shall pay his *Bett*, and lose his Six-Pence; *Provided*, That every Man speak freely, before Judgment given, what he thinks thereof; and if any Man speak afterwards, he shall, for every such Offence in speaking, pay Six-Pence.

XI. *Item*, That all Betts, made either within or without the Pit, shall stand good; and that one cannot go off without Consent of the other, and all Betts undemanded before the next Battle fights, to be lost.

XII. *Item*, If *any* Man, have made a *Lay* or *Bett*, and cannot tell, or call to mind, with whom he laid or betted such a *Lay*, then if he desire openly in the Pit, that the *Party* with whom he laid would give him the one half of the same, if he doth not confess it, and give him the one Half of the same, then it is allow'd, any one that knows the Bett to declare it, and the Party so *refusing to confess it*, shall pay the whole Bett, *Provided*, That no Man may tell before the Party said he is contented to take as aforesaid; but if any Man do tell him before the Party said he is content to take the Half of his Bett, then the Party, so telling, is to pay the said Lay or Bett.

XIII. *Item*, if any Man lay more Money than he hath to pay, or cannot satisfy the Party with whom he laid, either by his Credit or some Friend's Word; the which if he cannot do, then he is to be put into a Basket, to be provided for that purpose, and to be hang'd up in that Basket in some convenient place in the *Cockpit* that all Men may know him, during the time of Play that Day: and also the Party so offending never to be *admitted* to come into the *Pit*, until he hath made satisfaction.

XIV. *Item*, That if any Man in a Pit shall proffer a *Bett*, and the *Party* that lays with him say *Done*, and he answers *Done* to him again, it shall be judged a lawful *Bett*.

XV. *Item*, It is ordered, That Persons of the better Rank and Quality of the *Cockers*, *Cock-Masters*, and *Gamesters*, such as are appointed to set too Cocks, and put them fair in, and no others (*without Permission of the Master of the Pit*) shall set in the lower Ring; and that the said Master of the Pit shall have Authority at all times to remove such as he thinks not meet to set in the lower or second Ring; and also to make room for those that are of the better sort, and to place them there at his Pleasure, according to his own Discretion.

XVI. *Item*, It is ordered, That all *Controversies* which arise, or come by means of the *Sport of Cock-Fighting*, upon any of the Orders above-written, or otherwise, between Party and Party, shall be determined by the Master of the Pit where the said *Controversy* did arise, with Six or Four of the ancient and best experienced Gamesters there, being called, *by the Consent of both Parties*, to assist him therein.

XVII. *Item*, That none shall strike, or draw Weapon to strike any Man, upon pain, for every time so offending, to forfeit *Forty Shillings*.

XVIII. *Item*, For the better Observation of all the Orders before written, *It is ordered and agreed*, That if any person shall offend in *any* of the said *Premises*, *he presently pay his Forfeiture;* the which, being adjudged, if he shall refuse to do, then the *Party* so refusing to be banish'd, until he *satisfy* the Forfeiture by him so committed, or the *Party so offended*.

XIX. *Item*, It is ordered, That the Forfeitures aforesaid shall be equally divided, the one Moiety thereof to be paid to the Use of the Poor of the Parish, and the other Moiety to be distributed and dis-posed of, as the Master of the Pit shall think fit, unto such Feeders and ancient Breeders of Cocks as are or shall be decay'd.

(The modernity of Rule XIX is in interesting contrast to the provision of Rule XVII, that skewering with your sword a man with whom you were disputing cost you only £2.)

The analogy with horse racing can be carried a little further. The breeding of gamecocks, like thoroughbreds, was the passionate en-thusiasm of a small minority of gentlemen, usually with a strong family tradition. The most famous examples are successive Earls of Derby, who at Knowsley bred black-breasted reds which they esteemed quite as high as their horses; their tenants were obliged by the terms of their leases to walk cocks, as those of other landlords walked hound puppies.

A considerably larger minority of gentlemen bought cocks and engaged feeders. (Both the preparing of a cock for its match – 'feeding', as in racing – and its handling during a battle – 'setting' – were regarded as most delicate and arcane arts.) A great majority of country gentlemen went to matches, and most of them betted when they got there.

It was widely and sincerely believed that the courage of the fighting cock was a valuable example to the true-born Englishman. Dr Johnson said to Boswell, 'A fighting cock has a nobleness of resolution.' (This point of view was still seriously held by so able and sensible a man as Admiral Rous, in the third quarter of the 19th century, long after cocking had been made illegal in 1840.) Another argument was that the scientific breeding of gamecocks (as of thoroughbreds) was teaching gentlemen the laws of heredity, and so was valuable to husbandry. There is probably some force in this, especially since the great cradle of gamecocks, as of agricultural improvement, was East Anglia. A third argument was that gamecocks existed only to fight, and could be seen doing so, or trying to do so, naturally; the logic here is weaker, since the gamecock was the artificial result of selective breeding directed principally towards aggressiveness and fortitude. Arming with artificial metal spurs was approved because it ended the fighting more quickly.

Among gentlemen, however, contrary feelings grew. From perhaps 1790 a humanitarian uneasiness with the sport was beginning to be voiced (the same spirit which recoiled from trolling a live gudgeon or frog in front of a pike); this is well pictured by 'Nimrod' in *The Life of a Sportsman*, although 'Nimrod' was fully alive to the force of the favourable arguments. Secondly, the sums won and lost in betting were truly frightening. In individual histories it is hardly possible to separate losses on the turf from losses (perhaps to the same man on the same day) in the pit, or both from losses at the tables, especially at hazard and faro, respectively dice and cards; certainly fortunes were lost, estates broken up, manors sold, families ruined and dispersed: especially after 1800. Thirdly, while English sport had always prided itself on a heartily democratic and informal atmosphere, the cockpit carried this a shade too far, in spite of Cheny's Rule VX. Pepys had shrunk from the unseemly democracy of the cockpit; the fastidious exquisites of 1800 began to do so too.

The sport nevertheless remained enormously popular, and lost no social caste.

The racecourse attracted cockfighting because it collected great numbers of sporting gentlemen with money to lose; for the same reason it attracted boxing. Boxing was re-introduced to England (with classical precedents freely if defensively quoted) early in the 18th century. Jim Figg was the vastly admired Champion of England in 1719. The boxers themselves were esteemed – exactly as gamecocks were – for the

example they gave of pluck and bottom, and their battles attracted similar betting. The sponsoring of boxers by gentlemen was, indeed, not far removed from the ownership of cocks or racehorses: with the difference that many boxers were extremely dishonest.

The prize ring (so called quite early in the century) attracted large crowds, and gentlemen of the highest class went regularly to Broughton's Amphitheatre in London in the 1740s. There were also fights arranged (gentlemen matching their boxers against each other) all over England, often in gentlemen's parks, not infrequently at race meetings: the bouts were sometimes held in the middle of the racecourse during the actual running of the races. At a race meeting in 1791 the *Morning Chronicle* expressed amazement that no fight was held, 'notwithstanding Hooper, the tinman, Green, Sale and several other boxers were present'.

(xxx) Country House Games: Cricket, Bowls, Archery

Cricket, like cocking, found a place in the 18th century racing Calendar.

The ancestors of the game were played by boys in villages all over England, and varied in detail and in name from village to village; the common denominators were a ball or other missile thrown at a person with a bat or other weapon, the latter sometimes defending a wicket or other goal. (Baseball has the same remote ancestry.) In the very early 18th century a certain uniformity appeared among the yeomen and tradesmen of Kent and Hampshire, and within a generation the gentry were joining in. By 1743 'noblemen, gentlemen and clergy' were playing side by side with 'butchers, cobblers and tinkers'. This was village and country-house cricket, in atmosphere (if not in detail) perfectly recognisable today. In 1769 the Duke of Dorset captained a team of the Knowle servants and gardeners, an event quite typical of the game. (G. M. Trevelyan, in *English Social History*, remarks that if French dukes had done the same their chateaux would never have been burned.) The most celebrated ground was Broad Halfpenny, on Windmill Down near Hambledon, on which the Little Hambledon team (all of yeomen) played All England in front of a crowd of thousands: 'Punch that would make a cat squeak!' said John Nyren (in *The Cricketers of My Times*), lamenting the good old days, 'Sixpence a bottle!' The Hambledon Club had been founded, perhaps, as early as 1740.

There was a constant association of cricket with both racing and hunting, simply because many gentlemen who liked one sport liked another; a number of hunt servants were notable cricketers; and Sir Horace Mann in Kent was one of many leading turfites who had cricket-pitches adjoining their stables. This association explains the use to which Newmarket Heath was put in June 1751: 'Three grand cricket matches played at Newmarket between Eton and All England.' Each match was of two innings; England won the first and third by 37 and 95 runs, Eton the second by 70. The Earl of March was Captain of England – later Duke of Queensberry, the notorious 'Old Q', as great an all-round sportsman and jockey as he was sharper and roué; the Earl of Sandwich was Captain of Eton. There was £1,500 on the match; the whole was reported in Mr John Pond's *Sporting Kalendar*.

There were at this period two stumps, two foot apart and a foot high, with a bail across them. The space between was the popping-hole: the bat had to be popped into it before the wicket-keeper popped the ball through it if the batsman missed; the ball was bowled fast along the ground; the bat was curved like a hockey-stick. In 1776 a meeting was held at the Star and Garter in Pall Mall (where twenty-five years earlier the Jockey Club had briefly had its headquarters) which transformed the game. There was no longer a popping-hole, but something for the bowler to try and hit: three stumps instead of two, slightly narrower and shorter than the modern wicket. The straight bat perforce followed almost at once. What did not change, amid these changes, was the atmosphere of the game, or the limitless social spectrum which played and watched it.

Another country-house sport of undiminishing popularity was bowls. Many manors had excellent greens, some groomed, like those of Oxford colleges, for many generations. All towns had greens, and at the places of resort, like Tunbridge Wells and Epsom, the bowling-green was as much as ever the centre of daytime society.

Archery died as a sport in the 17th century; but in Scotland it was revived with some réclame by the Royal Company of Archers in 1676. This precedent was followed in England in 1781 with the foundation of the Royal Toxophilite Society; the moving spirit was apparently the eccentric and original Sir Ashton Lever, who took up the sport for his health. Gentle archery became a country-house diversion, especially of ladies (who were debarred from almost every other sport); the standard of marksmanship is said to have been extremely low.

(xxxi) Yachting

A minority of very rich gentlemen had yachts. The pleasure yacht had been invented by the Dutch in the 16th century, and came to England, with Charles II's return, in the 17th. Peter Pett built the first English yacht, on a Dutch model, and the first race was held in 1662. There was at once plenty of racing, seen and described by John Evelyn; the Isle of Wight was the headquarters from the beginning.

In the 18th century there began to be yacht clubs and there continued to be races; most of the latter, like contemporary horse races, were matches between two, and for comparable wagers. The 'Cumberland Fleet' under the patronage of the Duke of Cumberland developed ulti- mately into the Royal Yacht Squadron, established at Cowes in 1812. The first Commodore was Lord Yarborough, ennobled head of the Pelham family of Brocklesby, and hereditary Master of Hounds. His yacht was a frigate called the Falcon.

CHAPTER SIX

Waterloo to Sarajevo

(i) Depression and Reaction

Two factors sharply changed the life of the countryside in 1815, and dominated it for many years. The first was severe agricultural depression, the second anti-Jacobin reaction. Other important circumstances were the enclosing of more land and the amalgamating of more farms and estates into large units, a new wave of rich townsmen buying into the country and into county society, the immense growth of pheasant-rearing and with it of poaching, and the even more startling growth of piety, decorum and evangelicanism.

The Napoleonic wars, like those of a century earlier, had occasioned massive exports of corn, which therefore had a high and stable price; this was excellent for the whole agricultural interest, at all levels, though disagreeable for the poor and the towns. The prosperity of agriculture both encouraged and financed improvement to land, enclosure, experiments in husbandry and stock-breeding, and mechanical invention. At the Woburn Sheep-Shearings, for example, in the time of the 6th Duke of Bedford (who succeeded in 1802) there were prizes for all kinds of livestock, for wool, for new agricultural implements, and for satisfactory trials, in fields of not less than 10 acres, between drill and broadcast sowing of cereal and feed crops: farmers, yeomen, squires and magnates came, learned, and went away to invest.

Slump came immediately with peace. Sheep, pigs and bullocks showed a loss to nearly every farmer who sent them to market; the price of corn tumbled. A large minority of farmers, both tenants and yeomen (a word which by now meant freeholder), were ruined within a year or two. County Agricultural Associations were formed by landowners all over England, the purpose of which was entirely to petition Parliament for protection – either a total embargo on imported agricultural products, or an immensely high duty especially on wheat and wool. Parliament scarcely needed to be petitioned: composed as it was overwhelmingly of landowners, it passed the Corn Laws in 1815 to protect the people it represented.

The effect of the Corn Laws was (and is) debatable. They kept wheat and barley artificially profitable, and bread artificially expensive: but this was no help to graziers. Very many small farmers, and some lesser gentry, were still ruined by the minimum agricultural wage and the poor rate. The latter was a tremendous burden because of the huge new numbers of rural indigent. Small farmers simply could not afford labourers' wages, and the cottage and village industries were rapidly disappearing as machines in Lancashire and Yorkshire did the same jobs more cheaply. There were also more enclosures, depriving cottagers of livelihood and often of dwelling. The purpose of these evictions was sometimes purely to relieve the landowner of the burden of keeping his paupers alive: this is spelled out by the Tory Disraeli in *Sybil*, and identified as a major cause of the violent Chartist agitations of the 1840s.

The effect of depression on the country gentry was often serious, sometimes catastrophic. The farms they had in hand showed a loss, even with high-priced corn; the farms they let paid a sharply reduced rent or none at all. Investment consequently dropped to almost nothing, except when the estate was financed – as many now were – from banking, jobbing, mining, manufacture, or government sinecure. Drains filled up and fences fell down because there was no income for their maintenance; stews and decoys were let go – very few of either survived into the 1820s.

There was widespread suffering, sometimes acute: ironically, but perhaps inevitably, it was most severe in the richest agricultural areas like Norfolk and Wiltshire, because there the greatest amount of common and sheep-walk had been enclosed by the gentry: and in those where cottage industries had accustomed the villagers to what had seemed everlasting prosperity. The landowning establishment naturally predicted unrest. The Luddite movement of machine-smashers struggled, like modern trade unionists but without the latter's almost total success, to save their jobs by halting the march of technology. The example of the French revolution was horribly near and sufficiently recent. Landowners were frightened of bloody revolution; they were more immediately frightened for their property than for their persons. Yesterday land had brought a large income: tomorrow it would do so again. It was still the *sine qua non* of gentility, in the countryside if not in London: 'You misled me by the term *Gentleman,*' said Jane Austen's Sir Walter Elliot (in *Persuasion*). 'I thought you were speaking of some man of property.' The sanctity of property became the obsession of the Tory squire in Parliament and on his local bench, and he gravely over-reacted to threats which he saw or imagined.

(ii) Game Laws: the Tory Squire in Parliament

The first and worst result was the Game Laws. These already, and anciently, contained absurdities. Now it became illegal to buy game, as well as to expose it for sale, on the presumption that game in a shop had been poached. It became illegal for anyone to take game (pheasant, partridge, hare in particular) even if qualified in the old sense by an income of over £100 p.a., even at the landowner's invitation, except a squire or his eldest son (a ludicrous provision, widely bypassed by the device of 'deputation', but not repealed until 1831). In 1816, by 57 George III ch. 90, anyone found with nets or other engines at night, even for catching only rabbits, was subject to seven years' deportation. Pheasant preserves were guarded by mantraps and spring-guns, which killed or maimed many innocent people, and which the High Court repeatedly declared legal until they were forbidden by a statute of 1827. According to Cobbett in 1823, a third of all the prisoners in English gaols were there because of the Game Laws, apart from those deported to Botany Bay; other prisoners, 'real' criminals, were let out to make room for them. 'Game spies' were sent by landowners (who were Justices) onto farmers' own land, and their unsupported testimony could and did get farmers transported or gaoled: 'if a hare or pheasant come to an untimely death, *Police-officers* from the Wen [London] are not unfrequently called down to find out and secure the bloody offender!' In the Spring of 1822, two men were hanged at Winchester for resisting the gamekeeper of Mr Assheton Smith of Tedworth (father of the great

M.F.H.), an event which aroused such fury that it perhaps began the serious return to sanity.

It should be added that rabbit, woodcock, snipe and quail were not game in the meaning of the act, and could be shot by any man on his own ground; that waste and common could be sported over by any qualified person with the permission of the lord of the manor; and that although the laws of trespass were strict, the punishments were not draconic. It should also be added that there were large gangs of violent poachers – twenty and more, armed with guns – who came out from towns perfectly prepared to murder gamekeepers and their masters.

On the heels of the Game Laws, and inspired by the Luddites and the unrest that followed hunger, came the Six Acts of 1819. The intention was to stamp out sedition where it began, in the countryside, and the method was to give J.P.s much wider powers of arrest and punishment on top of the considerable powers they already had. These powers were used with ferocity (though not everywhere) after the labourers' riots and rickburnings of 1830, a circumstance which was used to confirm the arguments of both sides in the national debate about the Reform Bill.

Corn Laws, Game Laws, laws of trespass and Six Acts were the children of a parliament quite largely appointed, or self-appointed, rather than elected. A few examples may illustrate its composition. Sir Watkin Wynn of Wynnstay, the richest man in Wales, was a member; his brother Sir Henry was a member; his other brother Charles, 'Squeaking Wynn', was a member for fifty years. High Wycombe, Buckinghamshire, had thirty-four voters on its electoral roll, all Sir John Dashwood's tenants; it sent him to Parliament with his friend Sir Thomas Baring, whose father Sir Francis had bought the Stratton Park estate in Hampshire from the Duke of Bedford. Colonel Hylton Jolliffe, a famous foxhunter and 'the hero of the chase', lived at Merstham, Surrey, but owned the town of Petersfield, which consequently sent him to Parliament. Before the 2nd Earl of Harewood succeeded to title, mastership of the Bramham Moor hounds, and Lord Lieutenancy of the West Riding, he was a spokesman in Parliament for the abolition of *habeas corpus* and against the abolition of slavery. Mr Thomas Assheton Smith (the younger) took time off from foxhunting to be a Member of Parliament from 1820 to 1841; in 1831 he raised a troop of yeomanry at Tedworth to quell the Reform Bill riots.

Parliament composed of such gentlemen continued to enact private enclosure bills, and it gave J.P.s the power to fix local poor rates, which were often miserably inadequate. For these reasons Cobbett concluded in 1826:

> There is in the men calling themselves 'English country gentlemen' something superlatively base. They are *I sincerely believe*, the most cruel, the most unfeeling, the most brutally insolent: but I *know*, I can *prove*, I can *safely take my oath*, that they are the MOST BASE of all creatures that God ever suffered to disgrace the human shape.

This understandable view has to be qualified by some thought about the frightening new world of sedition and revolution which seemed, to so many squires, to threaten not just their own security but the whole fabric of the nation. Indeed it was qualified by the intemperate Cobbett himself. He knew how difficult life was for the gentry. His friend Sir Francis Burrell was a noted agricultural improver in Sussex; he took many farms in hand because his tenants were unable to pay rent; he could not farm them without serious loss; he let them go again virtually rent-free.

There were, secondly, many excellent landlords who combined agricultural efficiency with far-sighted generosity: such were Lord Egremont, the Duke of Richmond, and Mr William Chamberlayne of Cranbury Park, Hampshire, all of whom vastly increased the estates they inherited; such was that passionate hunting family the Palmers of Bollitree, Herefordshire.

There was, thirdly, an important minority of Whig and even radical squires, who believed with Lord Grey and the unenfranchised citizens and merchants that the constitution must recover its balance by reform of Parliament, even though such reform might open the floodgates to the ultimate disaster of universal suffrage, and even though it would destroy the secure pre-eminence of landowners. Among many Members of Parliament of this dangerous complexion were the Sir Charles Burrell aforementioned, Mr William Poyntz of Midgham, Berkshire (and later of Cowdray Park, of which his wife was heiress), and Sir John Sebright. Mr Poyntz had his own foxhounds in the modern South Berks country, and was in 1793 manager of the Prince of Wales's short-lived foxhounds; he was a political ally of the Prince's friend, Charles James Fox, and to that eccentricity added an unseemly passion for giving dances for the daughters of farmers and yeomen throughout the hunting season. Sir John, a successful and experimental livestock breeder in Hertfordshire, spoke strongly against the Game Laws in Parliament; it was in his park that John Gully, champion of England, defended his title against the Lancashire giant Gregson. (Gully afterwards became, successively, publican, bookmaker, and the foxhunting squire of Ackworth, Yorkshire.) Comparable in the House of Lords was the 3rd Lord Suffield (succeeded 1821, died 1835); his father-in-law was Lord Vernon, many of whose excellent Sudbury hounds were bought by George Osbaldeston when he went to the Atherstone country; Lord Suffield was regarded as a radical, and led the parliamentary campaign which got the spring-gun made illegal in 1827. His son lost his fortune on the turf and was a brief and deeply unsatisfactory Master of the Quorn.

Mention should perhaps also be made of the substantial number of country M.P.s who made no impact on the chamber at all: Sir Charles Bunbury of Mildenhall, uniquely influential at Newmarket but totally silent throughout a long parliamentary career; Colonel Henry Lowther, 'the silent Colonel', younger son of the 1st Earl of Lonsdale (of the second creation), who managed his father's Cottesmore hounds, and sat in Parliament for 50 years without making a speech; Mr William Beckford of Fonthill, who inherited an alleged £100,000 *a year* from his father, once Lord Mayor of London, dented even this fantastic wealth with the gothic extravagances of his building, and who as M.P. for his own rotten borough never opened his mouth.

Much contemporary opinion identified the barbarities of these years not with the old squirarchy but with the new arrivistes. Of such were Mr Scott of Rotherfield, Hampshire, who bought that estate and the village of East Tisted from the Powlett family, who had had it since Norman times; Mr Scott was 'well-known as a brick-maker at North End, Fulham' who had grown rich during the war building houses for 'Jews, jobbers and tax-eaters . . . Go on, good 'Squire, throw out some more of the Normans: with the fruits of the augmentations which you make to the Wen, go, and take from them their mansions, parks, and villages!' At Upstreet, East Kent, the sign by the gate of a property read: 'PARADISE PLACE. Spring guns and steel traps are set here', evidence which declared that it was 'doubtless some stock-jobber's place'. This identification was completely unfair, as witness the well-documented liberality of such new squires as the Barings of The Grange and Stratton, and the reactionary ferocity of such old ones as the Lascelles family of Harewood.

(iii) Evangelicanism and Boredom

Sir Thomas and Lady Baring are examples of another phenomenon of the late years of George III which it is easy to think of as particularly Victorian: obtrusive piety and do-gooding. Their tenants came demurely to church, the children all dressed in a sort of devotional uniform, as a condition of the landlord's bounty. This was in 1820. Trollope mocks, in the Barchester books, the evangelical Bishop Proudie's disapproval of 'Sabbath-day travelling'; Anne Elliot, in *Persuasion*, had long before darkly suspected her scapegrace cousin of the same offence, in his unregenerate youth, against the Old Testament rules. Family prayers and prudery were creeping in; drunkenness and self-indulgence were beginning, here and there, to go out. This began in towns, among such evangelical bodies as the Clapham Sect, and among the drab flocks of Wesleyan clergy, but it spread to the country: 'Evangelicanism', said George Eliot in *Middlemarch*, 'has cast a certain suspicion as of plague-infection over the few amusements which survive in the provinces.'

The great sufferers in country houses were women, who were supposed in this new atmosphere of decorous refinement to be incapable of activity or movement; they were allowed short walks, to neighbouring houses or to cottages (with tracts or soup); few rode, and hardly a dozen in the whole of England are on firm record as riding to hounds; they could dance; they had 'accomplishments'. Whether unmarried like the Bennett sisters or married like young Mrs Musgrove, they were very bored indeed.

And this vacuity of day-to-day life in the manor house has to be set against the philistinism of many of the men. There were, of course, many like Sir Mark Sykes of Sledmere, a discriminating collector of books and prints as well as a turfite and Master of Hounds; there were also many like Sir Walter Elliot, who for his own pleasure opened no book except the *Baronetage:* like Cobbett's acquaintances among the gentry, who talked of nothing but sport because they had nothing else to talk about: whose sporting conversation was '*six times* as much as *all other talk put together*'. A case by no means extreme in this regard (though extreme in others) was Jack Mytton, squire of Halston, Shropshire, who in about 1815 had this conversation, reported by 'Nimrod', with his mother's chaplain:

Chaplain My good sir, you must go to Oxford; you must indeed, sir!
Mr. Mytton I'll see you —— first.
Chaplain Upon my word, sir, you must go. Every man of fortune ought to go to Christ Church, if only for a term or so.
Mr. Mytton Well then, if I do go, I will go on the following terms.
Chaplain What are they, sir?
Mr. Mytton Why, that I never open a book.
Chaplain Not the least occasion – not the smallest, I assure you.
Mr. Mytton Very well then; I don't mind going, provided I read nothing but the *Racing Calendar* and the *Stud Book*.
Chaplain Excellent books, sir; they will do very well, indeed.

Extreme provincialism also survived into the middle of the 19th century. Emily Hall recorded in her diary in 1841 that the Somerset squires she met at Hatch Beauchamp were uncouth and ignorant in the last degree: one, very rich, had been to London only once in his life, to visit the Smithfield Show.

The boredom of Jane Austen's country houses also survived. 'And I remember the conversations,' says Thackeray of about 1840. 'O Madam, Madam, how stupid they were! The subsoil ploughing; the pheasants and poaching; the row about the representation of the country . . . and a great deal of conversation about the weather, the Mangelwurzelshire Hunt, new manners, and eating and drinking.' 'What a dreary time is that', says Surtees of a few years later, 'which intervenes between the arrival of the guest and the dinner hour, in the dead winter months in the country.' This has all the despairing *ennui* of Russian landowners in Chekhov and Turgenev: and Thackeray's and Surtees's characters dined at six: or if they were trying to be fashionable 6.30: or if desperately pretentious, like Mr Jawleyford of Jawleyford Court, as late as seven.

It may be relevant that the gentleman was still, in his own countryside, supposed to be a sportsman. Plantagenet Palliser 'did not hunt or shoot or keep a yacht, and had been heard to say that he had never put a foot on a race-course in his life'. He was devoted wholly to politics. Palliser was courted as heir to a dukedom: but Trollope considered he was expressing the view of all right-thinking men in finding his own character a dead bore.

If women suffered from the new refinement (though few, perhaps, knew they were doing so) animals benefited. In 1831 R. S. Surtees closed the pages of his *New Sporting Magazine* to prize-fighting, bull-baiting and cocking as 'low and demoralising pursuits'. Bull- and bear-baiting were made illegal in 1835 (though not dog-fighting) and cocking in 1840.

Bull-baiting, 1816. One of the country town amusements against which 19th-century opinion revolted. Engraved by Joseph Strutt.

(iv) The New Men

Enclosures, agricultural depression and industrial revolution combined to depopulate the countryside of its lowest classes and a good many of its yeomen: but the industrial revolution also sent a great army of new-rich recruits into the gentry. There was nothing new about rich townsmen wanting to be landed gentlemen, nor about such people retaining, in the midst of their acres, commercial contacts and non-agricultural incomes. What was new was the scorn with which these upstarts were apt to be greeted.

This response is hardly to be glimpsed in the 18th century, but it is very clear in the early 19th. It is satirised by Jane Austen, in such persons as Darcy's aunt and Bingley's sisters (in *Pride and Prejudice*) and Anne Elliott's father and elder sister (in *Persuasion*). In Thackeray, writing of some thirty years later, we find Major Ponto and his wife (in *The Book of Snobs*) deriding a 'purse-proud ex-linendraper': but the point Thackeray makes is that this contempt was the naive pretentiousness of people themselves emerged from obscure and mercantile backgrounds. False airs and false claims are what angered Surtees, too:

> Mr. Marmaduke Muleygrubs had been a great stay-maker on Ludgate Hill, and, in addition to his own earnings (by no means inconsiderable) had inherited a large fortune from a great drysalting uncle in Bermondsey. On getting this he cut the shop, bought Cockolorum Hall, and having been a rampant radical in the City, was rewarded by a J.P.-ship in the country.

He rebuilt the house as a vast false castle, claimed crusader ancestors, lived in amazing pomp, and tried to buy popularity with bag-foxes from Leadenhall Market in his foxless coverts.

Late in the century an odious change took place: new men were despised not for their pretension but for their background. When du Maurier was drawing for *Punch* and Fox Russell was writing his dreadful sporting novels, the social errors of the *nouveaux riches* were good for any gentleman's derision.

There were two ways in which a rich townsman could get himself and his family accepted.

One was to spend money. Trollope's Sir Roger Scatcherd bought land, built a pretentious house, invited contempt, but stifled local criticism by the munificence of his subscription to the foxhounds. Lavish hunt breakfasts and coverts full of pheasants were other normal ways of buying acceptance. Sidney's *Book of the Horse* of 1875 gives full and fascinating instructions about the former: 'When a rich migrant from town to country life, with all his way to make in the country, settles down in a mansion to which a famous fox-covert is annexed, where it has been usual to precede the drawing by a breakfast meet, the arrangement of the entertainment becomes a matter of serious consideration . . . Six dozen of really good sherry at a hunt breakfast have been known to establish the reputation of a new resident.'

The other device adopted by thousands of would-be gentlemen was to send their sons to public schools. A wave of these was founded in the second and third quarters of the 19th century, in imitation of Eton and more particularly of Rugby, intended to produce the 'Christian gentleman' of Dr Arnold's philosophy: producing, in fact, a more priggish, philistine and games-worshipping type than Arnold himself would have approved, and influenced more perhaps by *Tom Brown's Schooldays* than by the great headmaster himself.

The rich migrants were accused of vulgarity and ostentation not least in the houses they built. Cobbett in the 1820s mocked both Mr Montagu's false medieval stonework made of carved softwood and the 'Gothick' absurdities of Fonthill; one wonders what he would have made of the grotesque palaces, replacing houses of moderate size and much beauty, built by the rich right up to 1914. In fact many long-established gentlemen also built the barracks which have so embarrassed their descendants: this was possible because many of them had become extremely rich from the coal, iron, lead, copper or slates on their land.

(v) Recovery and Relapse

There was also an immense revival of agricultural prosperity. This began, perhaps, with the Poor Law of 1834, which took the responsibility and the burden of poor relief out of the local J.P.'s hands. (He lost most of the rest of his powers by the Local Government Act of 1888.) A more important step was that the Parliament reformed in 1832 repealed the Corn Laws in 1846; so far from destroying the agricultural interest this had, in combination with other factors of some complexity and obscurity, exactly the opposite effect. Until the middle 1870s there was a large and steady *increase* in the amount of arable (which the Protectionists hardly expected), a heavy and profitable new investment in clearing, draining, marling, fencing, the development of mechanical ploughing, reaping and threshing, and a marked improvement in all branches of stockbreeding. Much credit is due to the Royal Agricultural Society, but more to the pride of landowners in good husbandry which exactly echoed that described by Arthur Young a century earlier.

It was once again possible for a landowner to live decently on an income derived purely from agricultural rents, like the Dales in the Great House at Allington, who held all their ancestral acres, and from them derived a steady £3,000 a year during this period of agricultural prosperity. It was not of course, on this rent-roll, a very great house: but Squire Dale was king of his own village and a great man in the local market and assize towns.

As much as the squire the substantial yeoman benefited: such as the worthy George Dallas of Wharfedale, Yorkshire, described with such affection by 'Sylvanus' in his *Bye-Lanes and Downs of England* in 1850 – a representative of 'those of our gentry who, – thrice happy lot! – take station between the squire and the farmer'. Dallas owned the land he farmed; he kept hunters, carriage-horses, and bloodstock; for his kind 'Sylvanus' coined the term 'gentleman-yeoman', who did not and did not wish to rank with grand-jurymen, bear arms, or call himself 'Esquire'. (Mr Dallas in the event lost all his money backing horses.) Many such men, more ambitious, had eased themselves into the squire class during the agricultural boom which ended in 1815; many more now did so. Trollope deplored the social pretension of Lawrence Twentyman, whose father had sent him to Cheltenham, who wore a scarlet coat in the hunting field, and who called himself a 'gentleman farmer' instead of a yeoman: but for once Trollope's attitude strikes a most uncongenial note: rural society had always been mobile in England, and the possibility of becoming a gentleman one of its enduring glories and its greatest protection against revolution.

Incompetent landlords without liquid capital or plentiful credit could still find life a struggle, even on large estates. Surtees suggests that in the booming 1850s and 1860s this was almost always their own fault. Mr Jawleyford of Jawleyford Court (*below*) was:

one of the rather numerous race of paper-booted, pen-and-ink landowners. He always dressed in the country as he would in St. James's-street, and his communications with his tenantry were chiefly confined to dining with them twice a year in the great entrance-hall, after Mr. Screwemtight had eased them of their cash in the steward's-room.

His neighbour, Sir Harry Swift, was also an unsuccessful proprietor, but for opposite reasons: he was open handed and much loved, and adored by his servants, who cheated him: he ended up taking asylum from his creditors in Boulogne.

In 1875 even the best of landowners, and all farming tenants, suffered from another savage depression. This was immediately due to the import of cheap American grain: the virgin prairies were worked by machine, and the crop brought by railway to the coast and by steamer to Britain. Parliament had been reformed again in 1867, and the Free Traders representing the towns overwhelmed the landed interest. A million acres of arable reverted to fallow between 1875 and 1885 (there was rarely money to reseed for good grazing), and another million by 1900. There were 100,000 fewer agricultural labourers in 1881 than in 1871. 'Brooksby's' *Hunting Countries* of 1882 and 1883 recounts, of almost every part of England, that almost no farmers could afford to hunt. A slight recovery in the middle 1880s was lost in the 1890s when frozen meat began to arrive in quantity from Australia, New Zealand and the Argentine. Charles Whatley's *Farming and Foxhunting* describes many sporting farmers with fine Wiltshire grazing land hard put to it to make a living in the 1890s; he himself could not afford the shooting of a farm he rented in 1905, although he hunted and even played polo (largely as an aid to horse-dealing).

Farmers had a struggle for bare survival, though fewer actually went bankrupt than in the 1820s, but the squires were far less hard hit because few depended on their land for their incomes; many had some urban property, and almost all the rest had invested in industry, railways or banking.

(vi) Countryside Revolutions: Railways and Ladies

Railways themselves affected the countryside in many ways after Stephenson's Stockton and Darlington was opened in 1826. The two great periods of investment were 1836–7 and 1844–8, and a great deal of money was made (as well as some lost). To railways in the physical sense, on their land, landowners were almost unanimously opposed – until they negotiated satisfactory terms with the railway company; this was Lord Marney's typical experience, involving a total change of heart, in Disraeli's *Sybil*. Hunting was thought likely to suffer fatally

from tracks, trains and fumes; in fact it benefited from visitors and subscriptions. What was killed was not hunting but coaching, both public
and long-distance private; Victorian England had carriages and all
kinds of small utility vehicles, used only locally. The inns suffered a
decline from which few have ever recovered; many had in fact already
gone down, since fast coaches on good roads stopped less often.

Two other great changes to the life of the country gentry closely
followed, in point of time, the transformation worked by the railways:
the emergence of women into activity, and the withdrawal of parsons
from it. Although Victorian ladies were exceedingly, even suffo-
catingly, decorous, they began doing things like foxhunting, quite
suddenly and in fair numbers, about 1860: a fact remarked on by every
sporting writer of the time with amazement, and with admiration
(Surtees, Trollope, Whyte Melville) or dismay ('Scrutator', the censor-
ious Mr Horlock). Soon they were fishing, stalking deer, and owning
racehorses. When bicycles were invented they rode them; when lawn
tennis was invented they played it. The unfortunate country parson,
however, was at the other end of the seesaw of opinion: most bishops

and many laymen began to deplore his presence in the hunting field, and the old fashioned sporting parson – even in Devon, where he most flowered – became extremely rare and (according to Trollope) guiltily self-conscious.

In spite of the qualified liberation of Victorian women, the life of country houses was often still extremely dull. House-parties, assembled by train, were the major diversion, but unless sport was available there was very little for anybody to do. Henry James, an outsider who crept inside, described in *The Real Thing* an ageing couple who showed 'the blankness, the deep intellectual repose of twenty years of country house visiting'. Many of 'Saki's' stories describe the suffocating boredom of Edwardian house parties, unless galvanized by some audacious out-rage; and V. Sackville-West paints house parties at Knowle (disguised as 'Chevron' in *The Edwardians*) as given almost wholly to gossip. There were, perhaps, only three major differences between Edwardian and Victorian country-house life: in 'Society' adultery was fashionable for the first time for 130 years; everyone played auction bridge; and the car had arrived.

(vii) 19th Century Foxhunting

The essence of foxhunting changed hardly at all between the final defeat of Napoleon and the murder of the Archduke at Sarajevo. The method was that devised in Leicestershire between, perhaps, 1760 and 1780: a fast, driving pack drew its first covert soon after 11 o'clock in the morning, pushed the fox out into the open, chased it if possible entirely in the open, and killed it above ground. The hound itself developed in the direction of uniformity, a process accelerated by the ease of communications, the influence of Belvoir and the Peterborough Show: but even in 1914 there were celebrated packs like the Berkeley quite outside the fashion (and it was often no more than fashion) for Belvoir tan and 'bed-post' forelegs. Visually hounds changed during the century with the disappearance of some colours (red and blue-mottled) and of 'neck-cloths' and broken coats, and with the weight and straightness of foreleg bone: in temperament, style of hunting, breeding, entering and hand-ling they did not change at all. The vast majority of hunters continued

(*Opposite*) Early Victorian Foxhunting

THE MEET

THE DRAW

FULL CRY

THE DEATH.

Early Victorian foxhound bitch: Lord Kintore's Nosegay. George Aikman after Barengar

Typical high-class halfbred hunter: Chance, property of Mr Rowland Errington, M.F.H. Quorn. George Aikman after J. Ferneley.

to be half-breds, varied in height and type according to the needs of different countries. They were ridden in a virtually identical style (leathers long, trunk upright, leaning back over jumps), though there was a tendency during the second half of the century to go back from the double bridle to the simple snaffle. Clothes altered early in the century in the direction of an inappropriate high fashion – skin-tight swallow-tails and high cravats – but reverted by 1850 into something very like the late 18th century, except in regard to hats.

The most noticeable change early in the century was the expansion into heathen areas of modern foxhunting. This usually meant the conversion of local sportsmen from harehunting, a process well described in the early chapters of *Handley Cross*. Foxhunting countries continued to be made in harehunting or pheasant-shooting wildernesses. In Devon, for pioneers like the Revd Jack Russell, this meant primarily the preservation of foxes, previously very rare; in North Wiltshire for Mr K. W. Horlock ('Scrutator') it meant interminable diplomacy with covert owners and their vulpicide gamekeepers; in the Tedworth country (West Hampshire and East Wiltshire) it meant for Mr Thomas Assheton Smith tree-felling on a gigantic scale. There were also a good many countries, especially in the West Midlands, where old-style foxhunting changed more or less painfully into new: new hounds, new horses, new hours, new clothes, new methods, all in imitation of Melton. Sometimes old and new existed side by side for years: Robert Vyner records (in *Notitia Venatica*) that you could hunt with the private pack of Sir Edward Lyttleton in Staffordshire, and after his hounds had gone home attend the 11-o'clock meet of an up-to-date hunt. 'Nimrod's' and Surtees's sporting tours, and the novels of the latter, are full of provincials aspiring to speed and smartness. But uniformity was really as far off in 1914 as in 1815. Whyte Melville's ambitious hero in *Market Harborough* was as dazzled by a meet in the Shires (*below*) as the first

visitors a century earlier: and in 1914 there were still bobbery, trencher-fed packs, in the West and North, followed by yeomen in gaiters on un-clipped ponies.

(viii) Sporting Portrait: George Osbaldeston

Pierce Egan, the first all-round sporting journalist, called George Osbaldeston in 1832 'The Atlas of the Sporting World . . . a complete portrait of the thoroughbred Sportsman'. 'Nimrod', Delmé Radcliffe, Robert Vyner, 'The Druid', R. S. Surtees, all the sporting writers and writing sportsmen who knew him agreed that he stood on a pinnacle of sporting achievement which dwarfed contemporaries. He was one of the best half-dozen amateur cricketers in England; he was a champion oarsman; he beat champions at royal tennis; he was a brilliant and fearless boxer; he was supreme among athletes; he was as good as the best game-shots on record – once killing 100 pheasants with 100 shots, once 97 grouse with 97 shots, once 40 partridges with 40 shots, all with a flint-and-steel 18-bore; with a pistol he could put 10 shots in the ace of diamonds at thirty feet; he was an outstanding amateur coachman of four-in-hand and tandem in an age of great whips; he was an all-con-quering trotting-driver, although trotting was a sport which, for some reason, attracted almost no other gentlemen; he was the best amateur flat-race rider of his time, and the best cross-country steeplechase rider of any time; he was considered in a class of his own as a Master of Fox-hounds; the turf ruined him.

He was born in London on Boxing Day 1786. His father died when he was six: he was spoiled by his mother, especially because he was the only son among several daughters, and the heir to large Yorkshire estates. He went to Eton where, though very small, he was *victor ludorum* in every arena. During holidays at Hutton Buscel or Bushell, in the Vale of Pickering, he fished, coursed and rode. He went from Eton to a tutor in Brighton; there on the downs he went out with the harriers and rode his first informal races and steeplechases. At Oxford he lived much the same life: he hunted with the Bicester and Duke of Beaufort's (Heythrop side), fought the 'Town' and excelled at every sport.

Just after his twenty-first birthday he built kennels at home 'on Beckford's plan' and bought a pack of blue-mottled Sussex harriers. These slow, line-hunting 'currant-jelly-dogs' soon bored him, and he replaced them with a pack of fast dwarf foxhounds from Lord Jersey, with which he hunted hares in what is now the Middleton country.

In 1809 the 3rd Lord Monson died, leaving the magnificent pack of hounds with which the family had been hunting the Burton for many generations. Osbaldeston bought the pack and the hunt horses from Lady Monson (with whom he later fell in love), moved with his mother to Lincoln, and took over the country. He was Master for four seasons, and showed magnificent sport. The reasons were: plenty of foxes, good

Mr George Osbaldeston. Drawing from *The New Sporting Magazine*, October 1840.

scent, a first-rate pack of small, quick, killing hounds, and his own experience with harriers. The country he hunted was enormous, including the modern Blankney and the Spilsby – normally then considered part of Brocklesby territory – which is now the South Wold. In 1812 he became a Member of Parliament to please his mother: 'I thought it was a great bore; I had no taste whatever for public life.'

During this period he led an amorous career almost as vigorous as his sporting one, and perhaps for this reason gave up the Burton in 1813; he took his hounds to South Notts, which Mr John Chaworth Musters had temporarily given up. He hated the River Trent and the huge coverts, and it is probable that his hounds were quite unsuited to woodland hunting. He also disliked Mr Musters, and despised him as a sportsman; he was unique in doing so – most people liked and admired the 'Squire of Notts' immensely. Musters was very handsome and a ladies' man, and Osbaldeston's sourness probably has a basis in some unrecorded boudoir defeat.

After two seasons Osbaldeston moved to Atherstone; he took over the country which Lord Vernon and the Revd George Talbot had hunted as the Sudbury, as well as that known to him as the Derbyshire, previously hunted by various small packs. This amalgamation was the foundation of the modern Atherstone. Two notable events occurred during his two seasons there. First, he issued his first recorded challenge, to Sir Henry Every of Burton, who had a pack of harriers, and tried to stop the foxhounds drawing his coverts (Sir Henry declined the duel and signed an apology). Second, he heard a gardener refer to a fox as 'Charley', which is the first known use of the Charles James Fox pun.

In 1817 Mr Thomas Assheton Smith decided he preferred the small fields and knowledgeable farmers of the Burton country to the large, jealous-riding, overdressed fields of the Quorn; Osbaldeston took the latter. Like his predecessors he bought Quorndon Hall and the kennels, and there moved his hounds and his mother. This interrupted mastership was the Quorn's greatest until Sir Richard Sutton took over in 1847. A typical day was described unforgettably (though here and there a little oddly) by 'Nimrod' in his famous piece *The Chase* in *The Quarterly Revue*; a very game, fast horse was needed to keep anywhere near the flying hounds; Lord Alvanley, Lord Waterford, Sir James Musgrave, Sir Harry Goodricke were among the top-sawyers; Melton and Quorndon were the twin Meccas of fox-hunting.

The problems of Leicestershire were those familiar to predecessors and successors: finance; pressing and jealous riding; the enthusiasm of weavers and stocking-makers, who surrounded the coverts with excited clamour; the really dangerous riding of a few first flighters. Worst of these, wherever he went hunting, was Sir James Musgrave, and in 1821 he jumped on the Master, who had fallen, breaking the latter's leg so badly that the bone (as gorily described by 'Nimrod', who was there) stuck clear through the boot.

The effect of this disaster was that Osbaldeston had to take his hounds away to a country less physically demanding than the racing grass and formidable oxers of High Leicestershire. He went far south to the Hambledon, promising unprecedented execution of its foxes. The expedition was the most abject failure. The superb grassland pack had not the noses for cold-scenting plough, nor the cry for big coverts, nor the feet for sharp flints, nor the temperament for a slow 'hunting thing'. By Delmé Radcliffe's account, the Master and his whipper-in, the younger Tom Sebright, were just as hopelessly at sea as their hounds.

Tom Sebright went away to Milton, to become Lord Fitzwilliam's huntsman and one of the very best in history; the Squire moved to the Thurlow for a season so wretched that in his autobiography he does not even mention it. The problem here was lack of foxes, which he had met on a more tolerable scale in both South Notts and Atherstone. In the Thurlow country (at that point separated from the Newmarket) the only way to get anything to hunt was to buy it, and Osbaldeston accordingly had cartloads of foxes sent down from Leadenhall Market.

In 1823 he thankfully repurchased Quorndon. It was noted that he did not cross stiff country with quite the dash of the old days – he hated timber ('that d— carpentry') and he hated anyone riding close behind him. Yet he still hunted hounds, which were faster and harder-driving than ever, and sport was again superb.

In 1827 he gave up the Quorn, moved his hounds to Brixworth, and took over the Pytchley from his enemy Mr Chaworth Musters. This mastership lasted seven years, and was the Squire's longest, last, and greatest. In spite of the depredations of gangs of poachers the country was well foxed (the poachers could get 10 shillings a head for cubs from London dealers; the latter would guarantee them foreign, and sell them back, dispirited and mangy, often to the Masters from whose countries they had been taken). In order to draw the country properly, the Master took to going out twice a day after Christmas, drawing fresh coverts with a fresh pack, so that he hunted not five or six but effectively eight or ten days a week; 'An unheard-of proceeding', said 'Nimrod'.

The Squire walked with a permanent limp after Sir James Musgrave's unforgivable riding. Yet it was in this period that he emerged as the outstanding cross-country steeplechase rider, better even than the professionals Becher and Christian. He was, said *The Field* in its obituary of him, 'quite at the top of the tree in steeplechasing when the courses were unflagged, for he could pick his country better than any of his contemporaries: it was to this as well as to his horsemanship that his victories with Clinker, Pilot and Grimaldi were due'. Dick Christian, quoted by 'The Druid', fully confirmed this view. On Pilot he twice defeated the celebrated Captain Ross on Polecat. Clinker, belonging to Ross and ridden by Christian, was not the Squire's, but was beaten in the most famous match of all by him and his Clasher.

The year of these matches (1829) was that in which he met the jocular diarist Creevey. 'Osbaldeston himself,' said Creevey, 'though only five feet high [actually about five foot four], and in features like a cub fox, is a very funny little chap; clever in his way, very good-humoured and gay, and with very good manners.' These last were still crucially important to a Master of Hounds: without them he had few coverts to draw, few foxes in those he did draw, and very few subscriptions indeed.

Two years later occurred one of his best remembered feats (*above*). Of the Newmarket Houghton Meeting of 1831 *The Racing Calendar* records:

> Saturday, November 5th. Mr. Osbaldeston having made a wager of 1,000 gs. that he would ride 200 miles in 10 hours, and the ground, forming a circle of 4 miles, having been marked out on and about the Round Course, he started about 7 o'clock this morning, and performed the distance in 8 hours and 42 minutes, without apparent difficulty. He changed his horse every 4 miles, and rode 29 different horses. A bet of 1,000 to 100 sov. was laid that he did not perform the distance in 9 hours.

Afterwards there was an Osbaldeston Plate of £50 for horses which the Squire had ridden in the match against the clock.

In 1832 he was umpire at St Albans, which had been since 1830 the place of the first recognizable modern steeplechasing, on a round course marked with flags. Moonraker, belonging to the great horse-dealer Elmore, beat a great little hunter called Grimaldi; Osbaldeston was one of many who blamed the latter's rider. He bought Grimaldi and made a match with Elmore, to be run over Elmore's land at Harrow, Moonraker to be ridden by the stable jockey Dan Seffert (shortly to be succeeded by the great Jem Mason), and Grimaldi by himself. Grimaldi won easily, but a barrage of objections and counter-objections had to be referred to Tattersalls.

In 1834 the Squire sold his hounds. 'To part from my dear children, as I called them, when I had reared and cherished and brought them to perfection (at least in my estimation), was most galling and painful to me; but circumstances had occurred which compelled me to take that fatal step.' He does not say what circumstances. It was not loss of nerve or of horsemanship – he was riding races against professionals for another 13 years and against amateurs for another 21. It was not shortage of money – he was still rich enough to lose over £200,000 on the turf. It was, conceivably, a woman.

Relieved of hounds and hunting, Osbaldeston devoted himself to racing. This dangerous arena provided, almost at once, the most dubious episode in his career. At Heaton Park, Lancashire, Lord Wilton held races annually in the week after the St Leger. Charles Greville praised them highly, but other visitors noticed that handicapper and judge were creatures of Lord Wilton's, and bent far over backwards to favour his and his guests' horses. Determined to have a tilt at this closed

Mr Osbaldeston's hounds. The four nearest are among those sold to Mr Hervey Combe in 1834: from the left, Clara, Figaro, Foiler, Crafty. A. Duncan after Laporte, *The New Sporting Magazine*, February 1835.

shop, Osbaldeston bought a good Irish four-year-old called Rush. The second day of the meeting he rode Rush into fourth place behind Lord Wilton's Lady de Gros. In a handicap the next day, Rush was a stone better off with Lady de Gros, was backed from 10 to 1 to 2 to 1 favouritism, but was laid against freely by Lord George Bentinck. Bentinck was the heaviest plunger in England and – though later the 'Lord Paramount' of the turf and the scourge of its villains – a man of dubious racing morals. Rush won, costing Bentinck £400 to Osbaldeston. A few days later, racing at Newmarket, Osbaldeston asked Bentinck for his winnings. Bentinck effectively accused him of cheating. The result was inevitably a challenge. First one, then another of Osbaldeston's friends refused to act for him, clearly agreeing with Bentinck (a view to which posterity is obliged to subscribe). Everyone tried to stop the duel, reminding Bentinck that his adversary was the best pistol shot in England, reminding both men that a death would now, in law, be murder. But they met at 6 a.m. at Wormwood Scrubs. Bentinck, inexperienced, fired to hit but missed. Osbaldeston is said to have put his ball deliberately through Bentinck's hat. It is possible that neither pistol was loaded with ball, owing to a prudent conspiracy on the part of the seconds. For years the adversaries ignored each other, but settled, before Bentinck's death, into truce if not into friendship.

During the next dozen years Osbaldeston had a lot of racehorses, and some good ones. But it appears that the best were not as good as he thought they were, and they seem to have been ineptly placed and incautiously backed. The pathetic, inevitable result was the sale of the whole of the fine Yorkshire property in 1848, and a fairly simple life in London and various inexpensive places in the South of England. He was able out of the wreck to keep a few horses in training; he rode in amateur races until 1855, when he was beaten a neck at Goodwood at the age of sixty-eight. He died in his house in St John's Wood in 1866, not having done for many years any of the things he liked doing, but lucky in an affectionate and sensible wife who married him when he was already close to ruin.

(ix) Sporting Portrait: John Mytton

Jack Mytton was ten years younger than Osbaldeston. His family had become prominent in Shropshire in the 14th century, rich in the 15th, and added Halston to their other estates in the 16th. General Mytton and his wife had an only son in 1796. Two years later the general died; the boy was brought up, like George Payne and George Osbaldeston, by an adoring and indulgent mother. By the time he was ten he was impossible; Sir Richard Puleston, a great Master of Hounds and at that time a neighbour, called him Mango King of the Pickles. He already had his own pack of harriers. Expelled from Westminster he was then expelled from Harrow; he was sent to a private tutor but knocked him down. Plans for his future education resulted, as already described, in his agreeing to go to University on condition that he should be allowed to restrict his reading to the *Racing Calendar* and the *Stud Book*. He never in fact went up, even for this course of study.

In 1815, at the age of nineteen, he went into the 7th Hussars, joining them in France soon after Waterloo; he was forced to leave the army three years later because he gambled so wildly. The same year he married: a fashionable wedding at St George's, Hanover Square. His bride was elegant, delicate, and rather a snob. (Mytton was alleged in contemporary gossip to have thrown her lapdog into the drawing-room fire, and to have pushed her into a deep part of the Halston lake; both stories are denied and neither is terribly likely).

At the time he married he was already a Master of Hounds. Mr Cresset Pelham had united the two countries of Shropshire and Shifnal, the latter being approximately, though not exactly, the subsequent Albrighton. In 1817 Mr Pelham retired; Mytton, who had just attained his majority, took over both countries, which he hunted five days a week for five seasons. He had a big establishment – two separate packs, and over two dozen hunt horses. He kept the Shropshire pack at home, but left the Shifnal pack at its old kennel at Ivetsy Bank, forty miles from Halston. (This had been Sir Richard Puleston's kennel when he had the Shifnal country; he moved there from Flintshire when he married the daughter of John Corbet of Sundorne Castle.) On Shifnal days Mytton usually hacked from Halston to Ivetsy, and to coverts far beyond, hunted all day, and hacked home for dinner.

His packs were terrible. He was far too impatient to be a hound breeder, and too tolerant of advice to get good drafts. The hounds varied in size from small harrier to large staghound; they cannot have carried much of a head, or hunted as a pack. The Master never knew any of their names, although he often hunted them himself. They were not, however, often called upon to draw for a wild fox; this was also too time-consuming a business for their owner. He liked bagmen and always took out two. The first was often killed; as he got 'greyhound foxes' from the Welsh hills the runs were sometimes tremendous. But the second was turned down after luncheon, taken at an inn, a break so long and strenuous that the Master was often incapable of staying on his horse and always incapable of hunting his hounds.

He hunted, in fact, for the ride and the party. But if he was one of the most celebrated carousers of his era, he was also one of its most admired horsemen. He had a large number of falls, for two reasons: he crammed his horse at utterly impossible obstacles; and he fell off because he was drunk. He was as daring a driver as a rider: this had the added charm that it often imperilled a passenger as well as himself. He once turned a gig over deliberately because his passenger said he had never been upset. 'What a damned slow fellow you must have been all your life,' said Mytton, and ran the near wheel up a high bank. Like many of the top-sawyers, he liked driving tandem (a pair with one horse in front of the other, *opposite*): tricky because of the difficulty of controlling the leader. He once drove his leader at a turnpike gate to see if it would jump timber; it did; the wheeler, the gig, Mytton and his passenger were all left on the take-off side. Only the gig was badly damaged. In order to defend the proposition that a good whip could have perfect control over the leader of a tandem, he once drove half a mile across country, negotiating a three-yard haha, a deep drain, and two stout quicksets with ditches on the far side; this was in the dark.

He started racing as soon as he attained his majority, at the same time as he became a Master of Hounds. Two of his first three horses were called Hazard and Neck-or-Nothing. He spent a great deal of money on good horses and usually broke them down. He was totally unsuccessful as a breeder. Besides having far more horses than he could afford, he entered them in a ridiculous number of races and so forfeited huge numbers of stakes. This was a major outlay, since 'added money' was far in the future.

For a few years all went merrily. He was immensely popular locally, owing to good nature and liberality. He entertained constantly, although his wife snubbed their simpler sporting neighbours. He was a generous landlord at a very bad time, and himself a successful and scientific farmer on a small scale. He made Halston a sort of sporting paradise, with some of the best shooting and fishing in England. And he was a public figure. In 1819 he stood, like so many of his ancestors, for Parliament, and was returned Member for Shrewsbury. He made little recorded impact on the Chamber, and failed to be re-elected although, in his last attempt, he spent £10,000. He was also for a short time High

Sheriff of Shropshire, and for a long time Major of the North Shrop-shire Cavalry.

His public prominence surprises posterity, but not contemporaries. Regardless of personal quirks, public office went with his name, his inheritance, his estate. And in spite of his scrappy education he was a man of unexpected culture. He read very fast, and had an almost photo-graphic memory; he could quote not merely tags of Greek or Latin, but whole passages, pages long, accurately and appositely. Not many Masters of Hounds since the learned Beckford, even sober ones, have been able to match this.

He already had eccentricities, besides those he showed in the saddle or on the box-seat: some of the more memorable concerned his jokes, his animals, his clothes and his fights.

He might have been a wit (he was certainly clever enough) but for being deaf: which caused his humour to take a crudely practical turn. He liked dressing up as a highwayman and robbing his guests as they rode home after dinner; he robbed his own butler in the same way. He also liked putting red-hot coals into the pockets of men who stood in front of the fire and talked too much.

He was fond of animals, and especially his bear. Once he put a drunken guest to bed with the bear (a large female) and two bulldogs. Another time, in full hunting costume, he rode the bear into the drawing room; he touched her incautiously with a spur and she bit him severely in the leg. He also had a monkey, which used to go hunting on horseback; it was fond of the bottle, like its master, and died after emptying in error a bottle of boot-blacking. (Mytton himself once drank a bottle of lavender-water, in a barber's shop, when he was thirsty and nothing else was available.)

He possessed more clothes than anybody else: hundreds of every-thing: but nothing lasted long; he always wore very thin boots and shoes and the finest silk stockings for fishing, hunting, shooting and work on the home farm as well as in the drawing room. He never wore under-clothes. He went shooting in midwinter in a thin jacket and white linen trousers; he once went duck shooting naked on a sheet of ice, so as not to get his clothes wet. He never carried a handkerchief, wore gloves, or had a watch.

If an active outdoor life ruined his dainty clothes, so did the fights he was perpetually in, and nearly always started. He was only five foot nine inches tall, but with powerful and well-developed muscles and a great barrel of chest. He never learned the first rudiments of boxing, but simply waded in; he took a lot of punishment, but gave more. His longest fight was twenty rounds against a Welsh miner, who offended him by holloaing a friend's hounds onto a fresh hare. The miner cried 'Enough'; Mytton gave him ten shillings; he was not a man who bore grudges.

He fought dogs as well as people, but, matching his technique to his adversary, used his teeth. His method was to clamp his teeth over the dog's nose; he defeated at least two dogs of exceptional strength and savagery in this logical way.

His first wife died, and two more serious foibles began to destroy him.

From about 1822, when he was twenty-five, he started to drink heavily. His drinks had been of orthodox type, and taken at normal times, but he began concentrating on vintage port, starting early in the morning; by evening, day in day out, he himself drank a regular seven bottles. One of the reasons for his thirst was a passion for nuts. He had filberts sent out in cartloads from Shrewsbury by a sporting hairdresser who collected them for him all over Shropshire.

His other serious error was extravagance. His long minority had built up more than £60,000, and his rents were about £10,000 a year: not a great fortune, but he spent as though he were a nabob. His agent told him that if he could keep his spending inside £6,000 a year he would be out of debt and no property need be sold. He regarded this suggestion as the wildest folly: it was impossible to live on so little. In the last fifteen years of his life, says 'Nimrod', he spent half a million pounds. His hounds, maintained without subscription, might have accounted for £25,000 of this; his domestic expenses, in spite of port and hospitality, were quite reasonable for his station (he never, for example, had a 'man-cook'); shooting and game preserving, including the planting and up-keep of his plantations, could hardly have cost £50,000; he probably lost money on farming, but probably not very much; racing must therefore have cost him at least £400,000, of which the great bulk (although 'Nimrod' denies this) must have gone to the 'blacklegs'.

It appeared, in the midst of this rush to ruin, that his second marriage might save him. His wife was Caroline Giffard, niece of the Earl of Devon and sister of the first Master of the Albrighton under that name. For a time she had a good effect on him, but a vicious spiral set in: drinking threatened his marriage; misery at the threat to his marriage made him drink. And he turned from port to brandy. Caroline fled back to her family; he was heartbroken. He made desperate attempts to get her back, once burgling her family's house: but a look-out had been posted and he was tackled. He knocked down eight men before the constables got handcuffs on him.

He loved his first wife and adored his second: but like a large minority of sporting squires of his time he was an inveterate womaniser. Much less fastidious than John Chaworth Musters, somewhat less so than George Osbaldeston, he pursued innumerable drabs. He once sent a singer a cheque for £500, as payment in advance, which she thought must be false; she sent it back; she would have believed, and been happy with, a ten-pound note.

His debts piled up. He gave up first one pack of hounds, then the other. In 1830 he had only two racehorses. He had to sell all his effects at Halston (the house itself was entailed) – all his animals and sporting equipment outside as well as everything inside. It was not enough. He began to sell off his unentailed estates; he fled from the bailiffs to London and then to a small hotel in Richmond.

In the autumn of 1831 he followed dozens of others (including, notably, George Brummell and Charles James Apperley, 'Nimrod') and fled to France, just ahead of the duns. He was in a bad state – bloated, round-shouldered, tottering, decrepit. His mind had not gone but it was going; he believed that he was, any day, to be rich again; Halston would return to its former glory; he would have another pack of hounds and another string of racehorses. A few weeks after he arrived he had an attack of hiccups when he went to bed. 'Damn this hiccup,' he said, 'but I'll *frighten* it away.' He set fire to the tail of his nightshirt with his bedroom candle; it was cotton, and went up like a torch. Though badly burned, he might have recovered completely; but he drank brandy to deaden the pain, and never really got over this adventure.

He was persuaded back to England to sign legal papers. There was something odd about this; he must have known, if he could still think, that he would be arrested for debt. And he was – at Halston, to which he made a sort of sad pilgrimage. He was taken to Shrewsbury Gaol and thence to the King's Bench Prison. His health was worse; one of his legs was almost mortified owing, it was supposed, to brandy. After a period his friends and lawyers got him out; immediately he acquired a young person of nineteen whom he met by chance on Westminster Bridge and to whom, within seconds, he offered £500 a year. She accepted, and came with him to Calais. She was in fact a respectably-connected girl who had been seduced, deserted, and thrown out on the streets. She looked after him carefully and kindly, and his mother wrote her thanks; but Mytton's besetting jealousy soured and eventually destroyed this relationship.

He drank more and more, always brandy. He began to revile the French; this tactlessness obliged him to leave. Some madness sent him to London, and straight back to the King's Bench Prison. He died, very ill and only intermittently sane, in March 1834, aged 37. His funeral at Shrewsbury was attended by 300 people, with a guard of honour of his own Yeomanry; he was buried among his ancestors in the family vault at Halston.

(x) Sporting Portrait: Sir Tatton Sykes

Fourteen years older than Osbaldeston, twenty-four years older than Mytton, was a squire of comparable fortune, similar tastes, and a history at once profoundly different and equally representative of the times: Sir Tatton Sykes of Sledmere.

His elder brother, Sir Mark, had succeeded in 1801: a notable collector of books and pictures, a thoroughbred breeder and turfite, and from 1804 Master of what were then called the Castle Howard or Eddle-thorpe Hounds, their country being the modern Middleton and part of the Holderness. In 1806 an interesting arrangement was made. Sir Mark was joined in the mastership by Mr Richard Watt, squire of Bishop Burton, and they appointed Mr Digby Legard manager of the hounds (he was the younger brother of Sir Thomas Legard of Ganton, a near neighbour). Sir Mark subscribed £1,000 a year, Mr Watt £2,000, which in relation to figures quoted earlier suggests a large establishment.

Sir Talton Sykes of Sledmere; artist unknown. *By Courtesy of the National Portrait Gallery.*

Mr Watt was then only nineteen, so he had either a most exceptional control over his fortune, or else very sporting trustees. In return for his £3,000 a year, Mr Legard was bound by a legal deed:

> to keep and provide a proper Huntsman and two proper Whippers-In, together with twelve able horses, to hunt with the said Hounds for the said term of five years, in such manner, order, and condition, that the said Hounds may be regularly hunted during the several seasons in the said term, at least three days a week (and more frequently if required by the said Sir Mark Masterman Sykes and Richard Watt), with such a district of country as shall hereafter be agreed upon, and fixed by the said parties.

In 1811 Sir Mark resumed active mastership, joined by his brother

Tatton. The latter succeeded to Sledmere, baronetcy and hounds in 1823, and immediately bought Lord Middleton's Warwickshire hounds. Lord Middleton had bought this superb pack from John Corbet in 1812, and tried very hard to continue Mr Corbet's success with the Warwickshire sportsmen: but he was an outstanding example of a hard-working, generous and honourable man who lacked the gift of being liked, and his Warwickshire mastership is remembered (by Osbaldeston, 'Nimrod' and Surtees) as a period of gloom. Sir Tatton's mastership of the Eddlethorpe lasted until 1853 (interrupted by a single season), when he sold the hounds back to Lord Middleton. He was then eighty-one.

In addition to foxhounds, Sir Tatton had a very large thoroughbred stud in which he took a passionate interest. It had two oddities: practically no horse was ever named, and no filly was ever run. If the former quirk caused confusion, the latter guaranteed failure: considering the scale of the operation it produced very few good horses and only one outstanding one – Grey Momus, sold to Mr Bowes and by him to Lord George Bentinck, for whom in 1838 he won the 2,000 Guineas and other races, and was third in the Derby. When Sir Tatton's son of the same name dispersed the stud in 1863, 309 lots were sold by Tattersalls at Sledmere, over three days in September, for a total of 24,171 guineas: a miserable average of just over seventy-eight guineas.

Sir Tatton's connection with racing included both attendance and riding. He saw seventy-six runnings of the St Leger at Doncaster, and was the best known and easily the most popular figure there; in 1847 he led in the winner, which had been named after him by its owner and jockey Bill Scott, who would have won the Derby too had he not been so drunk that he got left at the start. As a race rider Sir Tatton may not have rivalled George Osbaldeston for success, but he surpassed even him for keenness: he many times hacked scores and even hundreds of miles to ride in a single race. He also rode from Yorkshire to London to have his portrait painted, in 1805 by Sir Thomas Lawrence and in 1848 (aged seventy-six) by Sir Francis Grant.

In the tradition of his family he was also, and pre-eminently, a landowner and farmer. In this regard he was followed by his son, who died in 1913 aged eighty-seven; the younger Sir Tatton had a small stud of high-class horses – a far more successful approach – and is locally remembered as a builder and restorer of churches: he built or rebuilt sixteen on his own estates, and then others further afield. His taste was fortunately better than that of most men of his time.

(xi) Sporting Portrait: Thomas Assheton Smith

Mr Smith was four years younger than Sir Tatton Sykes. His grand-father was Thomas Assheton of Ashley Hall, Cheshire, who took the additional name when he inherited the Vaenol property in Caernarvonshire. This had been given to a Smith who was Speaker of the House of Commons by Queen Anne; the gift turned out to be valuable because it included the Dinorwic slate quarries, opened about 1800 and the most important in Britain.

Thomas went to Eton, the youngest boy in the school, at the age of seven. Towards the end of his eleven years there he had a tremendous and never-forgotten battle with John Musters, whose father, Squire of Colwick, had founded the South Notts hunt. (Musters 'could ride, fence, fight, play at tennis, swim, shoot, and play at cricket with any man in Europe'; he married Mary Anne Chaworth, heiress of Annesley – to the dismay of the youthful Byron, who also loved her – in 1805, in which year he also took over his father's hounds and country. The 'Squire of Notts' was probably the best amateur huntsman of the early 19th century, and one of its most successful ladies' men.) At Eton, Smith acquired a love of literature which lasted all his life: his favourite authors were Ovid, Shakespeare and Pope. He indulged this taste at Christ Church, as well as hunting with John Warde, who then had the Bicester.

He spent his school holidays and university vacations at his father's house, Tedworth, Hampshire, already a sporting headquarters: the partridge shooting was famous; the squire had a pack of hounds, typical of the era and area, hunting hare and fox; young Thomas had his own pack of rabbit-beagles; and there were regular cricket matches in the park. Of the last Sir John Eardley-Wilmot remarked: 'For the purposes of social enjoyment, nothing can exceed a good cricket match in the grounds of an English country gentleman, if only the skies be auspicious.'

In his middle twenties, Smith was already famous for two accomplishments: he was the best and bravest rider across a country, and one of the greatest cricketers. The former reputation even reached Napoleon, to whom Smith was presented in 1802. As a cricketer he played for Surrey v. All England in 1802, for Hampshire in 1803 (the only amateur in the county side), for the M.C.C. v. All England in 1804, for England that year and the next, and in 1806 in the first Gentlemen v. Players match;

in 1809 he and Osbaldeston were both in the M.C.C. side v. England, and in 1810 in the England side v. Surrey.

In 1806, never having been Master or huntsman of foxhounds, aged only thirty, he was offered the Quorn when Lord Foley retired. Encouraged by his father (and by the fair but not enormous allowance his father gave him) he took the country. He collected a pack from various sources – principally from John Chaworth Musters, who after the fight had become one of his closest friends – and began hunting it himself, the first Master in the Shires to make this audacious decision. His horsemanship and courage continued to inspire the most ungrudging admiration, especially as he could not really afford good horses. As a huntsman he may not have been quite as successful: he was not admired by the great Melton roughrider Dick Christian, who as a horseman idolised him. Steeplechasing he would never have any part in, regarding it as cruel. At this stage of his life he gave evidence – amply confirmed over the next forty years – of combining generosity with strong prejudices and extreme, inherited obstinacy; he was quick-tempered, and in the hunting field exceptional for the force of his language in an age which was not mealy-mouthed (and in which there were no ladies hunting).

He had a great number of falls – more than Jack Mytton, but for a different reason: It was he who said, 'Throw your heart over and your horse will follow'; and, 'There is no place that cannot be jumped with a fall.' He was so tough that he hardly ever hurt himself. During his Quorn mastership he did have one bad fall, and put his enforced idleness to illuminating use: he observed a very pretty girl in the Melton Post Office performing mathematical calculations with wonderful speed and accuracy, and got her to teach him how to do it. The result was that when he took over the management of the Welsh quarries, he was able to supervise financial and engineering detail to a degree probably unique among gentlemen so placed.

In 1816 he went from the Quorn to the Burton, taking his pack, being followed in Leicestershire by Osbaldeston. It is not clear why he moved from the premier country in England to a good but far less celebrated one: probably he actively preferred the knowledgeable Lincolnshire farmers to the Melton thrusters. Money was not the problem, even in the agricultural nightmare of the time; the Dinorwic quarries were already much more valuable than the landed estates. And he was by this time a yachtsman, and had brought Lord Raglan (who lost an arm at Waterloo) home from Ostend.

In 1826 he sold his hounds to Sir Richard Sutton, a man with whom he had much in common, and went back to Hampshire. He established himself at Penton Lodge, near Andover, collected a scratch pack, and did a little hunting. This was intensely popular among the local gentry, with the single and startling exception of his father, who so violently opposed it that he closed his coverts to his own son. The older man's reasoning was that the younger had made an immense reputation in good hunting countries, and should not jeopardise it in a bad one; but he was brought round by the warmth of the countryside's welcome.

In 1827, at the age of fifty-one, Smith married; the next year his father died. He rebuilt Tedworth House (*above*) on admirable classical lines (being substantially his own architect) and bought a pack of his own blood from Sir Richard Sutton. He also built new kennels (*opposite*), all the work being done by his own estate labour, and particularly splendid stables. These housed fifty horses, including hacks and carriage-horses, all of which had loose-boxes, an unprecedented arrangement.

The requirement now was to make a foxhunting country. This involved the cleaning up of huge areas of woodland and the cutting of innumerable broad rides: Andover became, for a time, a single giant timber market. The new squire spent a great deal of money on this prodigious labour; but a lot of his neighbours, simple farmers as well as

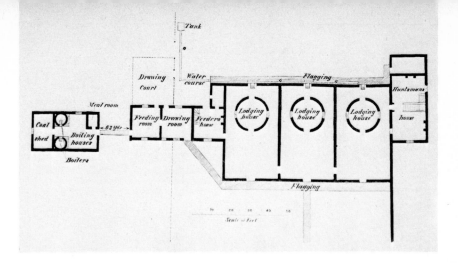

landowners, did so too, so great was their enthusiasm for the nascent
Tedworth hunt.

The hounds were maintained by their Master without a single penny
of subscription for thirty-two years. The breakfast meets at Tedworth
were the local high times of the year: 'What capital cheer within the
hall, what barons of beef, what interminable venison pasties!' Large
parties, of course, stayed in the house (of which the Duke of Wellington
was often a member) to hunt and to play billiards and pool: a billiard
room was one of the new amenities which country houses were coming
to have. The partridge shooting was energetically kept up, but entirely
for the squire's friends. He himself never shot latterly. Nor did he race.
As a friend of Lord George Bentinck he had embarked on thoroughbred
breeding and racing, and for a time was a member of the Jockey Club,
but he was not interested.

In 1840 there was an episode unique in sporting history, which showed
the unique place Smith had in the sporting world. He was invited, with
his hounds, by the Quorn and its Master, Mr Tommy Hodgson. Two
thousand horsemen came to the meet at Shankton Holt, together with
an immense crowd of footpeople and concourse of ladies in carriages.
There were too many people; there was not enough scent; as a hunting
day it was a failure; but what a tribute, what a celebration by the Shires
of the return of their greatest alumnus. Hounds and Master went on to
Sir Richard Sutton and the Burton for five days (they killed four foxes),
to the Duke of Rutland and the Belvoir for one, and to Lord Lonsdale
and the Cottesmore for two. Nothing like this round of visits has ever
been paid by another pack.

In 1842 Smith bought the Duke of Grafton's pack and engaged his
huntsman George Carter; the latter hunted hounds two days a week,

the Master four (he was sixty-six when this arrangement *began*). 'Oh dear,' said George, 'dear me, and he were an odd man, a very odd man were Mr Smith; why, he were unlike anyone else, and didn't care what he did or what he said.'

Mr Thomas Assheton Smith (mounted) with his huntsman Dick Burton at Tedworth. J. H. Whymper after J. Ferneley.

The Smiths spent their summers in Wales, where they had 47,000 acres of Snowdonia, including a stretch of coastline on the Menai Strait. As soon as he inherited, Smith began to increase the scale and yield of the Dinorwic quarries, investing heavily in a chain-driven railway system up the mountainside and a new harbour. By 1860 2,400 people were employed, among the highest-earning and most favoured workpeople in Britain. Good men were given land – ten acres each – on which they built cottages for their retirement; Smith also built schools and himself paid the teachers; he built a church and parsonage, gave glebe land and churchyard, and paid the parson; though a staunch member of the Church of England he also gave land and money to the Calvinists for their chapels, and supported their charities. Latterly the quarries earned £30,000 a year, and the agricultural estates in total another £15,000.

Wales was where he did his yachting after he left Lincolnshire. He had five successive sailing yachts, and was a member of the Royal Yacht Club. He then became enthusiastic about steam, which the Club debarred; he left the Club and had eight steam yachts built, the biggest of 400 tons, largely designed by himself and incorporating the revolutionary hollow-line principle in the hull. As a result of his trials this was later adopted by the Admiralty for gunboats.

His father had been a rigid High Tory M.P. for the family pocket borough. He himself stood unsuccessfully for Nottingham, in the same interest, in 1818, when he was Master of the Burton. His opponent was the popular radical Sir Francis Burdett, against whom a Tory fox-hunter had no chance in the furious turmoil of a town. He inherited the family nomination and sat until Parliament was reformed in 1832. His politics remained identical to his father's, to the extent that he raised a troop of militia to put down the agrarian disturbances of 1830. He was a conscientious Member, hurrying to London in a light chariot with four horses after hunting, in order to vote, and postponing the next day's meet until noon. He later twice represented Caernarvonshire.

He hunted until he was eighty, still getting a lot of falls not because his horsemanship had deteriorated but because his courage had not. He began drinking spirits moderately at this age, which he had never done in his life, on doctor's orders. Asthma, which had bothered him all his life, became a severe problem in his extreme old age, and he died in 1858, aged eighty-two, at Vaenol. His widow gave his hounds to the country, which owns them still.

(xii) The Changing Face of Hunting Country

There were large changes to the countryside, of which the most important were fencing, draining, steam-ploughing, fertilising, planting, railways, industrialisation and building.

Large-scale enclosing inside fences was, in Arthur Young's time, especially a phenomenon of East Anglia, but by 1815 – to Cobbett's rage and grief – it was everywhere. Almost every hunting country took jumping to cross: the only major exceptions were Exmoor and Dartmoor, parts of the North Riding and Northumberland, and the Lincolnshire wolds. The fences varied with the availability of materials, local custom and the scale of investment. The best grazing areas had quickset hedges of whitethorn or – more usually but less satisfactorily – blackthorn, started from rooted cuttings, pruned back hard after planting, then allowed to luxuriate until they were big enough to cut and lay. When young they were protected against the cattle by post and rail a yard away, the combination being the ox-fence or oxer, most formidable of hunting obstacles. Farmers with plentiful wood made deadwood fences instead of quicksets, which rarely lasted more than a few years. Where stones strewed the fields, drystone walls were easily built; in very few places was mortar used, or the tops of the walls coped. The South West had cops – hedges on banks – and in some places banks only, which put a great premium on Irish-bred horses.

Wire first appeared about 1860 and barbed wire twenty years later. Even hunting farmers were unable, economically, to resist it in sheep areas: but on the whole the spread of wire – and especially its presence during the winter, when much stock was in – was a result of two causes: an unpopular Master of Hounds, or a local race of selfish or unsporting landowners. History must be tolerant of some of the former: some of the most worthy and hard-working men have lacked a capacity to be loved, have been aloof at puppy-shows or inept at keepers' dinners. But nothing excuses the landowners, of whom there were thousands, who wired their own farms for economy and then did their hunting elsewhere.

Tile draining replaced simple ditching on a large scale as soon as agricultural recovery permitted substantial investment. It had long been accused of ruining scent by allowing the ground to dry up too quickly, especially in light-riding arable country like the East Riding; but in all countries of heavy clay soil – grass as well as arable – it made miles of country ridable which, after a week of rain, had before stopped whole fields of horses.

Steam ploughing was an important agricultural advance. The horse-drawn plough, even with a team of four or six, had seldom achieved more than an acre a day, and five inches was a good depth. But 'Brooksby's' hunting tours of the early 1880s execrate, almost everywhere he went, the 'villainous grooves' gouged by the steam-plough, which stopped horses like the ill-drained fields of fifty years earlier. Fertiliser, both fish and chemical, was equally important to agriculture but naturally unhelpful to scent. A fall onto chemical was also the cause of many ruined coats.

Throughout the 18th century and until 1815, tree planting had mostly been of hardwoods. The intention was often wholly aesthetic but sometimes partly commercial. Mr Thomas Tyrwhitt Drake of Shardeloes Park, (M.P. for the wholly-owned family borough of Amersham) had in 1822 several thousand oak trees 'worth, on an average, five pounds a-piece . . . which will be able to stand a tug with the fund holders for some time'. (Mr Drake was Master of the Bicester, with a private pack, from 1829 to 1851, in succession to the delightful migrant Welshman Sir Thomas Mostyn; he was himself succeeded by his son, of the same name, discontinuously until 1866.) But forestry meant a higher investment and a slower return than was possible between 1815 and 1850; and late in the century new plantations were almost wholly of rhododendron, laurel and pine, partly because Victorian taste preferred these dreary exotics, and partly as covert for pheasants. Nothing could be worse fox covert. At the same time there was a great deal of gorse planted specially for foxes. This had been necessary from time to time almost everywhere (even in Beckford's well-wooded Dorset country), and was needed on a large scale in such covertless countries as the South Wold. But it was carried much too far. Too many small coverts too close together, especially in the Shires, had the effect more than any other cause of making the long runs of 1800 impossible without repeated changes of fox.

Railways brought remarkably few accidents to hounds, and those few were caused more by deep cuttings than by oncoming trains. The fumes were transitory; hounds learned to ignore the whistles; the navvies went away after the line was finished to poach elsewhere. In the long term the effect was to open up remote countries to visitors, and increase the number of urban people hunting. Before railways, some of the most celebrated provincial countries had virtually no visitors at all, including the Brocklesby, Hoar Cross (Meynell) and Cheshire: hence the inward-looking local snobberies about such matters as the colour of boot-tops, hence the electrifying effect of the visits of the awesome 'Nimrod', hence the embarrassing episode when a Cheshire squire, of large acres and ancient family, was taken in the Shires for a farmer because of his buckskin breeches, and several gentlemen tried to buy his horse. Railways did not make hunts much more like each other, but they did make strange faces a normal part of the meet, and they did have a large effect on subscriptions. This was particularly true of hunts reachable by day-trip from large cities – from Doncaster, Birmingham and Bristol as well as London. A great many business and professional men kept a horse or two at livery near a railway station – it was as common, said Trollope, as to die – with the result that hunting for the first time became a sport of urban visitors as much as of country residents. Subscriptions and livery-stables profited; more hounds got broken backs; farmers had many more fences spoilt, gates left open, and turnips ridden over. These disasters were also, reportedly, the usual result of women hunting.

The building of factories and the digging of mines also cut both ways. They brought enormous wealth to certain landed families, who spent it munificently on foxhunting: the Fitzwilliams, the Lowthers, the Lamb-tons, the Assheton Smiths. They swelled the subscriptions of hunts like the Badsworth, Warwickshire and even the Quorn. But they destroyed a good deal of hunting country; and although colliers, navvies and workpeople were often the most sporting of foot-followers, their num-bers were awesome and their enthusiasm excessive. Building development was eating into hunting country in Cobbett's day, and did so steadily throughout the 19th century; but a good many squires, like the Dashwoods of West Wycombe, notably profited thereby.

The greatest single enemy to hunting was of equally sturdy growth: the hand-reared pheasant. Some squires – stupid men, very busy men, men often away – were probably genuinely ignorant of their keepers' vulpicide. Some turned a blind eye, thus keeping both their local popularity and their pheasants. Some secretly encouraged their keep-ers to destroy litters of foxes, either because they did not hunt, or because they hunted in smarter countries far from home. A few made no secret. In crack foxhunting countries this was extremely rare because violently unpopular; but the testimony of dozens of Masters of Hounds records the scandal in the provinces: of 'Scrutator' in North Wiltshire, of Captain Percy Williams at the Rufford, many Masters of the H.H., the Surrey packs, Worcestershire, Essex. Mr Francis Holyoake (later Sir Francis Holyoake Goodricke, owing to the never-quite-explained legacy he received from Sir Harry Goodricke) was Master of the Quorn for a time, calling it the Meltonian Hunt: his own coverts at home in Warwickshire were closed to the local hounds. Even Lord Fitzhardinge, who re-established the Berkeley, kept many of his own coverts strictly for pheasants; this was one reason he spent so much time hunting his 'out country', the Cotswolds, which was delightful for visitors to Cheltenham but annoying for his neighbours at home.

(xiii) Hunting Finances

From the hunting squire's point of view the greatest change was in finance.

About 1780, according to William Cobbett, there were five packs of foxhounds and ten of harriers, all wholly owned and maintained without subscription, within ten miles of Newbury. A foxhunting establishment had always been a good deal more expensive than a pack of harriers (except in the far North and the far South West), but it remained as well within the capacity of a prosperous squire as when Mr Darley of Aldby drew up his accounts about 1760. Between 1800 and 1815 there were more than fifty recognized packs of foxhounds maintained entirely at the expense of the owner. These included the great family packs like Belvoir, Badminton, Brocklesby, Goodwood, Berkeley and Alnwick; but also the packs of private gentlemen like Mr John Warde, Mr John Corbet, the latter's son-in-law, Sir Richard Puleston, Sir Thomas Mostyn (all mobile masters), and, of those who hunted at home, Lord Vernon of Sudbury, the Revd John Loder and his son-in-law the Revd Robert Symonds (Old Berks), Lord Monson of Burton, Mr Deane (Cotley), Mr Richard Hill (Derwent), Mr Bragg (Mid Devon), Mr George Templer of Stover (South Devon), Sir Mark Sykes, the Wilkinson family of Neasham (Hurworth), Mr Coke of Holkham (West Norfolk), Mr John Musters and his son Mr John Chaworth Musters (South Notts), Mr Chute of the Vine, Mr Selby Lowndes (Whaddon Chase).

An excellent sketch of a typical wholly-private establishment is to be found, improbably enough, in *The Water Babies* (Charles Kingsley was a keen hunting man at a time when it was still just possible for a parson to be so; he followed Mr Garth's hounds). Sir John Harthover of Harthover Place, somewhere in the North, had game reserves, salmon-fishing, and a pack of foxhounds; he employed a huntsman, first and second whippers-in, and a groom who 'looked so very neat and clean, with his drab gaiters, drab breeches, drab jacket, snow-white tie with a pin in it, and clear, round, ruddy face'. Sir John hunted four days a week (dining at five after hunting); the other two weekdays were given to the Bench and the Board of Guardians.

Sir John was evidently a very rich man: and by now it was accepted that only a rich man could maintain a pack of foxhounds, of any pretension, without financial help. Mr Thomas Ridge of Kilmeston began taking a subscription in Hampshire about 1780, and when he retired in 1795 the Hampshire Hunt was formed as a subscription pack. After Mr James Smith Barry quarrelled with the sportsmen of Cheshire in 1798, the Cheshire County Subscription Hounds were formed. Although its early history is obscure, it appears that the Bramham Moor was always a subscription pack, in spite of the wealth of the Lascelles and Lane Fox families who alternately managed it. In making these arrangements, gentlemen who were by no means poor were adopting the ideas of yeomen farmers (especially of Cumberland, Yorkshire, Shropshire and Wales) who formed the earliest subscription hunts. The idea spread, and rapidly after expenses went up and farming profits down after 1815.

In 1825 Colonel John Cook, who had been Master of the Essex, Hambledon and possibly Atherstone, thus listed the expenses of a four-day country:

14 horses etc.	£700
Hounds' food, 50 couple	275
Firing	50
Taxes	120
Two whipper-ins, feeder	210
Earth stoppers	80
Saddlery	100
Farriery and medical	100
Drafts and walking	100
Casualties	200
Total	£1935

This makes no provision for capital purchase or building, rent or up-keep of coverts, or the salary of huntsman or kennel-huntsman: the last at least £300.

Mr F. P. Delmé Radcliffe went out seven times a fortnight when he was Master of the Hertfordshire (1835 to 1839); he reckoned the expense at £2,000 a year. Mr Tom Smith ('Another' or 'Craven' Smith, not the squire of Tedworth) hunted the Craven four days a week for £1,400: but he was exceptionally economical, and quite unable to make ends meet in the Pytchley country where subscriptions were larger on paper but harder to come by. Lord Scamperdale (in *Sponge*) maintained the Flat Hat Hunt on £2,000 about 1850, hunting four days a week (a figure to which Jack Spraggon added, in conversation, another £500 because £2,500 sounded better); the establishment, like Tom Smith's, was respectable but economical. By this date, according to Trollope, a provincial hunt of middling status cost £2,500 a year, and a Shires pack at least twice as much. Sometimes, though not often, covert rents were a major additional item: Sir Harry Goodricke at the Quorn (1831–35) paid £1,200 a year. Under these conditions even the very rich Mr T. T. Drake, when Master of the Bicester, was stung into saying of an Oxfordshire neighbour: 'He doesn't know the first thing about hunting; he doesn't know how to subscribe.'

Gentlemen who took a country without subscription therefore became a very small class of very rich men. Sir Richard Sutton (Burton 1824–42, Quorn 1847–56) stopped taking a subscription at the Quorn because he did not want to be interfered with; his foxhunting career is said to have cost him a third of a million pounds. The few others to whom this sort of magnificence was possible included Lord Darlington (later Duke of Cleveland) in Yorkshire, Lord Elcho (later Lord Wemyss) in Northumberland and Berwickshire, and other territorial magnates of immense wealth; and of squires in the same period Mr J. J. Farquharson, Mr Thomas Assheton Smith, Mr Hervey Combe and Mr George Payne. Mr Farquharson was Master of the Dorsetshire (modern Portman, South Dorset, Blackmore Vale and Cattistock) from 1806 to 1859. This was possible because his father had been a prodigiously successful London merchant. The Smith fortune derived principally from slate quarries; the Tedworth was, inevitably, a subscription country with a country-owned pack after the founder's death. Mr Combe saved with his enthusiasm first the Old Berkeley, then the Old Berks; he was a brewer. Mr Payne inherited a large fortune, which a long minority increased; he spent it all on hunting (the Pytchley) and racing (everywhere), without, however, losing any of the esteem and affection in which he was held. A happier example was R. S. Surtees, who inherited Hamsterley, County Durham, in 1838, and re-established his father's and grandfather's pack; he paid all expenses himself, but with a two-day country in that part of England, and with his own detestation of extravagant show (a leading theme in all his books) they were modest. He was in addition a highly successful author and farmer, profiting greatly in the latter capacity from the agricultural boom of the 1850s.

One of the new-style Masters of Hounds: 'Mr. Puffington took the Mangeysterne, now the Hanby hounds, because he thought they would give him consequence.' His father was a great Stepney starchmaker, vastly proud of his son. John Leech in *Mr. Sponge's Sporting Tour.*

An established, resident squire like Surtees could, moreover, maintain a hunting establishment a lot more cheaply than any outsider. He had his own stabling, paddocks, forage; he had local sources of horsemeat for his hounds; he had plenty of walkers; he either bred hunters or could buy them locally; grooms, strappers, earthstoppers and other labour were easier and cheaper for him to come by. It was worth any country subscribing properly to such a man, provided he was liked. But the subscription never came near the expense, unless the country was being farmed by a professional M.F.H. like Trollope's Captain Glomax of the 'Ufford and Rufford United'. The difference between money received and money paid out has been the greatest cause, throughout foxhunting history, of the disaster of short masterships. Long mastership, even of subscription packs, meant wealth: hence the value to their countries of Mr J. T. Villebois in Hampshire (who inherited a brewing fortune), Mr G. S. Foljambe at the Grove (a highly successful sheep breeder and dealer at a time when farming paid well), Mr Henry (later Lord) Chaplin at the Blankney, and Mr Albert Brassey at the Heythrop (whose fortune came from railways).

In the agricultural depression of the 1880s, even the Dukes of Rutland and Beaufort began to take subscriptions: it was that or reduce the number of days they hunted.

Perhaps 2,000 19th-century squires were masters of subscription packs; the rest hunted and subscribed. Ideally they did rather more. They welcomed hounds and horsemen onto their land, and bullied their keepers into preserving foxes even though they preserved pheasants too. If the country needed them they planted gorse-coverts, often of five acres, a use of land valueless for anything except foxhunting. In a score of cases they gave land for new hunt kennels. And they played host to the hunt at breakfast meets: but the great disadvantage of this amiable custom (apart from its expense) was that many of the field and all the servants were apt to be drunk before the first draw. Tom Andrews ('Gin and Beer') in Worcestershire, Charles Whatley in Wiltshire, and Finch Mason in an uncertain region are all witnesses of this hazard.

An individual foxhunter could spend as much, and nearly as little, as he liked. In 1830 a groom cost £6 a month; the keep of two horses was £16 a month, nearly all of which a squire saved by having his own stables and forage. But a Melton first-flighter in 1815 needed (according to 'Nimrod', whose ideas were admittedly large) twelve hunters and two covert hacks for which stable expenses *alone* were £1,200 a year. For this reason the full-time hunting man who came to Melton for the whole season was practically unknown after 1850. But people who came out more or less regularly with their local packs increased steadily throughout the century (farmers in times of depression aside): and have increased ever since.

(xiv) Hare, Greyhound and Deer

Harehunting remained far cheaper, in terms of participation as of establishment. Many squires still liked doing their own harehunting in their own way: a writer remembers, in about 1820:

> an old Somersetshire baronet, who used to take his post on a fat cob in the middle of a hundred acres of grass almost surrounded by coverts, and spend the morning in listening to and watching a pack of queerly-bred beagles chasing hares out of and into the coverts. On rainy days the groom who stood at the cob's head completed the picture by holding a huge gig-umbrella over Sir Edward's head.

(Except for the umbrella, this is virtually a picture of American 'hill-top' foxhunting, as so lyrically described by men like Colonel Birdsong and Colonel Trigg; of course the American grey fox runs much like a hare, and the old American foxhounds were descended from English harriers.)

On the whole, harriers became an unpretentious poor relation in countries with established foxhounds. According to 'Scrutator', in the 1850s and 1860s many harrier packs attracted a very low type of sports-man, and were given to hunting poached foxes out of sacks; as a general view this is doubtless as unfair to the harehunting farmers of the times as many of 'Scrutator's' other judgements – on, for example, hunting ladies, or the Duke of Beaufort. One of the best harrier packs was the Prince Consort's: he adored them.

Informal coursing for the chase and the pot is not much recorded after Cobbett's time (he did it constantly), but an immense number of farmers kept a brace or two of greyhounds, besides the ones they entered in the local match-coursing meetings (*overleaf*). The latter sport received an important addition with the formation of the Altcar Club, near Liverpool, by the Earl of Sefton in 1825. Mr Lynn, of the Waterloo Hotel, Aintree, established the Waterloo Cup, coursing's blue ribbon, with Lord Molyneux's help in 1836. (Mr Lynn had already opened a racecourse at Aintree, and in 1836 put on its first steeplechase; this was the race that developed in 1839 into what is regarded as the first Grand National. With Mr Tommy Coleman of the Turf Hotel, St Albans – who invented modern steeplechasing – Mr Lynn is the most important inn-keeper in sporting history.) The National Coursing Club was formed

GOING OUT

THE CHASE

THE DEATH

Early Victorian Harehunting.

in 1858 to regularise the complex rules that had been causing so much confusion and ill-feeling. To a surprising extent it remained true that foxhunters did not own greyhounds, or coursing men go hunting, although they were in other respects identical.

The wild deer was hunted (*below*) only by the Devon and Somerset (and that intermittently) until the proliferation of deer enabled the Tiverton (1896) and Quantock (1902) to be established. The New Forest Buckhounds chased feral fallow deer from 1854. All four hunts attracted strong support from local squires and farmers. But a much more popular sport throughout the century was the hunting of carted

deer. Few packs attracted gentlemen in numbers; the one which attracted most was Baron Rothschild's, in the stiff Vale of Aylesbury country, which Whyte Melville so much admired; most of the rest, including the Royal Buckhounds, were remarkable for the obtrusive vulgarity of their fields.

(xv) Gentlemen and Others on the Turf

Squires had played a major part in the invention of modern racing and the creation of the thoroughbred. During the 18th century they were eased – very properly – out of total control of their local racing: but a minority continued to be the backbone of the sport as local stewards and as owners and breeders. Alongside them during the 19th century three new sorts of men became quite as celebrated and influential: jockeys, trainers and bookmakers. Rogues among jockeys and trainers helped ruin some gentlemen; bookies ruined many more. Among their famous victims were Mr George Payne (already mentioned as Master of the Pytchley), the 4th Lord Suffield and the 3rd Marquess of Hastings (both briefly Masters of the Quorn), Mr George Osbaldeston and Mr John Mytton.

In contrast to these ill-advised plungers, the prudent Sykes family lost no money by their racing: but they made none to speak of, either. It was (as it remains) extremely difficult for an honest man to do so, without prodigious luck. This is illustrated by the measures taken by Squire Thomas Thornhill of Fixby, Yorkshire and later Riddlesworth, Norfolk, a member of the Jockey Club, who weighed almost 24 stone in 1825 and probably more later. He won the Derbys of 1818 and 1820 and the Oaks of 1819 with horses trained by Bill Chifney and ridden by Sam Chifney the younger, brilliant and crooked sons of a brilliant and crooked father. What Mr Thornhill reportedly did was to offer Sam Chifney even more to win than the bookmakers ('blacklegs' or 'pencillers') offered him to lose. But Mr Thornhill was a sophisticated man, an habitué of London clubs and gaming houses; he was himself (perhaps

Mr Thomas Thornhill driving his phaeton; pen-and-pencil sketch by R. S., *The New Sporting Magazine*, June 1835.

quite unfairly) accused of sharp practice in a lampoon of 1826; he was, at any rate, an insider: a far cry from the simpler racing squires on whom the blacklegs preyed.

Two of the very few gentlemen of undoubted integrity who were really lucky on the turf were Mr John Bowes of Streatlam Castle, Durham, and Mr Henry Chaplin of Blankney, Lincolnshire: neither, for different reasons, typical squires.

Mr Bowes was the son of the Earl and Countess of Strathmore, but was born (in 1814) nine years before their marriage. He inherited a fine estate, made finer by the discovery on it of extensive coal. He owned racehorses for fifty years and was a member of the Jockey Club; of his four Derby winners, two were home bred. He lived most of his life very quietly in Paris, not County Durham (his wife was a French actress for whom he actually bought the Comédie Française); he never used to visit his horses at work or in stable, latterly never went near a racecourse, and can have seen very little of his stud. If his success was not due to luck – and he always denied that it was – then it relied on his choosing good servants and letting them get on with it: not the characteristic method of most resident country squires in any branch of sport. Mr Bowes is remembered in artistic as well as turf history: he founded the Bowes Museum at Barnard Castle, a prodigious collection of pictures, furniture and objets d'art, assembled by him with an enthusiasm which sometimes outran his taste as far as his horses outran those of his rivals.

Mr Chaplin, born in 1842, was also lucky, though not consistently so. His father was a Lincolnshire parson; he inherited the superb Blankney estate from an uncle. As a boy he hunted with and learned from the great Lord Henry Bentinck (brother of Lord George), Master of the Burton from 1842 to 1862. He came of age in 1863 and began racing on a moderate scale. The following year he was jilted, shortly before the wedding, by Lady Florence Paget ('the Pocket Venus'), who made a romantic but ill-judged bolt with the Marquess of Hastings. (The latter was neither evil nor stupid, but he was very, very silly.) This seems to have impelled Chaplin into an immediate and massive involvement in both racing and hunting.

He bought Lord Henry's hounds; known by now as 'the Squire' almost as widely as a previous Master of the Burton, Osbaldeston, he went out six days a week, hunting hounds two days, a magnificent horseman in spite of weight and bad eyesight, and among the best amateur huntsmen. But the country was too big even for him, and in 1871 he divided it by an east-west line through Lincoln; he kept the southern half, naming it for his house and kennel. He was then, for six years, too busy in Parliament to manage his hounds himself (a decision which would have been incomprehensible to an earlier generation: to Ralph Lambton, Osbaldeston, Assheton Smith and dozens of others); his brother managed them. He returned to active hunting, and to carrying the horn, in 1877, but for only four years; the death of his wife, another Lady Florence, sent him on travels abroad. He continued in public life, and his contribution in the First War (when he was very old but still very formidable) earned him a viscountcy in 1916.

He bought a number of racehorses in 1865, including a yearling called Hermit, picked by his astute but misanthropic racing manager Captain James Octavus Machel. Hermit's victory in the 1867 Derby, at the long price of 1,000 to 15, was almost miraculous, as he had broken a blood-vessel a week before. Chaplin won nearly £120,000 on the race; Hastings lost about the same, having laid against Hermit from injudicious if comprehensible motives; to Chaplin personally Hastings lost £20,000. Hastings, dying not long afterwards, said Hermit's victory broke his heart: 'But I didn't show it, did I?' Chaplin thereafter bred as much as he raced, and the Blankney stud produced such cracks as the Duke of Westminster's Shotover, which won the Derby of 1882.

Picnic party at Ascot Races, 1844

But he never again won a large sum of money, or owned an outstanding horse. He had contributed £1,200 a year to the Burton hounds (as had his uncle) and his outlay on the Blankney must have been much more. He entertained munificently. Blankney itself had to be mortgaged, and the mortgage was foreclosed in 1897. Like Osbaldeston he died, having lived for many years quietly in London, very much poorer than when he inherited.

Throughout the first half of the 19th century racing was consistently and violently dishonest; gentlemen had made it so a century before; gentlemen now cleaned it up: Lord George Bentinck, Admiral Rous, Lord Durham, Sir John Astley, and the other noblemen and squires of the Jockey Club. Meanwhile two-year-old races, handicaps and sprints grew; heat-racing and extreme distances disappeared. Amateur racing remained moderately buoyant in private parks, at hunt races, and at the unique Bibury Club meetings at Burford and later Stockbridge. The whole had shrunk to nothing by 1914, but its place was taken by point-to-point steeplechases. There was some trotting racing early in the century, mostly in East Anglia, under saddle and then in harness; there was pony racing everywhere throughout the century; neither sport attracted the gentry.

Nor, except for a dashing and celebrated minority, did steeplechasing.

In the early years, those of the unflagged cross-country races (*above*), a very few names (Osbaldeston, Ross, Lord Clanricarde) crop up again and again in the scrappy records; more names, but still not many, appear in the 1830s and 1840s when modern steeplechasing, mainly professional, spread from St Albans to Cheltenham, Aintree and elsewhere; and few gentlemen were involved in the great growth of the sport in the 1850s. The reasons are to be found, a hundred times, in the comments of 'Nimrod' and Surtees. Landowners and farmers (though not innkeepers) hated 'chasing because ignorant crowds did so much damage; hunting squires (for whom 'Nimrod' spoke) detested it because it put the countryside against hunting. What Surtees recorded (in *Sponge*, for example) was ill-management, scruffiness, complete dishonesty, and this view was echoed repeatedly in the sporting press. The National Hunt Steeplechase, invented by Dr Fothergill Rowlands at Harborough and then Cheltenham, was intended to bring hunting gentlemen back into the sport; this succeeded, but only in regard to one annual race. Other races for 'gentlemen' produced some very queer candidates. But Rowlands's rules were eventually adopted officially, and steeplechasing gradually became respectable. There were a few great amateur riders, like George Ede and Roddy Owen, but very few. Jumping racing only became a squires' sport when hunts started their own 'chases – known ludicrously as point-to-points – for their members and farmers: this began about 1872 and was almost universal by 1900. (For the atmosphere and detail of a pre-First-War point-to-point – as for accounts of the Eridge, Southdown and Atherstone – the reader is referred to Siegfried Sassoon's *Memoirs of a Fox-Hunting Man.*)

(xvi) The Great Age of Coaching

In 1800 every considerable squire had a coach, drawn by two or four strapping 17-hand horses for short journeys. The appalling roads called for at least six horses on longer journeys, ridden by postillions rather than controlled from the box. 'These vast, costly, unwieldy vehicles', says Sidney, 'were to be met at races, on nomination days of country elections, assizes, and every gathering of country magnates in every county, drawn by six horses.' The coaches themselves were extremely expensive: they were built to stand up to the roads, and often lasted for generations. Gentlemen also had chariots, brought out on a few ceremonial occasions.

The turnpike companies made possible the brief great age of coaching by having their roads engineered by Telford and surfaced by Macadam. A gentleman's coach immediately became a good deal more flamboyant; as four horses instead of six could tow it, it was controlled from the box instead of a leader's saddle. 'Nimrod' thus describes Andrew Raby's pretty typical vehicle:

> The coach was a bright yellow, neatly picked out with black, and a plain crest on the upper door panel. The mountings were, of course, of brass, to suit the furniture of the harness; there were roof-irons to the front roof, which held three persons, and a comfortable dickey behind, to carry the two servants. The box was likewise on the true coaching principle, made to sail forwards towards the wheel-horses, with a good roomy footboard, and well-cushioned seat, allowing plenty of elbow-room for two.

A gentleman might also have a curricle, the most conspicuously extravagant of all vehicles: two seats only, up to four horses, sometimes two grooms. It was largely replaced by the phaeton in various forms and by the gig. The latter became popular in the Regency (1810 sq.); the principal designs were the tilbury (after a coachbuilder), the dennet

Dennet gig and harness.

Sir St Vincent Cotton, of Landwade and Madingley, Cambridgeshire, on the box of The Brighton Age, where he was to be seen every day. *The New Sporting Magazine, June* 1837.

(after another, whose name, however, was Bennet) and the stanhope (after its inventor). The most dashing whips drove their gigs with the pair in tandem. A gentleman might also drive himself in a whiskey or a cabriolet, but not much outside big towns.

Cabriolet.

What is best remembered about the first forty years of the century is the amateur driving his own or a public coach-and-four, the 'passion for the ribbons' being much encouraged by the Prince of Wales (even before he was Regent) whose own tutor was the merry but impossible Sir John Lade. A young hopeful began by paying a good deal extra for the place on the box beside the coachman, whose skill he learned by observation. He then did one of two things: he horsed a coach by contract with the coachmaster who was licensed for the route or 'ground', in return for the privilege of sometimes driving it; or he bought a drag.

A very few gentlemen became celebrated amateur coachmen of stagecoaches – Sir St Vincent Cotton and Charles James Apperley ('Nimrod') among them. It was proper to ape the speech and dress of the professionals (Sir St Vincent made himself indistinguishable from them) but the effect of this apparent slumming was thoroughly salutary: the professional coachmen themselves became more gentlemanly, more skilful, less obtrusively greedy for tips, and much less drunken, when they had prolonged personal contact with, and knew themselves closely observed by, really competent amateurs.

It was far more usual to get a drag built by Henry and William Powell of Bond Street, get harness from Whippey or Laurie and whips from Crowther of Swallow Street, and drive on private expeditions with, or to, friends. The drags were bright-painted and crested, and carried liveried grooms outside. The guard had a blunderbuss until highwaymen stopped being a menace; afterwards he had the 'yard of tin' (which was often, in fact, a key-bugle instead of the straight coach-horn). Enthusiastic amateurs even took horses on good roads, like that between London and Holyhead. Typically they had two matched teams of four for the drag with two spare horses. The horses themselves were ideally between fifteen-two and sixteen hands (much smaller than those needed a few years earlier) with some blood but a lot of substance on short legs; top-class leaders cost £200, wheelers a little less. 'Nimrod' said the coach-stables should be quite separate from the hacks and hunters, but Mr Thomas Assheton Smith was probably typical in having his whole 'stud' together. A gentleman owning a drag would also have a chariot 'for church and dinner work', a brake, and a gig. The total annual expense was reckoned about £1,200 in the Regency.

It was inevitable that expert amateurs with expensive turn-outs and fine teams wanted to show off to each other. For this purpose the Benson Driving Club was formed, named for a small town in Oxfordshire where they used originally to meet: several famous Masters of Hounds were leading members, including Mr John Warde, Lord Sefton, Sir Bellingham Graham and Sir Thomas Mostyn (of whom only Sir Bellingham took a subscription when he had hounds: the others were very rich men). The Benson was joined by the showier Four-Horse Club (called also the 4-H, Four-in-Hand, or Whip Club) in 1808; the members met four times a year in London and drove in resplendent convoy to dinner in the country.

Long-distance coaching, commercial and private, was killed almost totally by the railways; the last four-horse coach going into London went out of business in 1845, and by this date there were (said Sidney, thirty years later in his *Book of the Horse*) hardly half-a-dozen private drags on the road. Only the Four-Horse Club survived, exclusive as ever: but according to its President, Mr Morritt of Rokeby, few of its members were by now competent to do more than wear the uniform.

(xvii) Victorians on Wheels

Horse-drawn wheeled transport remained, of course, both a necessity and a diversion. A squire's coach-house would have a barouche, usually replaced by a landau in about 1850 and then by a victoria (*opposite*); a chariot for state occasions; a brougham, which replaced vehicles like the cabriolet because it was far cheaper and more practical, and came in country versions costing only £100 as well as in daintier and dearer town versions; and for sporting use a stanhope phaeton, described as a stanhope gig put on four wheels, a less showy and much cheaper replacement for the mail phaeton; a pony phaeton, for governess and children, made by 1850 in every country town, often of basketwork; and above all a park phaeton, dog-cart (*below*) and wagonette.

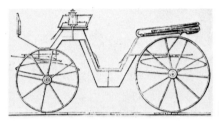 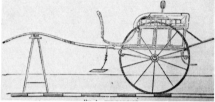

Victoria.   Dog-cart.

The park phaeton (*below*) was the lady's vehicle, comfortable and pretty expensive, seating two with one groom behind; it was the conveyance above all in which a lady drove herself to the covert-side to see hounds throw off. The dog-cart's advantages were very high clearance

Park Phaeton.

for broken ground and plenty of space for dogs or luggage; it was often driven to covert and very often to a shooting party; it was made for strength and utility, without ornament, and was used a good deal by injured sportsmen who wanted to follow the hounds.

Wagonette.

The wagonette (*above*) was probably the most used vehicle in the coach house, the normal 'second car', the late Victorian Land Rover, shooting brake or station wagon. It was invented in 1846, in general use by the 1860s, and thus described about 1870:

It is a combination of all the best parts of an Irish inside car, the French sportsman's *char-à-banc*, the English brake, and the modern stanhope phaeton; it may be constructed so as to suit one pony or one full-sized horse, a pair of cobs, or a four-in-hand. It may be driven by a groom or gentleman, to convey, besides the driver and his companion on the box, either two, four, or six, sitting face to face in pleasant converse, with two grooms hanging on spoon-like receptacles outside the door. It may be what is called 'reversible', and converted into a stanhope phaeton; or, by letting down hinged slats, into a *fourgon* for luggage, or a wagon to bring home fodder from a home farm. With the addition of a sort of cover, which may hang suspended from a pulley in the coach-house, it may be turned into a comfortable omnibus. It may afford ample space for the lockers for wine, ice, and all the provisions of a picnic, or to stow away the tackle of a shooting or a fishing party.

The date of this description saw a large revival of sporting coaching.

Throughout the 1870s it was common to see a hundred private drags in Hyde Park; private coaches, owner-driven, were used for expeditions to nearby resorts; livery, less and less seen for many years, came gorgeously back; but this was a fad (and a very expensive one) and had a short life.

Meanwhile it became more and more normal for a country gentleman to drive himself, in an unpretentious wagonette or brake, owing to the tyranny and expense of coachmen.

I have often felt amused in English country houses [said Mrs Burton, who knew other countries and their horses] where the host has sixteen or twenty horses, to hear the hostess say almost timidly to the fat powdered coachman – 'Barker, do you think that I might have the carriage to-day?' Barker (very crisply) – 'No, my lady, you can't.' Lady (timidly) – 'Oh, never mind, Barker; I didn't know.' Know what? The sacred mysteries of an English stud. That the horses are choking with food till it bursts out in disease. That their chests and consequently their forelegs are so affected by being pampered that they cannot do the slightest work with impunity. That the stables are kept so hot that it costs a fatal cough to take the beast outside it.

Trollope more than once remarks that huntsmen became the masters of their Masters; evidently coachmen became the masters of their mistresses. Since they were usually in charge of ordering the feed, they also did very well out of bribes.

(xviii) The Modern Shotgun

The sport of shooting – nearly every kind of shooting – changed completely during the 19th century, the causes of change being legal, financial, agricultural, scientific and social, as well as matters of technique and taste.

Early in the century the vast majority of birds were shot by a man on his own over two pointers (*below*); not many were shot flying; partridges (and hares) enormously outnumbered pheasants; coverts were natural and preserving simple. At the end of the century most birds were driven as high and fast as possible over a party of guns, whose only dogs were retrievers; as many as half the birds shot were hand reared; bags were enormous, competition desperate, costs daunting.

Early 19th-century partridge shooting. The nearer dog 'has the point'; the shooter is advancing stealthily. J. Webb after A. Cooper, *The New Sporting Magazine*, June 1831.

The gradual revolution in the gun – which took most of the century – was one of the things that made modern shooting possible. (It may be compared to the revolution in the foxhound, which made modern foxhunting possible, but not that in fishing tackle, which only made fishing easier.) By 1815 the detonator had been invented, but it was not yet satisfactory and had not generally replaced flint and steel; double barrels were usual; barrels were made of horseshoe nails of the best

Swedish iron; the efficiency of powder was becoming calculable; shot was round and regular.

Loading, 1842: 'be careful to hold your gun in a *safe* position.'

The urgent improvement was to the detonator. In 1825 'Mr. Purdey (a rising gunmaker of extraordinary merit) is acquitting himself most admirably in the detonating system.' In 1820 the fulminating powder was contained in a cap, and this was shortly fixed to the back of Eley's patent wire cartridge. The advantages were speed of loading (Johnson in 1838 reckoned it took a quarter of the time), reliability, and a better pattern at a longer range. Even the conservative Colonel Peter Hawker was converted, although no edition of his great book is late enough to record the fact. A convincing match was held in November 1828, on Lord de Roos's rented manor at Mildenhall, Suffolk, between Colonel Anson and Captain Ross, both celebrated match pigeon shooters, both using detonating guns. They walked forty yards apart, from sunrise to sunset, with four dogs. A big crowd made the partridges wild and shy,

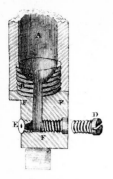
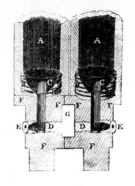

A's – Calibres
B's – Male screws as they go into them
C's – Chambers which fill with powder
D's – Screws for getting at & counter-
sinking touchholes
E's – Touchholes
F's – Solid Iron

Joseph Manton's breechings for single and double guns. Drawn by Colonel Peter Hawker, engraved by Wilson Lowry.

Percussion-lock, 1840.

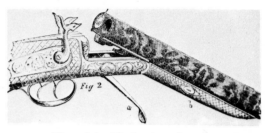

The original Lefaucheux breech-loading gun, with Damascene barrel.

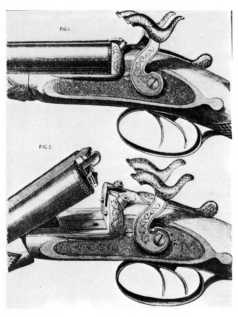

The central-fire breechloader.

SIDEVIEW

SECTION

Ely's cartridge, designed for use with the central-fire breechloader, almost universal by 1875.

and most shot were at fifty and sixty yards. The bag was small but the demonstration conclusive.

The Damascus barrel was invented in 1818, lighter for its strength because the horseshoe-nail iron was entwined with strips of steel; in the 1820s all the good gunmakers adopted it. The pure steel barrel was very slow in coming and very slow of acceptance (hardly before the 1880s) partly because it could not be given so elegant a finish.

The breech-loader was invented in France in 1850 and seen in London two years later. In 1857 the 'Old Shekary' said it was safer as well as faster, had less recoil, reloaded noiselessly, and made it quick and easy to change charge and shot for a different bird. Exhaustive trials in 1858 showed that it was no less accurate at equal ranges, and it came into general use in the 1860s.

The choke bore was already familiar in America; the first effective English example was made by Greener in 1874. The principle was a slight narrowing of the barrel just back from the muzzle, which had the effect of throwing a more concentrated pattern. More game was killed by good shots, but less by indifferent ones, who were recommended by Sir Ralph Payne-Gallwey to stick to the old cylinder barrel. The first satisfactory hammerless gun was invented in 1871 and the self ejector four years later. Both were virtually perfected (especially by Holland and Purdey) by 1890. Smokeless chemical powders under various brand names began to appear in 1878; they were completely satisfactory by 1900, relieving the shooter's eye of a pall of black smoke which had sometimes made his second barrel useless.

The skill of shooters improved steadily: especially, it would seem, in the first quarter of the century and the last. In a late edition of *Instructions to Young Sportsmen* (1825) Hawker inserted a remark which had only recently become appropriate: 'The art of shooting has of late been so much improved, that although but little more than half a century ago one who *shot flying* was viewed with *wonder*, we now frequently meet with *schoolboys* who can bring down their game with the greatest dexterity.' The almost fantastic achievements of George Osbaldeston at about that date would have been impossible, even for a sportsman with his 'eye', a few years earlier. They remained highly unusual. Stevenson's *Birds of Norfolk* of about 1870 says, 'he is no ordinary shot who can account satisfactorily in "feather" and "fur" for one in every three of his empty cartridges.' Lord Walsingham and Sir Ralph Payne-Gallwey (*Badminton Library*, 1892) call two cartridges per bird a very

Colonel Peter Hawker (on pony) and the gunmaker Joseph Manton (beside him) after shooting at Longparish on 1 September 1827. 'Mr. Childe [the artist] attended as a strict observer.' The bag was forty-eight partridges and one hare.

good average; they were two of the best shots in England. Sidney Buxton (*Shooting and Fishing*, 1902) recorded that within his memory shooting had immensely improved:

> A 'gun' who a few years ago would have been considered a fine shot, would now be but one of the ruck. . . The fact is that more care is taken in the fit of the gun, and the gun itself is handier and shoots better. Then the modern explosive carries the shot more quickly up to the object than ever did the old black powder, thus simplifying the aim; while the smoke no longer obscures the vision. The ordinary man, moreover, gets more shooting than he used to; and all these causes combined enable him to make better practice, though the bird itself has, in most cases, been made a more difficult object to hit.

(xix) Battue and Drive

The bird was more difficult to hit because it was driven. When Osbald-eston killed 100 pheasants with 100 shots he was shooting birds which had just been flushed: they were low, slow, close to him, flying directly away from him, and probably shot in October. Johnson (*The Shooter's*

Preceptor, 1838) when walking up pheasants, 're-approached the spot, when, throwing my foot into the bush, the bird rose, and was bagged as a matter of course'. Sometimes the bird was given thirty yards law (for sport, or to make it acceptable on the table), but the shot was still a very easy one. The same applies to Osbaldeston's records with partridges and grouse. Shooting the last he may have been with a friend or two; shooting pheasant and partridge he was quite likely alone with his pointers. This style of sport was largely a consequence of the ancient Game Laws which restricted game shooting to the financially 'qualified', and of the recent one which further restricted it to squires and their eldest sons; but it was also a matter of taste. Hawker hated parties (and therefore the grand shoots of Norfolk); in 1836 the *Oakley Shooting Code* remarked: 'the shooter seldom seeks for any other company than his dogs when out'.

The pheasant battue (*above*) was the first consequence of better guns, hand rearing, and the abolition in 1831 of the old and new qualifications (1 and 2 William IV, passed by Lord Grey's reforming ministry). But the battue was not a drive but a walk in line through the covert with the beaters: still easy shooting of birds going away and taken early. It aroused violent criticism, recorded by Lord William Lennox in 1858 and by Trollope as late as 1868: but by this time driving was much more usual. Driving in the modern sense – the guns remaining station-ary, where placed – is said to have begun about 1840, although there is confusion and disagreement about this date. Like the battue it depended on plentiful birds, sensible organization and stern discipline; much more than the battue it depended on the breech-loader, and above all on the shape and position and nature of the covert, not only to harbour the pheasants but also to get them flying well.

Flying well was – certainly by the 1860s – supposed to mean flying high and fast. But this ideal was subjected to contrary pulls from a num-ber of directions. Some landowners wanted big bags at any cost in quality of sport, either for *amour propre* or in order to let more profitably; some keepers wanted big bags for big tips, while others wanted small bags so that the covert could be revisited and the tips, though equivalent-ly smaller, made more frequent. Low and easy birds were sometimes the result of mismanagement (in the planting or clearing of the covert, the direction taken, the placing of the guns) but sometimes of intent. East Anglia swarmed with birds, owing to agricultural methods and the wealth and enthusiasm of the landowners: it was in some places genuinely impossible to get them flying high and fast, and this was a major reason for the almost obscene size of late Victorian and Edward-ian bags. 'The numbers killed', said Buxton in 1902, 'depend simply on purse, keeper, covert, and purse again.'

To an extent this had always been true. Jack Mytton established three miles of new plantation at Halston from about 1817, to afford 'shelter to the superfluity of game which it was his ambition to possess'. His extravagance in this as in most other departments of his life bears out Buxton's remark of eighty years later; at Halston in the 1820s, 'the average *annual* slaughter was – twelve hundred brace of pheasants, from fifteen hundred to two thousand hares, partridges out of number! We have turned into the preserves after luncheon, where the pheasants were as thick as sparrows on a barn-door and the hares running about like rabbits'. Some gentlemen continued on these lines, more modestly, throughout the century, especially after drives replaced battues. Planting specifically for sport received, ironically, a great boost from the agricultural depression which lasted from 1875 virtually until 1914: sporting rights were more valuable than agricultural rents, and there-fore attracted more investment. 'Coppices' were extensively planted of spruce, hazel, holly, laurel and gorse, all purely for covert, all useless. The need for broad rides, as Carnegie noted in 1885, was a frequent cause of dispute between shooting tenants and non-shooting landlords of existing woodland; this was another argument for new plantation. Yet another was that vermin could be much more easily controlled.

Among good sportsmen, the difficulty of shooting hand reared birds was deliberately increased, from about 1870, by shooting later. Sporting owners sometimes left their coverts until December, and few shot them before November except for special reasons (the most usual of which was to stop birds wandering to a neighbour). This was absolutely right in regard to high pheasants, but it had the lamentable effect of driving yet another wedge between shooting and foxhunting gentlemen: a covert shot early was opened to the hounds at Christmas, a covert left till late was probably closed to them all season. In this respect as in others, meanwhile, the obsession with enormous bags caused many immature birds to be killed with easy early-season shots. In these circumstances, as under more sporting auspices, a very good shot was welcome; and many men sharpened their skill by trap-shooting; they shot clay pigeons, live pigeons or sparrows.

There were some estates throughout the century where good shots were *not* welcome. Hawker reports:

> There are many '*squires*', however, so *hoggishly tenacious of their game*, that, in spite of *all reason*, they continue their prejudice against a *cracked shot* so far, as studiously to avoid his acquaintance; because there are *some* greedy destroyers, who take an *unfair advantage* of their *own skill* and their *host's indulgence;* and, on the other hand, *correct men*, who have been known to kill an immense bag of game, *at his particular request*, for the supply of an *election dinner*, or some other *reasonable purpose*.

Hawker elsewhere notes (in an equally furious rash of italics) that when coverts were under-shot they were always over-poached.

(xx) Hand Rearing

Pheasant shooting became, like racing, an industry as well as a sport; and the pheasant industry depended very largely on hand rearing. This was introduced on a small scale about 1800. Many landowners resisted it, like 'Nimrod's' Andrew Raby, because a preserve full of hand-reared pheasants called for an army of 'night-watchers'; its growth was quite slow and patchy. It was a complete novelty to William Cobbett when he saw it on the Duke of Buckingham's estate at Avington, near Winchester, in 1823: 'a gamekeeper lives in the farm-house, and I daresay the Duke thinks more of the pheasants than of the corn.' (Well might he, with the respective prices as they then were.) John Mayer (*The Sportsman's Directory; or, Park and Gamekeeper's Companion*, fifth edition, 1828) gives one of the earliest exact accounts of the method of his day: 'Let your pheasantry be well constructed with perches, hiding places made with reeds tied round with stakes put up along the centre, and boxes round the sides.' There should be six hens to one cock, and the eggs collected into a clutch for a setting of seventeen to nineteen. 'Silk hens' were the best sitters, as common hens were too hot and shell-baked the chicks in the eggs. (Turkeys could sit on very large clutches, but broke too many eggs.) In the covert shelters of wheat sheaves should be made, tied at the top and spread out below, plenty of grain and peas provided, and white clover planted in the adjoining fields. The reason for the barnyard hen was that the pheasant was believed a bad mother: wrongly, according to such naturalists as T. A. Coward: but it is true that she cannot hatch as many as she lays.

By the middle of the century hand rearing was very widespread, and by 1880 almost universal where the squire took his shooting at all seriously, or saw any chance of a good let. Incubators were occasionally used in the 1880s.

It was hand rearing which more than anything else aroused the furious contempt of old-fashioned sportsmen. As late as 1886 'Stonehenge' in *British Rural Sports* deplored the driving of clouds of tame birds, hardly to be distinguished from farmyard poultry, over batteries of guns. This was not always altogether rubbish, and certainly the scale did become monstrous. Payne-Gallwey reckoned 1,000 birds a day normal for a good shoot, 2,000 not out of the way, and 10,000 a season a fair average. Lord Walsingham quotes the gamebook of a typical Norfolk estate: in 1821 they shot 39 pheasants, in 1845 1,011, in 1865 2,887, in 1875 5,069. He says that, of the last figure, about half were hand reared, but the proportion was sometimes much higher. There were three principal defences to the attacks of those whom these figures outraged. First, hand reared birds were just as difficult to shoot if things were properly managed. Second, great numbers of men were given employment which depressed agriculture could hardly provide. Third, pheasants sold for only 2s. in London, and even at this price the value of the game could pay all preserving expenses.

To an extent, the growth of pheasant shooting was at the expense of partridge shooting. At Lord Stamford's shoot, Bradgate Park, Leicestershire, four days in January 1864 produced four partridges and 4,045 pheasants, a proportion unthinkable not many years earlier. But partridge shooting was also transformed by rearing and driving.

(xxi) The Partridge

Partridges themselves had increased with the agricultural revolution of the late 18th century, and shooting them also became easier: turnips and long stubble allowed a shooter and his dogs to come right up to a covey on the ground. Hawker says that many squires shot partridges every single day in September on their own manors, going out alone with one keeper and often only one pointer. This early, solitary shooting retained its charm for many people. Lord William Lennox said in 1858:

> There is nothing more calculated to raise the spirits than an early walk in the bright month of September: and to those accustomed to pass the largest portion of the year in a crowded town, to inhale the noxious atmosphere of a pent-up city, to turn day into night, the effect produced by the freshness, elasticity, and clearness of the morning air is exhilarating to the greatest degree.

It was also gratifyingly easy to get within a few yards of the birds.

Partridge shooting began to change, like pheasant shooting, when the law allowed a squire to ask whom he liked to shoot, and to let his shooting to whom he liked. This encouraged the method of a walking line of guns, especially where roots had been sown in rows rather than broadcast. It immediately became desirable to increase the partridge population, and a good many were hand reared in exactly the fashion of pheasants.

Partridges began to be driven not long after pheasants: perhaps about 1850. The efficient breechloader made this sport more popular in the 1860s. Soon after this the mechanical reaper replaced sickle and scythe, shaving the stubble to a few inches and making walking up impossible. For this reason driving became more and more usual, and by 1900 'wherever it is possible to drive, partridge driving has generally superseded walking'. To good sportsmen it had the merit of far greater difficulty: driven partridges swerve at the sight of the guns, and a shooter hiding below a hedge or hurdle does not see the birds, as he does a driven grouse, from a distance. Driving was also said to have the effect of increasing the partridge population because the old birds came to the guns first; walked, they got away at the front of the covey, and survived to fight each other, breed badly, and reserve far more territory than young breeding pairs. Walked or driven, partridges were commonly shot much later, and rarely in September.

A drawback mentioned by Carnegie in 1885, especially in regard to rearing and preserving, was that keepers were only interested in pheasants, and disdained the humbler bird. Another drawback to many people was the presence of 'Frenchmen', which sometimes flew when driven but hardly ever when walked. But Charles Arlington recorded in 1904 that partridge driving (to him a very recent invention) caused a startling recovery in the importance as well as the population of partridges, especially as pheasants could never be made to fly well from some coverts in flat country; on many estates partridges became the first care of squire and keeper, for the first time in fifty years or more. To this writer the worst enemy of the partridge – worse than reaping machine or fox – was the small farmer: his land was heavily shot by himself or a shooting tenant, and acted as a 'drain' to suck up birds from the preserved estate next door.

(xxii) The Grouse

Grouse were shot in Yorkshire, the far north, and parts of Wales by a few landowners and a lot of poachers. To Hawker this was 'muir-game', and he used Number 3, 2 or even 1 shot on his August visits to Yorkshire. (He believed Scottish grouse shooting was better, but the inns were intolerable.) The birds were rather infrequent and rather tame, and were still walked up with pointer or 'down charge' setter (*below*), or stalked on a pony. As with pheasant and partridge, there is wide disagreement even among contemporaries about the date of grouse driving. It was tried perhaps in 1850, and grew rapidly in Yorkshire in the 1860s. The hides were hedges or peat-stacks. Previously, two or three guns worked hard all day to get a dozen brace (and Johnson in 1838 saw the need for the shooter's refreshment, but warned against wine: 'give me brandy. On no account must cold water be drank [*sic*] – fatal results have been more than once produced by it'). By 1868, according to Trollope's collaborator, 150 brace of driven grouse was a normal day; a real fear was expressed that the combination of driving and breechloader would shortly make the bird extinct. By 1880 all Yorkshire moors were driven, although in Scotland most were only walked before 1900. (Englishmen came to Scotland in much greater numbers for their sport after William Scrope and Charles St John wrote their mouth-watering accounts of the fishing, stalking and shooting there; after Queen Victoria established herself at Balmoral; and perhaps because the mechanical reaper had spoiled the partridge shooting which had occupied them before the pheasant and the foxhunting seasons.)

Grouse did not approach extinction, but, on the contrary, became enormously more plentiful, entrely owing to the treatment of the heather. Yorkshire moors were regularly burned by graziers, and Yorkshire bags by 1892 were in hundreds a day, 500 brace being known, if exceptional. In Scotland burning was surreptitious and illegal, and violently opposed by lairds and keepers: and Scottish bags were still tiny. It was discovered that old heather is valueless to grouse as food and poor as shelter, and that burning on about a 15-year cycle produces the optimum conditions for the birds. This was infinitely more important than attempts at rearing, which were almost wholly unsuccessful.

(xxiii) Shooter and Beater in Peril

Driving all these birds increased the size of shooting parties and sometimes, in consequence, their danger. General Calley, an officer of unquestioned gallantry, refused all invitations to shoot with Mr C. A. R. Hoare when the latter was Master of the V.W.H. (1879–86); Mr Hoare's nursing of the farmers included parties where his guests, over-generously entertained, drunkenly shot each other. Nor was danger derived only from alcohol. In about 1860 'Lord Cardigan, of Balaclava fame, was once heard abusing his keeper for extravagance in using men instead of boys for "stops". "Beg pardon, my lord," was the matter-of-fact reply, "but your lordship will remember that last year you shot down all the boys".' About ten years later the bag from one shot consisted of 'one rabbit (the cause of the shot), one beater, one onlooker (a French cook), a boy, and a dog'.

Jealousy and competitiveness had always been part of shooting. The great Peter Hawker was not above it; William Cobbett far preferred hunting men to shooters because they praised hounds, horses or fox instead of themselves (this does not accord with other reactions to hunting men after dinner). The drive increased competitiveness to an unattractive and sometimes perilous extent.

In shooting, [said Buxton, who adored it] perhaps more than in any other sport, rivalry often leads to jealousy, selfishness, and want of consideration . . . The only remark – a fact – made by a 'gun', who, in the middle of a splendid partridge drive, badly shot his neighbour, was, 'What a —— nuisance! I should have been cock score this time.'

'The Right Sort'; 'The Wrong Sort' from *Shooting*, by Sir Ralph Payne Gallwey and Lord Walsingham.

(xxiv) Woodcock; Duck, Ground Game; Dogs

Woodcock were a lot commoner in 1815 than a century later; on many estates they were a lot commoner than pheasants. Hawker said, 'The pursuit of woodcocks, with good spaniels, may be termed, the *Foxhunting of shooting*!' (*overleaf*). (Before the days of driving, pheasants were often shot in the same way, by a man on his own, in covert, with a pack of spaniels.) As a delicacy, woodcock were often taken for the table – by squires themselves, or with their approval – by drawnets, snares of twisted horsehair, or bundles of limed twigs stuck in the ground. Battues and drives had the effect of including a few woodcock in most sizable bags of pheasants, just as a brace or two of blackgame often joined the driven grouse.

Duck shooting was of two completely different sorts: coastal and inland.

Hawker called the former 'gunning' or 'water-shooting': 'Wildfowl shooting' was 'not quite an obsolete term among the fraternity who understood it.' The fraternity were almost all professionals, whose methods are far outside our subject: Hawker himself was one of the very few gentlemen who had a punt-gun for sport. His Hampshire punt was fourteen foot long, two foot wide, ten inches high, flat bottomed, holding one man only, propelled by punt or paddle. The gun mounted in the bows could be up to 140 lbs, have a gauge of $1\frac{1}{2}$ inches, and fire up to 2 lbs of shot.

Inland duck shooting was and always had been a gentleman's sport. Jack Mytton crawled out over the ice at Halston, in nightshirt or naked; Hawker prowled up the river with a Newfoundland or a mute

'Commencement of a Cripple-Chase, after firing 2 lbs. of Shot into a Skein of Brent Geese, & Two Wild Swans.' Colonel Hawker's drawing of himself in *Instructions to Young Sportsmen.*

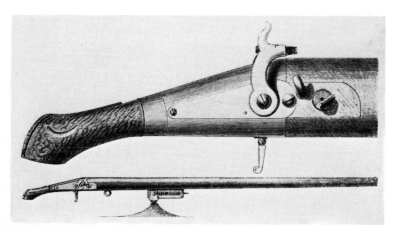

One of Colonel Hawker's punt-guns: 8′ long, $1\frac{1}{2}''$ bore, $128\frac{1}{2}$ lbs.

water-spaniel (*below*). The latter also went flight shooting from camouflage, finding that he had to shoot three feet in front at a range of sixty
yards with his flint and steel. A method introduced from France was to
tie tame ducks to pegs in the water to decoy the live ones; Lord Rodney
had great success, with tame French ducks as decoys, on his water at
Alresford.

Duck shooting in various forms grew in popularity, especially as
decoys (in the old sense) fell into disuse. The speed of detonating guns
made it much easier. It was usually very sporting, but not always. 'Tell
me, keeper,' said Philip Geen when duck shooting with a friendly
squire about 1880, 'why don't your duck mount and clear off instead of
making flights a moorhen would be ashamed of?' 'Well, sir, you see,
they are a pinion short; we cut the first joint from one of their wings
when they are young.' Geen used artificial decoys, very carefully made
and lifelike.

It is depressing to read the list of other birds which Hawker and his
contemporaries shot: godwits and redshanks; curlews and whimbrels;
gulls and terns (for soup); landrails and larks; coots and moorhens
(never inland, but good sport and good eating when shot on the shore);
bitterns (shot in the fens with pointer or springer); bustards (approached
in a cart, or with a gun concealed by a carried hurdle); mergansers and
great crested grebes (whose skins 'make excellent tippets and travelling
caps'); fieldfares and redwings (the game of schoolboys during the
Christmas holidays); golden plovers, dotterels, stone curlews, auks. One
feels less concern about the rooks (rook pie was 'worthy the notice of the

most scientific gourmand'), the starlings (also eaten: the trick was to pull off the head as soon as the bird was killed, which prevented a bitter flavour), or the pigeons. Wood pigeons were shot from hides in turnip fields, exactly as they still are, or sitting, as they also still are, and always will be.

Rook shooting, 1840.

Ground game was also treated much as now: hares were an expected part of rough shooting and of some driving; rabbits were bolted from warrens with ferrets and from hedgerows with terriers, beagles or spaniels. Hare and roe deer were sometimes driven, and sometimes shot over beagles or bassets in the French fashion.

With the change from walking to driving, the pointer went almost wholly out of use, and was joined in obsolescence by the setter, springer and pack spaniel; by about 1875 the retriever was virtually the shooter's only dog. The Newfoundland, in the two varieties of St John's and Labrador, was the great discovery of the beginning of the century. Some spaniels retrieved, and poodles were also tried (they got seasick in a punt). It is slightly surprising that when Mr Samuel Whitbread put on the first field trial on his estate near Bedford in 1865 the contestants were pointers and setters; this emphasis inevitably changed as shooting practice had done.

Wavy-coated Retriever; Irish Water-spaniel. After L. Wells, 1875.

(xxv) Poacher and Keeper

It was unfortunate that the considerable introduction of hand rearing coincided with the new Game Laws, and both with an agricultural depression which brought many humble country people close to starvation. The squire had three principal defences against poaching: protection of his game and coverts, observation of suspects and their accomplices, and personal popularity.

Coverts were guarded by spring-guns, mantraps, night-watchers, geese or guinea-fowl (both excellent watchdogs) and armed gamekeepers, who often carried pistols at night instead of shotguns, with ferocious dogs. A serious weakness of all these arrangements was that the keeper was often a poacher himself. Observation meant watching the houses of known poachers, back doors as well as front, and unlicensed ale-houses: and watching stage-coaches and wagons. Guards often smuggled game away, as railway employees later did; wagoners sometimes actually employed poachers, whose quarry they smuggled to dealers in towns. The squire's local popularity was crucial; a bad landlord was poached far worse than a good one, and with a general local approval that made the poacher's life pretty easy. This was, writ small, exactly the situation of a Master of Hounds in regard to fox-preserving, poultry and damage claims, and, later in the century, wire. All field sports rely on the goodwill of the countryside: good sport depends on the country people being actively and cheerfully co-operative, not merely cowed into a surly or spurious acquiescence.

The worst excesses of the 'Poaching War' generally quietened with the relaxation of the Game Laws, and the situation eased further with the return of prosperity to the countryside in the late 1840s. But it remained a problem to squires both as proprietors and as magistrates. Trollope's shooting collaborator tells of many rural murders in the 1850s and 1860s, and says that in 1868 there was still a 'frequent occurrence of severe combats or affrays between gamekeepers and poachers, attended, as they too frequently are, by fatal results'. It was a real moral dilemma to late Victorian game preservers whether they should put their employees at such risk. Gangs were still coming out from towns, by night or audaciously by day, dressed as respectable farmers, in the 1890s and 1900s; the local village poacher, says Sir Ralph Payne-Gallwey, was meanwhile 'with scarcely an exception, a cowardly, drunken ruffian', treated far too often with leniency owing to soft, romantic ideas derived from *It's my delight on a shining night*.

The keeper's honesty, vigilance and tactical skill were, with the squire's own popularity, the best weapon against poaching: as his knowledge and care were crucial to the whole success of the shoot. Mayer

'Crossing the Line.' W. Radclyffe after Henry Alken, *The New Sporting Magazine*, February 1841.

instructed his keeper pupil in the 1820s that his duties on a shooting day included: checking and cleaning every gun before going out, having quantities of powder, shot, wads, and the necessary tools, carrying gins in case vermin was spotted; 'Do not forget the sandwich-case, and flask of brandy, to hand to the gentlemen, when their nerves get a little affected.'

Hand rearing put far more long-term responsibility on the keeper, driving far more onus on him for the success of a given day. 'The ideal keeper', said Buxton three-quarters of a century after Mayer wrote,

> is a man of tact, who will get on well with the farmers, the labourers, and the tenants. A man of intelligence, who understands how to show his birds, as well as how to rear them. A man of action, who can control and manage his beaters and his underlings, and train them in the way they should go.

He should also be enough of a naturalist not to destroy all predators. Mayer put down arsenic and ground glass in his coverts to kill foxes. Johnson, only fifteen years later, urged his fellow keepers to spare foxes if there were plenty of rabbits, since they killed the predators (such as polecats) which were far more destructive of young pheasants. 'Scrutator' ten years later again found it impossible to persuade many covert owners and their 'velveteens' that they could preserve both foxes and pheasants. His cry rings down the decades: and there are plenty of shooting landowners today who support their keepers in the same ignorant and antisocial philosophy 'Scrutator' met.

Buxton ends his remarks about keepers with a warning: 'the host should be master of the man.' Head keepers, like huntsmen and coachmen (and butlers, cooks, gardeners, chauffeurs and nannies), have horribly often become tyrants.

Another enduring problem was the gentleman poacher. Hawker describes how an elegant stranger would stop his carriage, have a few shots, and when challenged explain that he was an intimate friend of the squire: or, stammering in broken English, convey that he was a foreigner of high degree. This was an awkward situation for a keeper to deal with, in case the story was true. So was the shot taken just over the boundary. Mr Thomas Assheton Smith's father was baffled in his dealings with a deaf-mute neighbour who shot hares on the wrong side of the line: they stood bowing to each other, interminably, like mandarins, unable to communicate; Thackeray's friend Ponto (in *The Book of Snobs*) was humiliated by his greater neighbour's keeper, but there was nothing the keeper could do; prosecutions were naturally rare. Even greater ill feeling was caused by a man, who did not preserve, shooting the birds of a man who did. The feud on this issue between Mr Passenger and Major Fosdick about 1930 (in Anthony Powell's *From a View to a Death*) could have taken place anywhere in England at any moment during the previous century, and caused the most intense hatred; and the author knows a West Country landowner, of high but patchy probity, justly resented by his neighbours on precisely the same grounds today.

'Sportsman Accoutred', 1842.

(xxvi) Clothes and Medicines

Shooting clothes changed a good deal more than hunting clothes, but a good deal less than might be supposed. 'We all know', said Colonel Hawker, 'that a jean, nankeen, or any kind of thin jacket, is the pleasantest wear for September, one of fustian for October, and one of velveteen for the winter.' Many men wore shoes and gaiters, Hawker boots with trousers pulled down over them, which were usual for some years after 1825. Kid gloves were recommended in order to prevent roughened hands, 'not quite in unison with the general appearance of a perfect gentleman'. For wildfowling the colonel wore seaboots or 'galoches', a swanskin waistcoat, and an overall waterproofed with linseed oil, ideal also for fishing with a casting net; he carried an umbrella which doubled as a mizzen-sail for his punt. (It is a lasting grief to the writer that Hawker's marvellous illustrations to his *Instructions to Young Sportsmen* do not include one of his punt being propelled by this sail.)

Lord William Lennox in 1858 has moved a little towards modernity, except as regards his hats:

> For August, shooting jacket, waistcoat, and trowsers [*sic*] of tweed, a broad-brimmed straw hat, or drab-coloured 'wide-awake', and a pair of strong, easy shooting-boots, doubly leathered over the toes. For September, a jacket of jean, nankeen, or merino, waistcoat to match, tweed trousers [*sic*], strapped to the knee with thin leather to turn the thorns in scrambling through a hedge. For October and winter shooting, nothing can be better than a velveteen jacket, lined with fine flannel, a dark kerseymere waistcoat, cord trousers, strapped with leather as above-mentioned, plain or waterproof beaver hat, according to the season.

The late Victorians made more extensive use of tweed, put deer-stalkers or peaked caps on their heads, and wore knickerbockers with stockings or gaiters.

Hawker has notes which should not be omitted about stimulant medicine and dental hygiene:

> Huxham's Tincture of Bark as an effectual stimulus to brace the nerves of a bad shot. The sportsman has only to take a dessert spoonful in a glass of water before he goes out ... BRUSH your teeth every morning, with Spanish Sabilia snuff (which may be had in perfection, from Fribourg and Treyer, Haymarket), and every night with a little arquebusade, or brandy; and keep, in the bottle containing it, a small piece of *camphor*. This will not only make it a tenfold greater preservative, but will prevent the vassals of the place from drinking it.

(xxvii) Trap Shooting and Dovecote

The trap shooting of live birds (*opposite*) was a sufficiently popular and gentlemanly sport also to require mention. It began about 1790. Hawker called it 'a glorious opportunity for assembling parties to gamble and get drunk', but by the time he said so many serious sportsmen and fine shots were in fact enthusiasts. There were clubs all over the country, but the headquarters was Hurlingham and then the London

Gun Club; crowds were large and betting heavy, but if anyone got drunk it was certainly not the shooters. The birds were specially bred blue rocks, very pampered and strong. There was much criticism on predictable Victorian lines, but the R.S.P.C.A. made a thorough investigation and approved the sport as not cruel. In 1875 the Ranelagh Club introduced 'inanimate birds' (long familiar for private practice); in 1909 live pigeon shooting from traps was made illegal, and trap shooting took its modern form.

Trap Shooting, 1830.

Decoys almost everywhere disappeared, but dovecotes remained an invariable part of a complete country house. Varieties kept and carefully bred, listed by Mayer in 1828, included: 'carriers, croppers, powters, horsemen, runts, jacobins, turbits, helmets, nuns, tumblers, barbs, petits, owls, spots, trumpeters, shakers, turners, and finikins'. There were also hybrids or bastards, such as the dragoon, a cross of tumbler with horseman. Some gentlemen shot some of their pigeons as a way of practising for covert shooting. Most ate some of them. A proportion of the stock was pinioned to grow fat, and they were best eaten young. A few people amused themselves with carrier pigeons, but they were not raced early in the century. The dovecote was part of the gamekeeper's responsibility.

(xxviii) Fishing: the Dark Ages

Fishing changed almost as much as shooting during the century, but the change was of a different sort. For one thing, it was not so much tackle that changed, or needed to change, as philosophy; for another, much that was regarded as revolutionary had, in fact, been known and stated long before. What happened was that methods familiar to a few men in remote places were brought to the attention of influential men on famous rivers, and they and their disciples (against bitter and derisive opposition) converted most of the rest of angling England.

The most obvious example is fishing upstream, fully described as accepted local practice in the North Country by Robert Venables and John Worlidge in the late 17th century. The flies so fished were sunk, and there were two or three of them, but they were careful attempts at exact imitation; as were closely similar flies described in the 15th-century *Treatyse*. Because they were imitations they were small. But on the Test, known for centuries as the very best of trout rivers, always difficult because of the clarity of the chalk-filtered water, the most sophisticated sportsmen of the early 19th century were totally unaware

Fly fishing: J. R. Scott after A. Cooper, *The New Sporting Magazine*, June 1831. It is assumed editorially (by R. S. Surtees) that all expert fishermen tie their own flies, and some still make their own rods.

of the upstream method: they had never heard of it: it never occurred to them. This is amazing, but it is put beyond doubt by a mass of documentary evidence – the fishing diary of Colonel Peter Hawker of Longparish, which covers the seasons 1802 to 1853; that of the Revd Richard Durnford of Chilbolton, 1809 to 1819; and the Chronicles of the Houghton Club at Stockbridge, which start in 1822.

Trout trolling tackle, 1844, fished with a 20-foot rod.

Hawker (as arrogantly yet disarmingly forthright about fishing as about shooting) says that everybody fished but most people did it very badly. He started in January, fishing two flies downstream. In April and May he used an artificial grannom, in June the mayfly. A few sophisticates on the chalk streams used artificial mayflies (of which dressings perfectly acceptable today had been known for perhaps five centuries) but most the natural fly on a blowline. From July onwards the principal fly was the caperer. Worm and minnow were used throughout the season, by the most sporting and scientific anglers, especially when large hatches of olives made fishing 'impossible' by other means. Hawker's fly-rod was twelve foot long and weighed fourteen ounces (exceptionally small and frail); he had two flies on a nine-foot cast, usually a yellow dun and a red palmer dropper or 'bob', both large, neither a deliberate imitation of anything. He had a multiplying reel from which – a new technique – he actually played his fish.

He spun a dead natural minnow with an eighteen-foot, double-handed, whole cane rod, and wormed at night.

Parson Durnford was in some ways slightly more modern. He only used a dropper on windy days to help him see what was happening to his tail fly (a method favoured by short-sighted nymph fishermen today), and his flies were much more varied. He used a number of naturals besides the mayfly, including bluebottle, daddy-long-legs and sedge; these were fished on a blowline if there was enough wind, a crossline if not. The latter device, involving a friend or servant on the far bank, was very common, although dismissed by March (*The Jolly Angler*, 1833) as a 'poaching, destructive method and unworthy of the honest angler'.

The rest of the Test, including the Houghton Club water, was fished quite as much with worm and minnow as with fly. The Itchen seems not to have been fished at all: Cobbett, a sportsman as well as everything else, knew the whole river well, and the only fishing he mentioned was in the ponds at Alresford (those, presumably, where Lord Rodney decoyed wild duck with his tame ones).

There was a great deal of good fishing elsewhere, on rivers since

'The Trout Stream', 1837; Mr Charles Elliott of The Holm, fishing the Hermitage Water, Liddesdale. The length of the rod suggests he is fishing with a minnow. J. W. Archer after G. Balmer, *The New Sporting Magazine*, May 1837.

polluted by industry or drained by the water-hunger of cities. All methods went, as in catching birds, including the netting and spearing of all species. An extremely keen fisherman, who would never have considered himself unsporting (and was, in truth, only impatient, slapdash and perhaps greedy) was Jack Mytton of Halston, whose sporting equipment came up for sale in 1830:

> Catalogue of effects sold at Halston when the establishment was broken up. The furniture of the net house, for instance, included three bush nets, twenty-six or twenty-eight yards long, five deep; two small mesh nets for bushes; three larger mesh nets; two drag nets, with large tunnels; four trammel flue nets, of various sizes; one minnow net; one minnow net and pole; three gutter nets; two casting nets; two drum nets; one cleaching net; one large salmon net; one gudgeon, or fine meshed brook net; four landing nets, of various sizes; six fishing poles; four bait cans; two large fish cans; two angling chairs; two coracles, or small fishing boats; two eel spears; two trout spears; one salmon spear; fishing cases and rods of every description.
>
> In the engine house and aviary there were six pheasant nets; three rabbit nets, and several purse nets; two pairs of lark nets; one partridge net; various rabbit traps, in lots; one hundred and twenty-eight vermin traps, of every description; one badger cub; two fox cubs; thirteen dog kennels; fourteen ferret boxes; three cages for wild animals; nine birdcages; sixteen pairs of quoits; two sets of bowls; sundry cricket-bats and balls.
>
> The guns ran to six rifles of various bores; nine double-barrelled guns; four single; with some dozens of powder-flasks, shot-belts, and gun-cases.

Mytton was probably ill-equipped in personality for the niceties of fly fishing, but to daintier anglers exact imitation was being preached with more authority than ever before. In 1836 Alfred Ronalds published his admirable *Fly-Fisher's Entomology*, in which natural insects are exactly observed and faithfully imitated: but Ronalds fished downstream and wet. It seems that even in the Borders and Lowlands, so far ahead of England, upstream fishing was limited to a few places, and may even have been forgotten during the 18th century. It is difficult otherwise to explain the contemporary impact of Stewart's *The Practical Angler* (1857), a book of the utmost merit, hailed as revolutionary, which does no more in essence than restate the ancient gospel of the upstream wetfly.

(xxix) The Coming of the Dry Fly

But a real revolution was quietly under way. In 1838 appeared William Shipley's *A True Treatise on the Art of Fly-Fishing, trolling, &c.;* unexpectedly, and in passing, he says: 'the quick repetition of casting whisks the water out of your flies and line, and consequently keeps them drier and lighter than if they were left to float a longer time in the water.' The word 'float' is probably misleading, and Shipley's flies and line were dried only to make them fall on the water more lightly. But George Pulman, in *The Vade Mecum of Fly fishing for Trout*, mentions in 1841 a fly intended to float, and in 1851, in his third edition, false casting to improve floating.

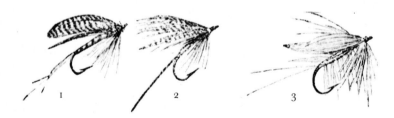

Exact imitations, but fished wet: 1 & 2 Mayflies; 3 Stonefly.

The purpose of fishing upstream with a floating, drag-free exact imitation was that it caught more fish (not that, as F. M. Halford and his disciples sometimes suggested, it was the only gentlemanly way to fish): yet how slow the idea was to catch on! Francis Francis, writing in *The Field* in 1857, mentioned using a dry fly on the Itchen, but no more than mentioned it in *The Book of Angling* of 1867, and still no more than glanced at it in passing in the third edition of 1872. Charles Kingsley's *Chalk Stream Studies* of 1858 recorded the introduction of tiny northern flies to the Hampshire rivers; he fished them upstream, but he fished them wet.

Five events changed fishing on chalk streams: the invention of the divided-wing dry fly, by G. S. Marryat and H. S. Hall, which fell lighter, floated higher, and imitated better; the invention by the latter of eyed trout hooks, which reduced weight and enabled the gut to be changed to suit conditions; the production and adoption of satisfactory fine-drawn gut; the invention of the oil-dressed silk floating line; and F. M. Halford's *Dry Fly Fishing* of 1889, the first book on the subject and arguably the most influential sporting treatise since Hawker on shooting and Beckford on hunting. Halford was followed by George Dewar's *Book of the Dry Fly* and Sir Edward Grey's (later Lord Grey of Falloden) *Fly Fishing*, which preached to a largely converted world.

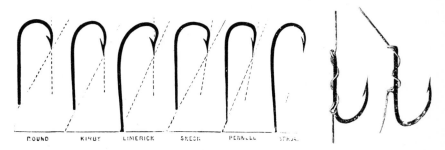

ROUND   KIRBY   LIMERICK   SNECK   PENNELL   UPRJS.

Hooks, old and new. The 'lip-hook' was of major importance in the development of modern dry-fly fishing.

Away from the chalk streams, the premier trout-fishing regions were considered Devon and Derbyshire. Cutliffe's *Trout Fishing in Rapid Streams* of 1863 deals with fly fishing in the former, and very well, but Philip Geen – himself fishing two very small flies upstream, a March brown and a blue upright – records that at just that date there was very little fly fishing in Devon. (He used a single brown horse-hair for a cast, and a twisted colt's-hair line made by the local sweep.) Geen sometimes deliberately dried his flies in midsummer; but when Edward Grey used a dry blue upright in Devonshire not long afterwards, it was so strange, and so successful, that local anglers considered it unsporting. The dry fly was introduced to the Derbyshire Wye during the 1860s by John Ogden, and worked so well that the owner of the water immediately forbade the blow-line. On some Scottish waters it was unknown before 1900: Sidney Buxton tried it on the Deveron, where it was previously unheard of. In 1904 W. Earl Hodgson, who did his fishing in Scotland, faced the new arrival and howled it down; his *Trout Fishing* is perhaps the silliest and most pretentious successful fishing book ever written.

The one other revolution in approach was the use of the nymph, systematised and made respectable by G. E. M. Skues, an Itchen fisherman, in *Minor Tactics of the Chalk Stream* in 1910. (As a scientific angler Skues was typical in being, not a squire or riparian owner, but a London solicitor and member of a syndicate.) In a sense history has exaggerated Skues's invention. Halford in 1889 speaks with detestation of using a sluglike sunk fly for nymphing fish, striking on the movement of the cast or on touch; and Buxton used a big wet fly downstream for tailing fish on the Kennet (he regarded bulgers as uncatchable). Skues made nymphing respectable, and his imitations were in general use until Frank Sawyer devised the dressings usual today.

(xxx) Rods and Tackle

Stewart and his northern contemporaries used a 10- or 12-foot single-handed rod, reel at the butt, for fly fishing; the butt was ash, the middle hickory, the top bamboo, lancewood or greenheart. A two- or three-piece split cane top was desirable but expensive. In most of England a similar but somewhat larger rod was usual; on the chalk streams, especially the big Test and Kennet, most anglers used very much longer rods, and some continued to do so until about 1900. Very much smaller and lighter rods, made of six-piece split cane, were introduced from America late in the century; they first found acceptance on the smaller chalk streams, and it was found, after an absurdly long time, that they were superior in performance as well as more agreeable to use. Brass ferrules, as a convenient alternative to splicing, were known to George Bainbridge of Liverpool, who wrote *The Fly-Fisher's Guide* in 1816; in 1850 (by which date very few anglers except the humblest made their own rods) the slip ferrule with a wire catch was replacing the screw type. Some people continued to prefer splicing because of the unbroken curve it made possible.

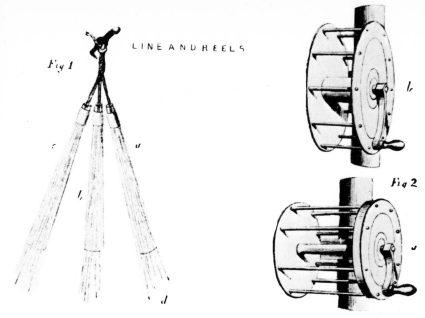

Fig 1

Fig 2

Method of plaiting a horsehair line, using transparent goose-quills.

The multiplier reel (*below*) and the large-spindle simple reel which replaced it for fly fishing but not for spinning.

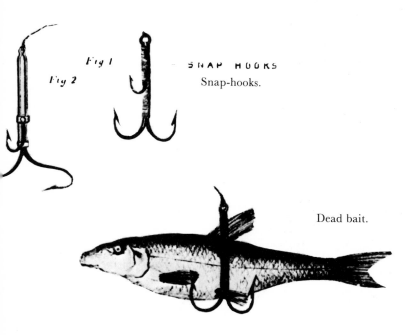

Fig 1

Fig 2

SNAP HOOKS
Snap-hooks.

Dead bait.

Fishing Apparatus.

The multiplying reel lost favour for trout fishing. High gearing was achieved instead by making the reel deeper and narrower, so that more line was wound in with each turn of the handle; at the same time the balance of reel to rod was better understood, and the weight of the multiplier was against it. A brake (on a ratchet or 'rack') was well established by 1850, but many people agreed with Stewart in preferring to break with a finger rather than risk mechanical seizure.

Silk lines were replacing horsehair everywhere by the middle of the century; they needed more care and did not last as long, but in other respects they were generally preferred for all kinds of trout fishing. Gut casts were slow to attract fishermen because so many bad ones were sold, but once drawn gut was reliable and properly dyed its advantages were irresistible; only a few diehards used horsehair after about 1870. Hooks, eyed and plain, proliferated in design – round, Limerick, Kirby, sneck – arousing arguments of surprising ferocity. The 'old' and 'new' numberings were both in use by 1850, the 'new' (upwards from 000) becoming general in England until, quite recently but almost totally, supplanted again by the 'old' (20 downwards).

Few 19th-century gentlemen tied their own flies; they bought them from tackle-merchants, as they did all the equipment which had once been homemade or improvised, or got them from a local enthusiast – parson, schoolmaster or tradesman – who was allowed to fish in return. Some households still had a resident sporting hanger-on, a sort of latter-day Will Wimble, like Lord Marney's Captain Grouse (in Disraeli's *Sybil*) who 'could sing, dance, draw, make artificial flies, break horses, and make everybody comfortable'.

(xxxi) Salmon and the Invasion of Scotland

Salmon fishing had been an important local source of income, reported by Defoe, in several parts of England in the early 18th century. But English salmon spawned in the big rivers, and big rivers attracted industry; the last Thames salmon was caught at Taplow in 1824, and many of the other traditional fisheries had lives even shorter, or scarcely longer, with only such exceptions as the Test, Hampshire Avon, Wye, and the Devonshire rivers. A salmon in the industrially revolutionised Trent became as unlikely as snipe shooting in Chelsea.

In Scotland the cradle of serious salmon fishing was the Tweed. It was the pursuit of artisans, part-time professionals, of whom the greatest was John Younger, the shoemaker of St Boswell's; he introduced gut to the Borders, devised and tied a range of original flies, and about 1820 wrote the first notes for his classic *River Angling for Salmon and Trout*, published in 1840. (This is a far more interesting and original book than Sir Humphrey Davy's *Salmonia* of 1828.) Though Younger fished for a living (nobody paid his shoemaking bills) he was totally against such methods as night-lining, netting, spearing, or using roe as bait.

The visiting Englishman: drawn and etched by W. Heath during a tour of the Highlands, *The New Sporting Magazine*, September 1835.

Then the whole circumstances of Scottish salmon fishing were rather suddenly transformed by English squires and merchants. William Scrope, a Lincolnshire squire who was the son of a Wiltshire parson, adopted Scotland as his playground; familiar with Kennet trout, he came north for grouse shooting, deer stalking and salmon fishing, taking for the last a property called The Pavilion from Lord Somerville, opposite Melrose and near Sir Walter Scott's Abbotsford. He was taught fishing by Younger's pupil John Haliburton, and in 1843 published his

Days and Nights of Salmon Fishing on the Tweed. Another significant new-comer was George Bainbridge, the self-made Liverpool banker who had already written a trout-fishing book. He bought the Gattonside estate from Sir Adam Ferguson: Walter Scott was entirely hostile until he met this uncouth new neighbour; when he got to know him he liked him very much. Younger commented: 'Scrope came round and suc-ceeded old John Wright and Geordie Sanderson, by trebling the rents of the Mertoun Waters, commencing what we may call the gentle epidemical mania for salmon fishing, which has the effect of those great lordly pikes driving us smaller fry out of the water.' An ironic result was that such diversions as torchlight spearing (*below*), execrated by Younger, came merrily back with Sir Walter, William Scrope and their grand friends: though not with Bainbridge, who was as much a purist as Younger.

An annual migration began: Englishmen and high rents went rapidly north and west from the Tweed. Trollope's collaborator in 1868 said salmon fishing had already become too expensive for any but the rich: £1 a day, and the visitor did not keep his fish. On the Lyon in West Perthshire in the 1880s Philip Geen found that every rod fishing was a paying visitor, and they had to book months in advance. They were spinning there with phantoms, minnows or spoons, using a Silex reel with a 'coiling tin' on the belt.

The torch and spear were made generally illegal in 1862. Fly fishing for salmon has thereafter changed extremely little, except for a growing understanding (still far from complete) of why a salmon takes a fly. Fruitful study of this subject began with an Irish book, the Revd Henry

Newland's *The Erne: its legends and its fly-fishing* in 1851; Newland's idea that a salmon fly is a shrimp, not a wasp or dragonfly, has gained gradual but general acceptance, together with Arthur Ransome's much later discovery (made, he says, by watching American soldiers chew gum in the Piccadilly Hotel during the Second War) that some of the best salmon flies are elvers. The tube flies derived from Richard Waddington's experiments are also assumed to imitate elvers. Spinning was transformed in ease, though not in essential method, by the invention of the fixed-spool reel and monofilament line: but until this often-deplored development it changed even less than fly fishing.

Unnamed salmon flies, 1875: 'gaudy' and 'very gaudy'.

Loch fishing was popular throughout Scotland throughout the century. Stewart used three or four flies, entirely modern, and a thirteen-foot rod; other anglers (deplored by him) used natural and artificial minnows and parr tails, sometimes with six or seven hooks (*below*). Visiting Englishmen enjoyed this sport, but it is doubtful if any came to Scotland especially for it.

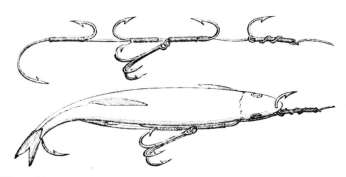

Pike tackle used for loch trout, incorporating the new triple hook, 1875.

They preferred, as they still do, big salmon in big rivers, and in pursuit of them they were remarkably tough. Scrope often found himself wading, where the banks were wooded and there was no boat to be had; he cut holes in the uppers of his hobnailed shoes to let the water out, and recommended wading as far as 'the fifth button of your waistcoat'.

Should you be of a delicate temperament, and be wading in the month of February, when it may chance to freeze very hard, pull down your stockings, and examine your legs. Should they be black, or even purple, it might, perhaps, be as well to get on dry land; but if they are only rubicund, you may continue to enjoy the water.

Stewart, made of softer stuff, noted a decade later that waterproof wading stockings were replacing heavy leather sea-boots.

The great problems in Scotland (besides the 'gentle epidemical mania') were pollution, poaching and commercial netting. The first had gone far to destroy some fishing, such as Gala Water, by 1850. Poaching was done everywhere, by spear and flare, by netting in low water, by using salmon roe (from poached salmon), by foul-hooking with big hooks sunk deep and dragged across a pool. Netting at river mouths became a valuable business in Scotland about 1850, and its effects on the spring run were immediately noticed. Some rivers suffered so badly that the science of pisciculture was at once studied; by 1868 the artificial rearing and stocking of the Tay, from the Stormontfield 'breeding boxes', was already considered necessary.

(xxxii) Stocking and Letting

Commerical stake-netting had long been important in the north of England. Sir John Harthover of Harthover Place (in Charles Kingsley's *Water Babies*) had in about 1820 'miles of game preserves' and 'a noble salmon river'. The former were heavily poached, the latter netted but not usually poached because 'the colliers disliked cold water'. When gangs did come out from the towns with spears and flares they had battles with the keepers as bloody as those in the coverts. Elsewhere in England pollution was a major problem in trout water as well as salmon; and late in the century 'the rapacity of some of the London Water Companies has of late years told severely on the trout streams of Hertfordshire and Essex'.

Stocking trout streams came later than the artificial rearing of salmon: partly because trout were not netted, principally because even the best dry-fly fishing attracted rents nothing like as high as those of the leading salmon rivers. (Sir Reginald Graham, a distinguished Master of Hounds and son of a very great one, said in his *Foxhunting Recollections* that in the 1860s almost all of both Test and Itchen were so cheap as to be almost free.) When stocking came it aroused mixed feelings. By some it was criticised, like hand reared pheasants, for creating a false and too easy sport. Sidney Buxton entirely welcomed the stocking of the Kennet with silver Loch Leven trout, which in 1900 were appearing to replace the yellow-bellied indigenous sort, because they fought better. But Buxton gives himself away. He caught forty trout on one occasion, on another thirty all on the mayfly, none of these as much as two pounds. This vast population of easy, smallish fish was what Skues objected to when he fought the rest of his syndicate about stocking the Upper Itchen (a story he tells with the unforgiving bitterness of old age in the posthumous *Itchen Memories*).

Between the 1880s and 1914 (and ever since) fishing offers a close parallel to pheasant shooting. Landowners found that it earned more than farming, and was worthier of improvement and investment. High paying fishing tenants or syndicates wanted quantity, hence heavy stocking and the large bags which justified still higher rents. It was also usual in expensive, well-stocked waters to overcut the weed in order to make things easier for the customers. Other comforts followed: the cutting back of all trees and undergrowth that might impede a back-cast, the mowing of banks like bowling greens, the provision of seats and shelters: so that some rented fishing could be managed quite well from a wheel-chair.

The Upper Itchen may have been overstocked from the stews, but at least it kept grayling out. This tiresome fish was introduced from York-shire to some southern rivers in, perhaps, Norman times; it spread all through the Test in 1816; was taken to Scotland about 1850; was put into Derbyshire rivers in the 1860s and the Cumberland Eden in the 1890s. Squires were presumably responsible for these follies; their descendants have regretted them.

(xxxiii) Faraway Sports: Yachting, Mountaineering, Golf, Boxing

An effect of the railways was to change attitudes to sport. With certain clear exceptions (of personalities as of pursuits) country gentlemen had taken their active diversions at home, or at least locally. The earliest exception was racing: a small minority of rich men came from all over England to Newmarket from the 17th century, and a very few had their own establishments there. The next exception in point of time was yacht-ing: an even smaller minority, of necessity even richer, transplanted themselves for part of the year to the Isle of Wight and their magnificent ocean-going pleasure craft. The next was foxhunting; Leicestershire attracted a few gentlemen from far away from about 1770, a good many more fifty years later, also necessarily rich, and able to be idle from November to March. Before 1840 a handful of gentlemen rode or posted

English racing yachts.

The schooner America.

great distances to shoot pheasants in Norfolk or grouse in Yorkshire. The railways made it easy for any squire who could afford it to race at Newmarket or Doncaster, sail in the Solent, hunt with the Quorn, accept shooting invitations anywhere, and follow William Scrope to Scotland with rifle, shotgun and salmon rod.

Racing was not really affected at all; hunting by the mixed blessing of larger fields; shooting and fishing, as we have seen – and stalking similarly – by the widespread conversion of personal sporting facilities into money-earning businesses. Yachting grew immensely in scale, as the ease of getting to the anchorage coincided with immense prosperity. There were many more steam yachts, many more pure racing yachts – some huge and dauntingly expensive – the fastest built on American lines. In 1868:

> Parliament and Downing Street, the Stock Exchange, the clergy, the bar, the medical profession, the army and navy, the civil service, the fine arts, literature, commerce, Manchester, and country squires, may all be found side by side in the club lists. Some of the boldest riders and best shots are the most adventurous and devoted of yachtsmen.

And the yacht itself became a means of travelling to sport hardly before attainable: 'Every summer sees a fleet of British yachts hovering round the coasts of Norway, while the owners are salmon-fishing in the fiords.' Though not snobbish, yachting remained exclusive for reasons made unconsciously clear by the beautiful Mrs G. A. Schenley in 1891 (in *The Gentlewoman's Book of Sports*): one of the first ladies to take the helm of her own racing yacht, she was followed at sea, in case of accident, by either her own steam yacht or her husband's steamer.

A sport (like deer stalking) almost created by easy travel was mountaineering. 'Some future philosopher may turn aside from more important topics to notice the rise and development of the passion for mountain climbing.' The passion derived from admiration of wild scenery – Gibbon's autobiography mentions the new fashion to 'view the glaciers' – and from serious scientific enquiry; sporting climbing started in about 1850, the enthusiasts taking fewer guides and less equipment than the pioneers. Snowdon, before this time almost as remote as the Matterhorn, claimed as many victims, because tourists swarmed up it in ignorance of the hazards.

An ancient diversion much encouraged by the railways was golf. The game had become popular in Scotland in the 15th century, in spite of an official view that it distracted the people from archery; it came to England in a small way with James I. The first English clubs started in the 18th century, the game being played on improvised courses on racegrounds or sheep-walks. The railways served the celebrated seaside courses of Eastern Scotland, and there was very widespread enthusiasm, among the English polite, in the last third of the 19th century; women joined in in numbers (to the scandal of conservatives, especially at St Andrew's) in the 1880s.

Apart from racing, the one spectator sport to which gentlemen had travelled was boxing. This received great encouragement from noble and even royal patrons in the late 18th century, and from a number of squires in the early 19th, such as Sir Thomas Mostyn when he was Master of the Bicester. Another advantage the sport enjoyed at this period was the character of the champions: good manners and modesty were ascribed to Jem and Tom Belcher, to Tom Cribb the 'Game Chicken', and to the subsequent coal-owning squire and Member of Parliament John Gully. Hazlitt (an urban intellectual after a rural boyhood in Shropshire) saw the fight between Tom Hickman (the 'Gasman') and Bill Neate: 'The crowd was very great when we arrived on the spot; open carriages were coming up, with streamers flying and music playing, and the country people were pouring in over hedge and ditch in all directions.' £200,000 was allegedly betted on this fight by the Fancy. Elsewhere (on *Notes of a Journey through France and Italy*) Hazlitt compares the knowledgeable and emotional involvement of an English country crowd in a prize-fight with the reaction of a Paris audience to Racine or Molière. Prize-fights were fully reported in the press, and attracted the attention of a leading sporting journalist in Pierce Egan.

Cumberland Wrestling, 1830, which never suffered the odium which boxing attracted.

The sport was then attacked from all directions; from above, by legislation which outlawed it, and condemned the perpetrators of the degrading spectacle to transportation to Australia; from one side, by local squires and townsfolk (as recorded by Emily Hall in her diary) dreading an influx of rowdies and sharks; from the other side, by R. S. Surtees and his colleagues on the *New Sporting Magazine* deeming it as bestial as bear-baiting; and from below, the boxers themselves making the 'cross-fight' or rigged match so normal as to be almost invariable. Boxing was reinstated into a qualified respectability by the Queensberry Rules (1867) and by the participation of Lord Lonsdale in the sport's management: but it was no longer anything to do with the countryside.

(xxxiv) Home Sports: Cricket, Archery, Croquet, Skating Tennis

At the beginning of the 19th century gentlemen held cricket matches in their parks, had archery grounds and bowling greens in their gardens, and in winter skated on decoy ponds or stews.

Cricket changed a little in detail and profoundly in organization. In 1817, batting being too easy, the stumps were raised and widened, and

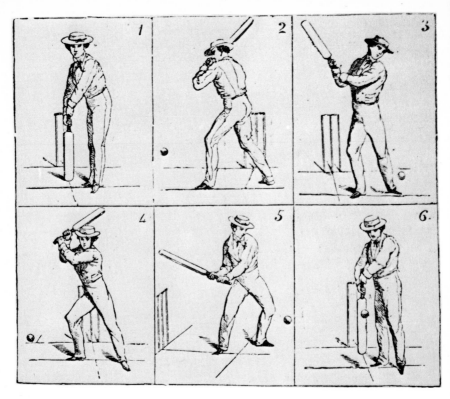

'Batting positions', 1875.

in 1822 spin bowling appeared, at first illegal. Meanwhile the emphasis steadily moved from private parks and village greens to Lords and to county and club grounds; and from amateurs to professionals. Village and country-house cricket absorbed the technical changes without being touched by the others. George Meredith's account (in *Diana of the Crossways*) of the estate match at Copsley, and of Sir Lukin the keen and hospitable squire, will stand for much of the country and most of the century; Siegfried Sassoon, 'Dornford Yates' and L. P. Hartley are among dozens of writers who confirm the unchangingness of local cricket. Ladies entered the game (much opposed) in the last quarter of the century, of whom Lady Milner remarked in 1891: 'A favourite form of fielding with some ladies is to stop the ball with their petticoats. This may achieve their purpose, but it is, to say the least of it, most ungraceful, and is very bad "form".'

Archery at the beginning of the century was practically the only outdoor sport available to women, and remained popular for most of the century. Many country houses had grounds very near the house, the targets staying up all the time so that any break in the rain, or gleam of sunshine, could be taken advantage of with no delay. Clubs were formed quite early in the century in many parts of the country, mostly meeting at a particular house or at several in rotation; tournaments ended in dances and often in betrothals. The Grand National Archery Meeting

was first held on the Knavesmire at York in 1844, and ladies participated the next year. The sport was very nearly, but not quite, killed by lawn tennis, a few passionate enthusiasts surviving here and there, as did falconers and players of real tennis.

Bowls was never in danger of death, but it moved from practically all the country houses, where it had flourished for so long, to the quadrangles of Oxford colleges and municipal bowling greens, thus becoming a much more and a much less exclusive pastime. Many bowling greens became croquet lawns. The ancestor of croquet was introduced as pell mell, or *palle malle*, from France, with the Restoration, but seems hardly to have penetrated outside London and to have died in the early 18th century. It was reintroduced as croquet, from France by way of Ireland, about 1850; the confusion of rules was systematised in the 1860s. Mr Walter Whitmore of Moreton in Marsh was in some sense champion in 1868, and partly as a result of a book he wrote the game spread to the lawns of nearly every country house in England. (Alice was not surprised to find a game in progress in Wonderland, though the local rules were unfamiliar.) The All England Croquet Club at Wimbledon became headquarters: but suddenly its lawns, like thousands of others, became tennis courts. Croquet was, however, too enjoyable, too skilful and too vicious a game to let die, and the number of lawns studded with hoops was shortly greater than before, and still is. It was even played at Renishaw, least sporting of English country houses, in the time of Sir George Sitwell, least sporting of squires.

Rackets, 1830; 'One of the most healthful Exercises connected with BRITISH SPORTS; and the principal Amusement for confined debtors in the FLEET and KING'S BENCH Prisons.'

Lawn tennis was bred by rackets out of real tennis: rackets itself being an adaptation of the older game, said to have been devised about 1800 by gentlemanly debtors in the Fleet prison. In 1869 Major Walter Wingfield took it out of doors onto grass, patenting some of the equipment needed. Rules were drawn up in 1874. Success was immediate and enormous, and tennis became the country-house game *par excellence*: it was quite cheap; it needed little space compared to cricket; it was healthfully vigorous compared to croquet; it lent itself, like the latter, to participation by both sexes. (Mixed doubles were the most popular country-house version.) By 1890 stop-netting was usual but by no means universal: many households had fox terriers trained to retrieve the balls. Mrs Hillyard in 1891 instructed ladies to wear sailor hats and urged a white underskirt (more fully and frequently revealed than the wearer realised); 'white shoes should be avoided, as they make the feet look large.'

Skating came, like yachting, to England from Holland at the Restoration: it was watched with admiration by Pepys. Appropriate pieces of wood and then of metal were fashioned by local craftsmen all over England, and skating became another classless country diversion. Wordsworth describes one of the sports of his boyhood (about 1785) in *The Prelude*:

> All shod with steel,
> We hissed along the polished ice in games
> Confederate, imitative of the chase
> And woodland pleasures – the resounding horn,
> The pack loud chiming, and the hunted hare.

At Dingley Dell about forty years later there were enough skates for everybody: after the ice had been swept Bob Sawyer inscribed figures of eight and Mr Wardle, the squire himself, went through motions he described as a reel. Mr Pickwick and Sam Weller – master and servant in merry democracy – then took to sliding, hurrying round from finish to start to 'keep the pot a-bilin'.' These jovial improvisations depended on the weather; the first mechanically frozen indoor rink in England was the London Glaciarium, opened in 1876; its echoing urban descendants, full of semi-professional children, are a long way from Dingley Dell.

CHAPTER SEVEN

Epilogue

(i) The Squire Transplanted

England's most important exports to the world – in the history of civilization, not of economics – have perhaps been language and literature, parliamentary democracy, and the sporting country gentleman. The one that has stood transplanting best, at least for short periods, is the last.

The idea went to Scotland before any English sportsmen went there; the hawking, deer-slaying, unintelligible lairds described by Defoe gave way to men like Weir of Hermiston, who about 1800 dined with and entertained their sporting neighbours and hunted with the local foxhounds. In the last hundred years the Scottish landowner has grown more and more to resemble the English, in some basic attitudes and some matters of detail – though by no means all of either – with the major difference that he was for a long time able to charge far more for his sporting rights.

The idea went to Ireland with a transplanted landed aristocracy, one of the most sporting societies in the world if resident; the Anglo-Irish have produced over the years people of the utmost charm and talent, and others remarkable for their drunken and provincial crassness: the situation, of course, among their English cousins, but a good deal exaggerated, owing to isolation among a near-foreign peasantry, and the absence of anything to do.

The idea went to America with another transplanted landed aristocracy, and flourished on a slave economy in Virginia, Maryland, the Carolinas and Georgia. It went to Australia, carried there by the adventurous younger sons of landed families, who re-created on their enormous estates the sporting establishments of home. It infected South Africa, Kenya, the Argentine. It was deliberately imitated, sometimes with a certain success, in Russia, Poland, Hungary and North-East Germany. Details have even been adopted in France and Italy, such as owning fox-terriers, carrying flasks of whisky, and wearing deerstalkers: as though these signs, by a kind of sympathetic magic, endowed the person so badged with a sporting life.

It is agreeable to contemplate the survival of the sporting squire, in however debased a form, in exotic places, because he scarcely survives in his birthplace.

(ii) Decline and Fall

Since 1918 England has been full of rich people disporting in the countryside: even since 1970. But a decreasing proportion of them have been the hereditary owners of land or sporting rights.

There have been three overlapping reasons for the squire's withdrawal. Taxes have reduced his disposable unearned income, often to vanishing point, while costs, especially of wages, have made it impossible for him to employ a staff devoted to his amusement, or forego shooting or fishing rents. Secondly, it was almost impossible between the wars to make agriculture pay, and only intermittently possible since the Second War. Thirdly, the operation of primogeniture has all but broken down. Time was, the whole of an estate and the bulk of a fortune went to the eldest son, so that what a gentle family had it held. Death duties have caused more estates to be broken up or put on the market than any other single disaster.

Gentlemen who have contrived to hold on to their ancestral acres, and even to inhabit their ancestral mansions, have nearly all been obliged to make their sporting facilities pay for themselves, if not show a profit. This applies most obviously to pheasant and grouse shooting, salmon and dry-fly fishing, and deer stalking. Most good shooting and fishing is let or syndicated, in whole or in part. Specialist agents now handle sporting rights; rents can be very high indeed, as can capital cost. Some landowners open their houses to the public to pay one lot of bills; far more open their coverts or rivers to customers to pay another lot of bills. Landowners who keep major sporting estates for the diversion of themselves and their non-paying guests are now a very small minority; they are very rich men; few of these fortunes are ancient.

A new phenomenon which has inevitably followed is the ownership of sporting rights by institutions. This can sometimes be justified as an investment, sometimes as a means of providing fringe benefits to directors or staff; it sometimes enables a financier to enjoy the sport of a millionaire duke at his shareholders' expense.

Hunting has been affected least by all this, since for a century and a half it has mostly been financed by the subscriptions of clubs rather than the munificence of individuals. What has altered hunting is physical and technological change: motorways, tractors and lorries, artificial fertiliser, wire, forestry. These developments have created new problems for the foxhound, and so for its breeder, which have been solved with a great deal of success, principally by the use of the Welsh cross hound.

Hunting continues to depend on landowners, although few of them provide its packs. Their land must be crossed, their coverts drawn, their goodwill kept. A few take down all wire in the winter; more punctuate it with jumpable timber. Some have given land for kennels; many have lent it for hunter trials, pony club rallies, cross-country rides, and point-to-point courses. Hunt balls are sometimes still held in private houses. The landowner who hunts continues to have advantages, and enjoy economies, denied the visiting townsmen or villa-dweller: he has his own stabling, forage, bedding, grazing and, from time to time, labour.

Organized covert shooting has changed very little, except in the proportion of guns paying to be there, and the frightening sums they pay. This is true also of grouse driving and deer stalking. The expense and commercialisation of organized shoots has led to a limited return to rough-shooting and also to the use of the pointer and setter. Many people, reliving Colonel Peter Hawker's shooting life, have found it enjoyable, and have left driven birds to stockbrokers, Americans and Arabs.

Fly fishing has been subjected to much technical experiment and a prodigious weight of literature. From America have come nylon casts and floating lines, from France new concepts of rod design. Various new flies have gained acceptance, such as Wulff dry flies and Sawyer nymphs. Spinning has been transformed in ease by the fixed-spool reel and monofilament line. On dry-fly rivers the biggest change has been the introduction of stock rainbow trout, reared in hatcheries and fattened in stews. They are on the whole found to fight and taste better than native browns, but their chief advantage is that they put on weight at three times the speed. The great growth has been in reservoir fishing, a classless sport in which large rainbows are caught, by chuck-and-chance-it methods, on miscalled flies which imitate shrimps and prawns. Many landowners have stocked ponds, many have made them by excavating and damming.

D. H. Lawrence wrote of the amorous career of a Derbyshire game-keeper in the 1920s, a fellow who still wore green velveteen and gaiters 'in the old style'; but of the traditional life of the landowners Lawrence said: 'The England of the Squire Winters and the Wragley Halls was gone, dead. The blotting out was only not yet complete.' It is still not yet complete, half a century of surtax later; the funeral oration was premature; but the patient is very ill, and not likely to recover.

BIBLIOGRAPHICAL NOTE

A conventional bibliography for this book was attempted, and proved impossible. It would have been either uselessly short or ludicrously long. The principal sources are: works of general and social history; books of tours and travels; biographies and memoirs; diaries and letters; fiction; sporting history; sporting and other journalism; and above all sporting treatises. A minority of the more important (or surprising) sources appear in the index. Most quotations are identified in the text, and an effort has been made to give authority there for the more contentious or least credible statements.

INDEX